Make It HAPPEN

Coaching With the 4 Critical Questions of PLCs at Work®

Kim Bailey & Chris Jakicic

Solution Tree | Press

555 North Morton Street
Bloomington, IN 47404
800.733.6786 (toll free) / 812.336.7700
FAX: 812.336.7790

email: info@SolutionTree.com
SolutionTree.com

Visit **go.SolutionTree.com/PLCbooks** to download the free reproducibles in this book.

Printed in the United States of America

Library of Congress Cataloging-in-Publication Data

Names: Bailey, Kim, author. | Jakicic, Chris, author.
Title: Make it happen : coaching with the four critical questions of PLCs at
    work® / Kim Bailey and Chris Jakicic.
Description: Bloomington, IN : Solution Tree Press, [2018] | Includes
    bibliographical references and index.
Identifiers: LCCN 2018026543 | ISBN 9781947604216 (perfect bound)
Subjects: LCSH: Professional learning communities. | Mentoring in education.
    | Teachers--In-service training.
Classification: LCC LB1731 .B236 2018 | DDC 370.71/1--dc23
LC record available at https://lccn.loc.gov/2018026543

Solution Tree
Jeffrey C. Jones, CEO
Edmund M. Ackerman, President

Solution Tree Press
President and Publisher: Douglas M. Rife
Editorial Director: Sarah Payne-Mills
Art Director: Rian Anderson
Managing Production Editor: Kendra Slayton
Senior Production Editor: Christine Hood
Senior Editor: Amy Rubenstein
Copy Editor: Ashante K. Thomas
Proofreader: Elisabeth Abrams
Cover Designer: Rian Anderson
Editorial Assistant: Sarah Ludwig

Acknowledgments

● ● ● ●

We dedicate this book to the memory of our mentors in this work, Richard and Rebecca DuFour. Rick and Becky, you exhibited the highest form of leadership—leading humbly with passion and persistence and ensuring that the right work continues even if you aren't there to guide us. Thank you for entrusting us to carry on this important work.

Solution Tree Press would like to thank the following reviewers:

Joanna Ayers
Instructional Coach
Clinton Middle School
Clinton, Iowa

Jennifer Cook
K–2 Literacy Collaborative Coach
North Greenville Elementary School
Greenville, Wisconsin

Jennifer Deinhart
K–8 Mathematics Specialist
Mason Crest Elementary School
Annandale, Virginia

Benjamin Dobes
Instructional Coach
Morton Freshman Center
Cicero, Illinois

James Dobrzanski
Instructional Coach
Morton East High School
Cicero, Illinois

Louise Donaghey
Elementary Instructional Coach
Singapore American School
Singapore

Jacqueline Heller
Literacy Teacher and Coach
Mason Crest Elementary School
Annandale, Virginia

Patti Henning
Literacy Coach
Longleaf Elementary School
Melbourne, Florida

Kathy Liston
Instructional Coach
Brookview Elementary School
West Des Moines, Iowa

Kristin Rice
Mathematics and Science Coach
Wells Road Intermediate School
Granby, Connecticut

Yessenia Santiago
Literacy Coach
Link Elementary School
Elk Grove Village, Illinois

Maria Schroeder
Instructional Coach
Lakeview Elementary School
Solon, Iowa

Melanie Sims
Instructional Coach
Highland Park Elementary School
Bloomington, Indiana

Deb Van Dalen
Instructional Coach
Hortonville Middle School
Hortonville, Wisconsin

Visit **go.SolutionTree.com/PLCbooks** to download the free reproducibles in this book.

Table of Contents

● ● ● ●

Reproducible pages are in italics.

About the Authors

● ● ● ●

Kim Bailey is former director of professional development and instructional support for the Capistrano Unified School District in Southern California. Her leadership was instrumental in uniting and guiding educators throughout the district's fifty-eight schools on their journey to becoming professional learning communities (PLCs). She also taught courses in educational leadership as an adjunct faculty member at Chapman University in Orange, California. Prior to her work in professional development, Kim served as an administrator of special education programs and a teacher of students with disabilities.

Kim's education background spans forty-one years, and her work at Capistrano has won national praise. The National School Boards Association (NSBA) recognized Kim's leadership in coordinating and implementing the district's Professional Development Academies. The academies received the distinguished NSBA Magna Award and the California School Boards Association Golden Bell Award. Kim has served on the Committee on Accreditation for the California Commission on Teaching Credentialing.

As a writer and consultant, Kim works with U.S. educators to build effective leadership of PLCs. She is passionate about empowering teams with practical, collaborative strategies for aligning instruction, assessment, and interventions with the standards so all students receive high-quality instruction.

Kim earned a bachelor of science and a master of science in education and special education from Northern Illinois University.

To learn more about Kim's work, visit kbailey 4learning (https://kbailey4learning.com) or follow @Bailey4learning on Twitter.

Chris Jakicic, EdD, served as principal of Woodlawn Middle School in Illinois from its opening day in 1999 through the spring of 2007. Under her leadership, the staff shifted toward a collaborative culture focused on learning and implemented formative assessment practices to shape their instructional strategies. Student motivation and performance increased. Chris began her career teaching middle school science before serving as principal of Willow Grove Elementary School in Illinois for nine years. At Willow Grove, she helped teachers develop high-performing collaborative teams to increase student learning.

Through her work with teachers and administrators across the United States, Chris emphasizes that effective teaming is the heart of PLCs.

She also shares practical knowledge about how to use data conversations to interpret classroom information for effective instruction. She has worked closely with schools and districts that want to use the power of common formative assessments to increase learning for all students. She provides specific, practical strategies for teams who want to make the best use of their limited common planning time to write effective assessments meeting the rigor of the Common Core State Standards. Teams can use the data from these assessments to effectively provide students with exactly what they need next.

Chris has written articles for the *Journal of Staff Development* and *Illinois School Research and Development Journal* detailing her experiences with common assessments and PLCs. She has worked as an adjunct instructor at National Louis University as well as Loyola University Chicago, where she earned a doctor of education.

To learn more about Chris's work, visit www .chrisjakicic.com or follow @cjakicic on Twitter.

To book Kim Bailey or Chris Jakicic for professional development, contact pd@Solution Tree.com.

Introduction

● ● ● ●

Throughout the literature on school improvement is a consistent call to enhance teachers' content knowledge and instructional practice to impact student learning. Generally speaking, a recommended strategy to improve schools is to provide teachers with more professional development (Darling-Hammond, 1997; Elmore, 2002; Joyce & Showers, 1981). Schools and districts responded to this recommendation by providing teachers with various forms of trainings, but not all have led to a positive impact on student learning. To examine the impact of professional learning, several descriptive studies identified effective versus ineffective practices (Guskey, 2003; Hill, 2009; Hirsch, 2005). Three common findings related to the effectiveness and impact of professional learning have emerged from this literature.

1. Professional development is most impactful when it aligns to the prioritized needs in student learning.

2. Professional development engages educators and promotes deeper learning when provided within meaningful contexts.

3. Professional development designed to provide ongoing and embedded support leads to greater implementation of new practices.

When these factors are in place, it is much more likely that professional development will systematically improve teacher practice and ultimately student learning. In contrast, professional development focused on ever-changing initiatives or practices, delivered in "drive-by fashion" without sustained and ongoing support, simply doesn't lead to systematic improvement in student learning—it leads to fragmentation of efforts and random impact on student learning.

In recognition of these factors, legislation contained in No Child Left Behind (2002) and its iteration the Every Student Succeeds Act (ESSA) specifically outlines indicators of quality professional development. ESSA section 8101.42 defines "'professional development,' specifically noting that the professional development activities are sustained (not stand-alone, 1-day, or short-term workshops), intensive, collaborative, job-embedded, data-driven, and classroom-focused" (ESSA, 2015). This more in-depth view of professional learning implies that in order to impact student learning, it needs to be systematic and continuous, rely on data as an indicator of its focus and effectiveness, and be learning focused and collaborative in nature.

These specifications have led to a lot of forward movement in our field, particularly in how districts and schools approach their design and implementation of professional development. Yet, while these guiding principles have generally led to many improvements, we still observe symptoms of initiative overload and delivery of professional development activities that seem random or fleeting. At times, the mere announcement of an upcoming professional development event is met with anxiety, sometimes eliciting responses such as "Uh oh, now what?"

Do teachers need ongoing professional learning to improve their practice? Absolutely! But they need access to professional learning that is meaningful and that aligns with students' needs. And rather than having a revolving door of workshops that focus on a new instructional strategy each occurrence, teachers need time and support to implement those strategies. They need embedded opportunities and a meaningful structure to examine the impact of their practice on students so they can continually refine their practice. Moreover, teachers need to learn alongside their colleagues who teach the same grade level or course, working in collaboration to implement these practices and study the results.

In their foundational 1995 research, Bruce Joyce and Beverly Showers conclude that there is little transfer from professional development sessions into classrooms without the opportunity for practice, feedback, and coaching after teachers engage in this new learning. Michael Garet, Andrew Porter, Laura Desimone, Beatrice Birman, and Kwang Suk Yoon (2001) surveyed teachers who indicated that their practice changed most when they received professional development that was coherent, focused on content knowledge, and involved active learning. In 2009, Ruth Chung Wei, Linda Darling-Hammond, Alethea Andree, Nikole Richardson, and Stelios Orphanos, in partnership with the National Staff Development Council (currently known as Learning Forward), identified the beneficial impact of sustained professional development (for example, study groups and coaching) on teacher practice and student learning because of programs of greater intensity, duration, and connectedness to the teachers' context. As a result of these findings and recommendations, many schools and districts have been providing support from coaches in a variety of forms, including peer coaching, collegial coaching, cognitive coaching, and mentoring, among others. This is where *instructional coaching* comes in.

The Coaching Movement

Numerous schools and districts have established instructional coaching positions as a specific vehicle to provide teachers and collaborative teams with *ongoing* support while learning about the curriculum and effective instructional strategies. In our work around the United States, we have seen a significant increase in the number of academic or instructional coaches within districts and schools. The specific titles of these positions and actual roles they fulfill vary depending on the site or district context, but in general, the individuals serving as coaches have been charged with providing ongoing and embedded support to teachers in order to raise student achievement. There are different versions of coaching roles, including how and with whom they interact at the school or district level. Depending on the context and expectations, instructional coaches may work with individual teachers, collaborative teams, or both.

One way the coaching role varies across schools and districts is the nature of the relationship between the coach and teachers or coach and team. In one role, for example, some schools expect coaches to work as an *expert*, that is, someone with greater knowledge about the anticipated outcome. This might happen when reading coaches help teachers implement strategies to improve student learning in English language arts.

In a second role, the coach does not necessarily have greater knowledge about the curriculum being taught but must facilitate meetings and processes, almost in a management fashion. Finally, in a third role, the coach supports teachers and teams as they think through ideas and decisions, provides questions to encourage them to reflect on their practices and the overall impact on student learning, and chooses resources and ideas to support the teachers' work. In this last example, the balance of knowledge and expertise between the teachers and the coach is equal. Sometimes, the expectations for how a coach relates depend on the teacher or team needs, and coaches move in and out of the three major roles based on the team context.

We further define the nature of coaching by looking at some foundational work around the topic. In their study of successful schools, Robert Garmston and Bruce Wellman (2009) cite four hats of shared leadership to define four major roles of instructional coaches.

1. Facilitating
2. Presenting
3. Coaching
4. Consulting

Using their terminology, a coach who *facilitates* may support teams by leading them through unfamiliar agendas and protocols. This coach may not have the same content-area expertise as the team members but has training on facilitation skills. A coach who *presents* typically is one who delivers content via some type of training. Garmston and Wellman (2009) use the term *coaching* to explain the role the

teacher leaders play when they take an unbiased view and help teachers and teams reflect on their work. They can support decision making, planning and carrying out instructional strategies, responding to data, and improving effectiveness of teams. These coaches might also seek out resources to streamline the work of teachers and teams in their classroom. Finally, Garmston and Wellman (2009) consider coaches who *consult*. These coaches typically have greater knowledge about content and skills teachers want to learn about. Rather than presenting new material, they work closely with teachers and teams throughout the implementation of new practices and ideas.

In our observations throughout numerous schools and districts, the roles of instructional coaches are not typically fixed on a specific approach; in other words, coaches are continuously shifting between the roles of facilitating, presenting, coaching, and consulting, depending on the context and the needs of educators they support. Yet, understanding how each role interrelates to support team work is crucial and provides coaches with a decision-making framework when approaching their work.

The increase in instructional coaching is an exciting and promising delivery model for schools to support the work of teams and impact student learning on a systemwide basis. But simply hiring more instructional coaches isn't the answer. We see three major variables impacting the effectiveness and ultimate success of instructional coaches: (1) capacity, (2) culture, and (3) context.

Capacity

If you are fortunate enough to have moved into a coaching position after having significant training and support, we congratulate you! However, if you are like many instructional coaches, you may have been assigned to your position having little to no training in coaching strategies or clarity about the role. Although there are limited data, one study examined the frequency of training of teacher leaders and coaches within urban districts. Marianna Valdez and Alexandra Broin (2015) point out that "research from the Council of Great City Schools found that 86 percent of urban districts have teacher leader roles, but only 32 percent offer specialized training for the responsibilities that go with those titles." Our observation as we work within districts throughout North America is that this tends to be far too common a reality for teachers hired in the role of instructional coach, regardless of the size or location of the district. They are often placed in the position because they are effective teachers, but the schools and districts provide little to no support or specific direction for their work.

Adding to this lack of knowledge about how to coach is the potential context a coach may find him- or herself in. For example, teachers who interact with multiple coaches at a school site may experience confusion about best practices, competing priorities, or mixed messages. Furthermore, coaches may be conducting their work without a firm framework or consistent vision for how to impact the school systematically.

Culture

The culture of a school to which a district assigns an instructional coach could impact the nature of the coaching or the approach. For example, if the district assigns a coach to a school because the school hasn't made significant progress toward accountability goals, this may result in heightened skepticism. In such a setting, staff may resist change or blame the lack of achievement on the school's demographics and its students. A toxic culture such as this could feed the impression that the coach is there to "fix" the school, making the coach's

initial work more challenging. Conversely, a school achieving at high levels could resist support from an instructional coach because staff feel they already know what they're doing and are complacent with their current achievement. In contrast, a school with a healthy school culture embraces the notion of continuous improvement as a way of doing business. The staff would likely welcome support from an instructional coach.

Each culture presents its own challenges and implications for how an instructional coach initiates support to its teams. Working with schools requires that coaches are attentive to the culture of the school *and* flexible in their approach.

Context

Schools bring in instructional coaches under a number of circumstances. Some coaches are directive, acting almost as extensions of the site administrator, building expectations with teachers, and monitoring whether teachers are using strategies. Still others are working with teachers by invitation only in order to avoid being viewed as evaluative in nature. Some coaches have one specialty area. For example, the literacy coach's focus is to empower teachers with effective practices to promote high levels of literacy; the mathematics coach's focus is to empower teachers with effective practices to support high levels of learning in mathematics, and so on.

Some schools have multiple coaches—for example, in addition to a mathematics or literacy coach, a school might also have a coach who supports practices for English learners or whose focus is instructional technology. Some schools don't have an official position of an instructional coach, but the site administrator provides the instructional coaching support. Consider the following four scenarios that represent common coaching roles.

1. Janice is highly trained in literacy strategies, and her students' achievement reflects their effectiveness. As a result of her apparent effectiveness, the district asks her to serve as a coach. It assigns Janice to four elementary schools in the district to share those strategies with other teachers. She works with each school one day per week. The fifth day is her prep day. During her sessions, she visits teachers' classrooms to observe or model literacy strategies and periodically meets with teams to train them in instructional techniques that support literacy or analyze data from a recent benchmark assessment. In addition, she works closely with the site administrator to discuss her observations. There is also a literacy and a technology coach within the school working with the same teams.

2. Mike is serving as a secondary mathematics coach, supporting a large middle school. He was hired specifically to improve mathematics scores in his school because of low achievement in this subject. He works with individual teachers and spends significant time modeling strategies in their classrooms.

3. Rachel is an aspiring administrator. She is currently completing her administrative credential program and is anxious to make an impact on the school. She works closely with the principal at one site, and her work closely aligns to the areas of student needs. She has a general elementary credential and emphasizes quality instructional practices that go across all content areas.

4. Matthew is an assistant principal at the middle school. As part of his role, he will be supporting the history and social studies and the English departments in their collaborative work.

Each scenario has different implications. A school that supports its teams with multiple coaches, as is the case with the first scenario, needs to help teachers implement clear communication systems so they aren't overwhelmed or getting mixed messages. In the second scenario, the mathematics specialist will likely emphasize specific practices that support mathematics while working with teams but needs to ensure he reinforces schoolwide practices and expectations. In the third scenario, the budding administrator might be more general in how she approaches teams but should ensure alignment with specific content areas outside her area of expertise. In the fourth scenario, the assistant principal should work with multiple content areas and provide more global support. Successful coaches take time to consider the context of the work they are doing. They recognize that a one-size-fits-all approach won't serve the teachers well and differentiate their work based on teachers' specific needs.

About This Book

Coaching is a professional development practice that has the potential for deepening the implementation of powerful instruction so students learn at high levels. Our purpose for writing this book is to provide instructional coaches and *anyone* supporting the work of teams with a guide they can use to engage in the right work—a collective focus on continuously improving a school's results in student learning. It's intended to marry the important role of coaching with the powerful work collaborative teams must accomplish.

To that end, the book goes beyond simply providing a menu of facilitation strategies from which coaches or other instructional leaders can choose. Rather, the processes and protocols in this book are grounded in a consistent foundation and framework designed to impact a system— the Professional Learning Communities at Work® (PLC) model. The major architects of this model, Richard DuFour and Robert Eaker, along with Rebecca DuFour, Thomas W. Many, and Mike Mattos (2016), operationalized this process by embracing and enacting three big ideas: (1) a focus on learning, (2) a collaborative culture, and (3) a results orientation.

Various coaching models exist, such as student learning–centered, teacher-centered, or relation-centered coaching (Sweeney, 2011). Yet these common coaching models are often implemented within the context of coaches working individually with teachers. Within the PLC model, one in which educators work in teams collaboratively and interdependently on behalf of student learning, coaches can best impact learning within a school by broadening their support from an individual level to a team level. Therefore, we advocate a hybrid model: *a team-centered, student learning–focused model of coaching.*

PLCs frame the work of collaborative teams around four specific critical questions that ensure clarity about what students need to know and do, the evidence teams seek of their accomplishments, the high-yield instructional practices, and the instructional responses to data that ensure all students learn at high levels (DuFour et al., 2016). These four critical questions are familiar to many schools that embrace

the PLC model and serve as the backbone of the work collaborative teams accomplish, as DuFour et al. (2016) describe.

1. What do we want students to know and be able to do? (In other words, what knowledge, skills, and dispositions should every student acquire as a result of this unit, this course, or this grade level?)

2. How will we know if they have learned it?

3. How will we respond when some students do not learn?

4. How will we extend the learning for students who are already proficient?

Notice that these questions are *we* statements, not *me* statements. The nature of this work is to build common clarity across teams about what they consider essential for student learning, to gather common evidence of that learning, and work together to support students who may struggle with attaining skills or require differentiation and challenge. These questions are also grounded in the mindset of taking action (DuFour et al., 2016). In *Whatever It Takes: How Professional Learning Communities Respond When Kids Don't Learn*, Richard DuFour, Rebecca DuFour, Robert Eaker, and Gayle Karhanek (2004) remind us that learning always occurs in the context of taking action, and that team members value engagement and experience as the most effective strategies for deep learning.

The instructional coach can play a vital role in supporting teams as they answer the critical questions and work in a continuous cycle of improvement. Use table I.1 to examine how instructional coaches can enhance the impact of teams through a collective inquiry process using the four critical questions of a PLC to focus the work.

Table I.1: Critical Questions and the Collective Inquiry Process

Four Critical Questions	Instructional Coaching Role Can Support
1. What do we want students to know and be able to do? (In other words, what knowledge, skills, and dispositions should every student acquire as a result of this unit, this course, or this grade level?)	Support includes: • Identifying and pacing essential standards • Clarifying "end in mind" for end-of-year and end-of-unit student performance • Unwrapping standards to identify learning targets • Identifying effective instructional strategies that result in high levels of learning in the identified learning targets
2. How will we know if they have learned it?	Support includes: • Developing or calibrating common end-of-unit assessments • Developing or calibrating common formative assessments • Recognizing that a balanced assessment system has the best opportunity to gather the right kind of data to support students
3. How will we respond when some students do not learn?	Support includes: • Analyzing assessment results to identify students requiring additional time and support • Identifying strategies for intervening with students who require additional support as well as those practices that seem highly effective
4. How will we extend the learning for students who are already proficient?	Support includes: • Identifying strategies for extending the learning of students requiring additional challenges • Designing units that embed differentiation

*Visit **go.SolutionTree.com/PLCbooks** for a free reproducible version of this table.*

In this book, we define leaders in the school as people beyond the identified administrators. A true PLC operates with the idea of shared leadership because one principal cannot realistically be the only person responsible for guiding this work. Schools typically have a leadership team made up of the principal and assistant principal, team leaders for each collaborative team, and other leaders in the building, including instructional coaches. Therefore, in some schools the coach or team leader might have greater influence on decisions than in other schools. Being familiar with the expectations around decision making is important in your role as a coach.

How to Use This Book

Make It Happen: Coaching With the Four Critical Questions of PLCs at Work® is designed to serve as a guide for instructional coaches, teacher leaders, and site and district administrators to support the work of collaborative teams. It contains practical processes and protocols coaches can use to guide teams as they engage in the real work and is focused on specific actions that propel and empower teams.

It is organized into five chapters. Chapter 1 provides information about how to get started as an instructional coach, and each remaining chapter addresses one of the four critical questions of a PLC and contains information about why and how teams answer them. These four chapters start with a graphic organizer that lays out the actions a team takes to answer the designated critical question. For each action, a corresponding tab in the book allows coaches to quickly access the information they need to consider. While many practitioners like to read a book from cover to cover, we know the value of providing easy access to a topic or idea and have intentionally developed the materials in the book to make this possible.

Each chapter begins with coaching background information, discussion about how the school's context may impact the work of teams related to that particular section, and a section that addresses the research around why teams should engage in this work. The chapters also include coaching tips, insights, templates, activities, and charts related to each action for coaches to use with their schools and teams and a vignette or two related to some of the most common issues a coach may face. Each chapter concludes with reflection questions for each action, which coaches can use to reflect on their work.

We encourage coaches to use these special features to jumpstart their work or to get deeper into implementation. Use them as is or make them your own. We know this work is difficult, but we also recognize its worth. We hope this book keeps you moving forward on the right course.

Ready, Set, Coach!

We've just reviewed several foundational elements that will assist you in charting your course as an instructional coach. Reflective questions you can use to summarize your learning and ponder the possibilities as you move forward in coaching follow in each chapter.

As you move through this book and the various actions in your coaching work, we encourage you to look back at this introduction periodically. We've discovered that with more time spent at a school, more insights

regarding some of these foundational pieces come to light. While a school may, for example, have a vision statement, it might not be a living document that school leaders continuously reference as they develop new actions and initiatives. This school might benefit from reviewing its vision as a school to ensure alignment with their actions.

Now, let's move forward by examining how to get started in your journey to becoming an effective instructional coach.

How to Get Started as an Instructional Coach

1

ACTION 1: Review the *Why* of PLCs and the Big Ideas Behind the Model

2

ACTION 2: Clarify the Foundation of the Work (Mission and Vision)

3

ACTION 3: Review or Develop Collective Commitments (Values)

4

ACTION 4: Identify Current Schoolwide and Team Goals

A C T I O N S

How to Get Started as an Instructional Coach

If you are in the role of an instructional coach or even oversee the work of an instructional coach, you should address some critical and foundational areas before jumping in. While this book is not intended to serve as an introductory PLC course, we will spend some time reviewing the main concepts so your coaching experience is aligned and impactful. We recognize that you may, in fact, already be immersed in your role as a coach. If you are in this position, we suggest you use this book as a tool you can refer to throughout your work to clarify concepts or strategies, affirm your approach, suggest potential alternatives, or simply provide food for thought.

We know the coach's role is multidimensional, one that must consider many factors such as a school's history, present culture, structure, or needs. Along the way, we make suggestions to address those considerations within the various contexts in which you may find yourself. To begin, asking yourself the following questions may bring initial clarity about your role.

- ▶ What are the expectations for my work? How will the school support me? How will I communicate with the site administrators?

- ▶ How does the school present my role to teacher teams?

- ▶ What are the current climate and culture of this school? How much experience does the school have in collaborating around student learning? What are the expectations for team collaboration?

- ▶ What commitments has the school made to support my efforts and help its teams implement necessary changes?

- ▶ Have teachers played a major role in creating the school's mission and vision?

Once the context for coaching is clear, you can move forward to assess and, if needed, establish some foundational actions that set the stage for coaching collaborative teams in a PLC. We know a school's needs may vary in terms of these foundational pieces—coaches may be supporting schools that have a history of operating as a PLC, while others may encounter schools just beginning the journey.

To ensure a coach is empowered regardless of the particular context he or she encounters, we provide specific insights, strategies, and tools for each piece. It all begins by setting the stage about the big ideas behind the work and engaging schools as they develop foundational elements on which PLCs anchor their efforts. Let's examine the four specific actions a coach would take to ensure these pieces are in place.

1. Review the *why* of PLCs and the big ideas behind the model.

2. Clarify the foundation of the work (mission and vision).

3. Review or develop collective commitments (values).

4. Identify current schoolwide and team goals.

Action 1: Review the *Why* of PLCs and the Big Ideas Behind the Model

The best source instructional leaders can use to support the development of shared knowledge about PLCs is *Learning by Doing, Third Edition* by Richard DuFour, Rebecca DuFour, Robert Eaker, Thomas W. Many, and Mike Mattos (2016). In this pivotal book, the term *professional learning community* is defined as "an ongoing process in which educators work collaboratively in recurring cycles of collective inquiry and action research to achieve better results for the students they serve" (DuFour et al., 2016, p. 10). The big ideas that drive that work are a:

▸ **Focus on learning**—Schools don't improve by focusing on teaching. They improve by focusing specifically on student learning of essential skills.

▸ **Collaborative culture**—Rather than working in isolation, educators are far more effective when they learn continuously along with their colleagues and work interdependently to merge their strengths to yield high levels of learning for all students.

▸ **Results orientation**—Educators know they are effective when students learn more. Rather than making decisions based on opinions, they actively study the results of their work regularly to make sure they are engaged in the right work. They strive to recognize collective efficacy.

Teamwork is cyclical in nature and follows a plan-do-study-act (PDSA) cycle, as shown in figure 1.1. Within this cycle, teachers work collaboratively to prioritize the skills and concepts they consider essential for student learning. They build clarity not only about the standards but about the smaller pieces of learning that staircase to the standard, in other words, the learning targets. Together, teams examine the level of rigor and the "end in mind" for student learning so each team member is clear about the journey for his or her students. They design meaningful end-of-unit and formative assessments and use them to monitor student learning of the essential standards. Then, they use those data in a formative fashion to learn about the effectiveness of their instructional strategies. Afterward, they collectively take action to further support students who didn't acquire the skills and concepts.

As a coach, you may find that a school is familiar with the definition of a PLC and even the four critical questions, but it is not yet clear on how it will put the model into action. The model itself isn't yet visible to the school. Its staff may need support through a number of vehicles, including visiting schools operating as PLCs, conducting a book study on key resources, examining resources offered through sites such as AllThingsPLC (www.allthingsplc.info), or watching videos, such as those offered

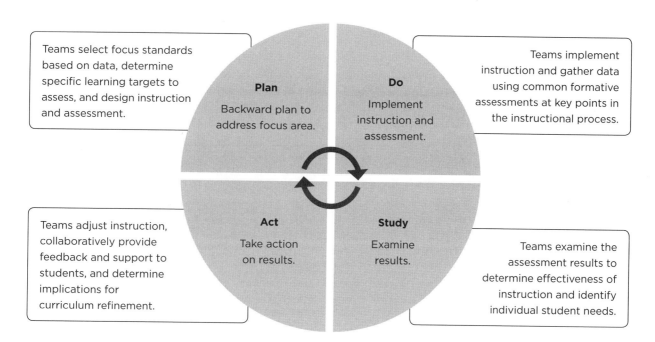

Teams select focus standards based on data, determine specific learning targets to assess, and design instruction and assessment.

Plan
Backward plan to address focus area.

Do
Implement instruction and assessment.

Teams implement instruction and gather data using common formative assessments at key points in the instructional process.

Teams adjust instruction, collaboratively provide feedback and support to students, and determine implications for curriculum refinement.

Act
Take action on results.

Study
Examine results.

Teams examine the assessment results to determine effectiveness of instruction and identify individual student needs.

Source: Adapted from Bailey & Jakicic, 2017, p. 3.

Figure 1.1: PDSA cycle.

through Global PD (www.solutiontree.com /video-library). (Visit **go.SolutionTree.com /PLCbooks** to access live links to the websites mentioned in this book.)

We also found it effective having teams model their work using a fishbowl strategy, which allows outside participants to quietly observe a process in action. After a specified period of watching, observers debrief and share notes about what they saw related to the process, culture, and focus during the collaborative team meeting. For example, observers may note strategies a team uses to ensure that they stay on topic during their agenda or how they make decisions around assessment planning.

Another aspect we found helpful is to clarify how teams within a school use their collaborative time. One helpful tool is an organizer that embeds the cycle of inquiry, the critical questions, and the actions needed within each phase. Figure 1.2 (page 14) shows an example

of this organizer. You'll note that there is an additional question embedded in the process. This question often relates directly to the roles instructional coaches play: What quality instructional strategies will result in high levels of student learning?

In tandem with the organizer, coaches may use a common agenda that embeds the continuous-improvement process so teams can focus their efforts within their collaborative meetings. Figure 1.3 (page 15) offers such an agenda. It embeds the simple steps of *focus it* (to establish the purpose of the meeting and what will take place), *do it* (to accomplish the plan), and *review it* (so the team is planning ahead to the next collaborative meeting and clarifying anything that should take place in between). The cycle is there to remind teams of the PDSA cycle. Team members can circle the appropriate action based on where the team is in the cycle.

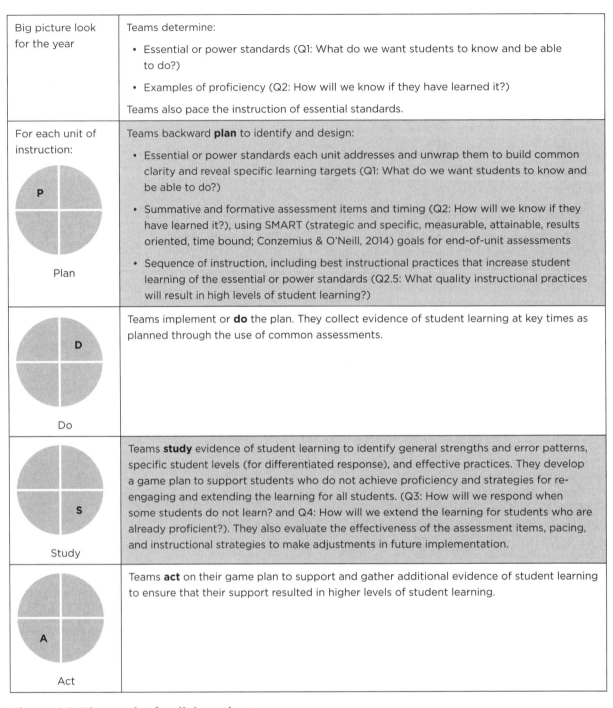

Big picture look for the year	Teams determine:
	• Essential or power standards (Q1: What do we want students to know and be able to do?)
	• Examples of proficiency (Q2: How will we know if they have learned it?)
	Teams also pace the instruction of essential standards.
For each unit of instruction: P Plan	Teams backward **plan** to identify and design: • Essential or power standards each unit addresses and unwrap them to build common clarity and reveal specific learning targets (Q1: What do we want students to know and be able to do?) • Summative and formative assessment items and timing (Q2: How will we know if they have learned it?), using SMART (strategic and specific, measurable, attainable, results oriented, time bound; Conzemius & O'Neill, 2014) goals for end-of-unit assessments • Sequence of instruction, including best instructional practices that increase student learning of the essential or power standards (Q2.5: What quality instructional practices will result in high levels of student learning?)
D Do	Teams implement or **do** the plan. They collect evidence of student learning at key times as planned through the use of common assessments.
S Study	Teams **study** evidence of student learning to identify general strengths and error patterns, specific student levels (for differentiated response), and effective practices. They develop a game plan to support students who do not achieve proficiency and strategies for re-engaging and extending the learning for all students. (Q3: How will we respond when some students do not learn? and Q4: How will we extend the learning for students who are already proficient?). They also evaluate the effectiveness of the assessment items, pacing, and instructional strategies to make adjustments in future implementation.
A Act	Teams **act** on their game plan to support and gather additional evidence of student learning to ensure that their support resulted in higher levels of student learning.

Figure 1.2: The work of collaborative teams.

*Visit **go.SolutionTree.com/PLCbooks** for a free reproducible version of this figure.*

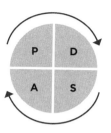

Facilitator:	Recorder:
Timekeeper:	Norms:

1. **Focus it (first three to five minutes):** Review the meeting focus and desired end result. Provide a brief description of the process.

   • Where are we in the cycle? What did we plan to accomplish today?

   • What will we walk away having done or created (for example, decisions, products, plan of action)?

   • What process will we be using (for example, brainstorming, examining protocol for reviewing student work, identifying assessment items)?

2. **Do it (majority of the meeting):** Discuss and determine actions (time allotted _____).

   • Facilitator guides the team through the process.

   • Recorder takes notes on key decisions or products made.

   • Timekeeper helps to monitor the progress of the team during the allotted time.

3. **Review it (last five minutes):** Discuss what the team accomplishes and determine next steps and assignments (time varies). Collaboratively establish the next agenda.

Figure 1.3: Sample meeting agenda.

*Visit **go.SolutionTree.com/PLCbooks** for a free reproducible version of this figure.*

Action 2: Clarify the Foundation of the Work (Mission and Vision)

As an instructional coach, it is important to examine existing mission and vision statements. If a school's mission and vision are clear, all stakeholders know their purpose and where they're trying to go. These drive their improvement process and the specific actions the school will take. Once the school establishes these two elements, it can implement a campuswide conversation to clarify the behaviors everyone must commit to in order to accomplish that vision. Finally, once the school defines the vision and values, it establishes specific goals (in other words, SMART goals) that close the gap between its current reality and the future it is trying to create (DuFour et al., 2016).

Figure 1.4 helps demonstrate the relationship of these foundational elements to the purpose and structure of a PLC.

Mission

A school's mission statement should reflect its purpose. It answers the question, "Why do we exist?" In a PLC, that purpose is simple: The mission is learning. Whose learning? The students and the educators. Most schools have a mission statement. We encourage you to review and reference it as you do this work.

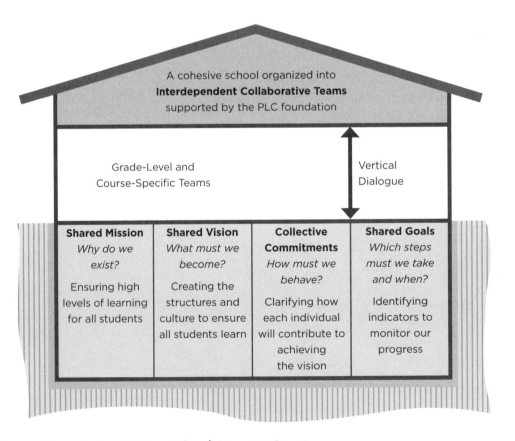

Source: Mattos, DuFour, DuFour, Eaker, & Many, 2016, p. 12.

Figure 1.4: The PLC structure.

Vision

A school's vision is a statement of where it is trying to go, answering the question, "What must this school become?" This question asks the school to picture itself in the future having achieved its mission of ensuring high levels of learning for all. The vision defines the evidence that would be in place—in other words, describing the culture within the school, its structures to support students, and the institutionalized actions that reflect a school that meets its mission. If your school doesn't yet have a vision statement that clarifies the future it is trying to create, try working with the site administrator to facilitate a conversation. This conversation ideally engages all stakeholders in defining the school they would like to see that reflects their beliefs.

Coaching Insight

Schools who develop a vision are creating a picture of what their ideal future will be. This vision should be inspirational and represent something that teachers believe is important and worth fighting for. We know working as a PLC includes difficult work, and it's easy for teams to give up if they don't perceive that the ultimate outcome is worth the work it takes. This means that it's important to involve as many people as possible in creating the vision so they each have some input into the outcome. Also, the more tangible the vision feels to teachers, the more willing they will be to participate in ensuring its outcome. This means that, if possible, the staff should be involved in developing the vision.

What if Our School Hasn't Established Its Vision?

We've created visions using different processes, but one of our favorites is a version of the process Timothy D. Kanold (2011) suggests in his book *The Five Disciplines of PLC Leaders*. In his process, he engages all stakeholders to create *Imagine* statements that describe a compelling picture of the school's future. The process starts with the facilitator asking teams to consider what their future school system would look like and offering some Imagine statements for teams to consider, such as the following:

Imagine a school where every student has access to and equal opportunity for success in each grade level and each course within the curriculum.

Imagine a school where every student has access to relevant, engaging, and meaningful learning experiences every day.

Imagine a school where technology strategies are integrated into the student learning experience and used as a tool for engagement and motivation every day.

Imagine a school where every faculty and staff member works interdependently and positively in a collaborative community to erase inequities in student learning.

Imagine a school where every administrator, faculty member, and staff member is fully engaged and enjoys his or her work.

Imagine a school where every teacher uses formative and summative assessments that inform, enhance, and motivate student learning and improve instruction. (Kanold, 2011, pp. 12–13g)

As participants consider this ideal school of the future, they begin to define what it will look like as they work together to make it happen.

What Is the Coach's Role if Our School Already Has a Vision?

More frequently than not, schools have already developed a vision for their ideal school. When this is the case, the coach's role may be to help the staff articulate specific steps they need to take for their vision to become reality. Or, the school may task the coach to work with teams to engage in the practices necessary to succeed in fulfilling the vision.

As a possible starting point, the coach may suggest that the staff use the continuum related to a school's vision included in *Learning by Doing* (DuFour et al., 2016). Figure 1.5 illustrates this continuum.

Indicator	Pre-Initiating	Initiating	Implementing	Developing	Sustaining
Shared Vision We have a shared understanding of and commitment to the school we are attempting to create.	No effort has been made to engage staff in describing the preferred conditions for the school.	A formal vision statement has been created for the school, but most staff members are unaware of it.	Staff members have participated in a process to clarify the school they are trying to create, and leadership calls attention to the resulting vision statement on a regular basis. Many staff members question the relevance of the vision statement, and their behavior is generally unaffected by it.	Staff members have worked together to describe the school they are trying to create. They have endorsed this general description and use it to guide their school-improvement efforts and their professional development.	Staff members can and do routinely articulate the major principles of the school's shared vision and use those principles to guide their day-to-day efforts and decisions. They honestly assess the current reality in their school and continually seek more effective strategies for reducing the discrepancy between that reality and the school they are working to create.

Source: DuFour et al., 2016, p. 48.

Figure 1.5: PLC continuum related to a school's shared vision.

To use this protocol, teachers read each description noting the terms and ideas that best articulate their current reality. For example, schools in the *implementing* category have a vision, and their leaders (coaches, administrators, and team leaders) refer to that vision regularly. If you are working in such a school, you'll want to ask yourself whether you are articulating these important connections when you're working with teams. To continue to move forward, read the next level's description, *developing*, to see what actions will help the school move forward. In this case, the vision is the foundation for school improvement and professional development. As a coach, you can help facilitate a plan for the steps teams must take and provide embedded professional development to increase teams' capacity.

Action 3: Review or Develop Collective Commitments (Values)

Collective commitments, or values, answer the question "How must we behave to create the school that achieves our purpose?" (DuFour et al., 2016, p. 41). In this process, school staff are making commitments to act in in a way that moves them toward their mission and vision. It embraces the notion that each staff member contributes to school success, and in order to maximize that success, they are willing to behave accordingly.

Ideally, commitments go beyond meeting norms and delve into deeper mindsets and practices. Compare two teams' differing sets of commitments in figure 1.6.

Team 1 Commitments	Team 2 Commitments
We will come to our meetings on time. We won't interrupt each other. We will not grade homework during the meetings.	We will work efficiently and focus on student learning at all meetings. We will work within a continuous-improvement cycle and commit to collaborative planning, monitoring, and using information about our students' learning to help them learn more. We will base our decisions on information or data around student learning, not on preferences or power. We will work interdependently using our individual strengths. If we disagree about an approach, we will build consensus based on what's best for students at that point in time. We will hold ourselves accountable for the work.

Figure 1.6: Two sets of team commitments.

Which team will benefit from its commitments? Team 1 focuses primarily on meeting norms and social behaviors—something we call *playing nice in the sandbox*. Its statements speak to issues of getting along, being respectful, and basically acting like a professional during a collaborative meeting. But simply being professional doesn't help a team reach its mission of ensuring high levels of learning for all students. Consider team 2's commitments. This team is committing to behaviors that will take it toward its mission. While these team members also address the notions of working professionally, the major focus is on their commitment to work collaboratively for their students' benefit.

How do teams establish their commitments? Coaches can facilitate the development of schoolwide or team commitments through the use of facilitating questions. The primary question we ask when developing commitments is: "What behaviors must we consistently demonstrate to ensure we reach our vision for our school? What behaviors will ensure our work is productive and effective?"

3

Teams can use more specific questions to prompt conversation and potential commitment statements, such as the following.

▸ How will we ensure a focus on the work?

▸ What commitments must we make that will lead us to ensuring a guaranteed curriculum for our students?

Schools and teams engaging in the development of commitments often embed a formal sign-off within their process.

Action 4: Identify Current Schoolwide and Team Goals

The power of writing goals is that the people involved take collective responsibility for the students they serve. The process generally starts with the school's leadership team that considers the district's goals, the school and team's current reality based on data they analyze, and the school's vision for the future. Note that data don't always mean test scores but can also include attendance; grades; student, teacher, and parent perceptions; observations; professional learning information; and so on. We know that when schools set a few goals for the year, this laser-like focus keeps the school moving forward. When schools set many goals, everyone loses his or her focus and it's unlikely the power of teamwork will help them accomplish these goals. Once the school has written its goals, it communicates these goals to all stakeholders.

However, schools must spend time examining and reviewing student data before beginning the process of writing SMART goals. Then, coaches can determine how to help with the writing of SMART goals and action plans.

Examine and Review Student Data

Educators can obtain data from a number of sources, such as high-stakes assessments, benchmark assessments, behavioral data, and so on. Coaches may be part of facilitating a schoolwide process to engage stakeholders

in analyzing these data systematically. We've had success using a whole-faculty protocol called PAVE IT (see figure 1.7). This protocol helps pave the way in establishing priorities for improvement, setting the stage for annual SMART goals.

The PAVE IT protocol begins by dividing a staff into mixed teams, each of which will study a category of data related to the school. For example, a team made of multiple grade levels and content areas might examine school discipline data, another team might examine attendance data, and still another might examine academic achievement data. The general goal of all teams is to examine their data, determine any patterns or trends, and develop recommendations for taking action.

The process each team works through is described in the protocol and includes clarifying the purpose for looking at the data, reframing the data visually to highlight any key facts that emerge, and identifying any additional information or questions that arise from their analysis. After each team completes its analysis, team members present their information to the rest of the school. The final result of the process is to outline specific actions to impact each area as part of the school improvement process.

Figure 1.8 (page 23) shows a note page for the PAVE IT protocol. Teams can use it to record individual or group responses in conjunction with the protocol.

Purpose: Build shared knowledge about relevant areas impacting the school and its students.

Structure: Teachers work in mixed teams to examine schoolwide data, communicate trends, and engage in developing action plans.

Preparation: Collect information and data sources in key areas. Suggested areas include—

- Demographic
- Achievement
- Perception
- Schoolwide processes
- Discipline
- Attendance
- Tardiness
- Referrals for additional services

Process

The process has two parts.

1. Instructional leader or leaders frame the purpose for the exercise and review norms prior to beginning the process.

2. Instructional leaders engage teams in the PAVE IT protocol. Each team should have a facilitator, timekeeper, and recorder.

Time Frame	Process	Description	Facilitator Notes
Five to ten minutes	**P**ose questions, make predictions, and identify any potential biases before looking at the information.	Discuss the why behind looking at the data; what questions do you want to answer? • "We are exploring these data to learn . . ." • "I wonder . . ." • "Some expectations I have before learning about these data are . . ."	Start with an individual reflection and then go around the room once allowing each participant to briefly share out. Record reflections on chart paper with a table. You don't necessarily have to have one response for each item, but the recorder should note their comments in the appropriate column. Purpose (or Why) / Questions / Possible Bias or Predictions

Figure 1.7: PAVE IT—A whole-faculty protocol for looking at schoolwide data. continued →

Ten to thirty minutes	**A**nalyze the information.	Spend time examining these data and identifying the information coming from these data. Examine these data from both a big-picture viewpoint and by looking at specific subgroups, including English language status, gender, grade level, and ethnicity. Describe without making judgments or imposing opinions. Guiding questions include: What information, patterns, or trends surface from these data? Any surprises? Any further questions?	Begin by taking five to ten minutes to individually examine data. During this time, take notes about observations, patterns, or any questions that surface during the examination. You can write these on sticky notes if desired. After individual reflection time, share out your observations using one of the following two options. 1. Implement a chart, collecting information from each participant by going once around the room for each to share. 2. Post sticky notes, arranging them around common theme and topics. Once you gather information, you can also identify any questions or need for further information.
Ten minutes	**V**isually represent the data.	Create a poster restating and summarizing these data.	Collaboratively recreate these data into a poster that communicates the findings quickly and clearly. Use infographics and other strategies to communicate the information, but remind members to represent facts obtained, not opinions. You can post questions if desired.
Five minutes for each area	**E**xplain the facts.	Take turns sharing out the team's data to the other teams.	Stick to the facts and what data show.
Five to ten minutes	**I**nfer from facts.	Discuss hypotheses for your current reality; identify any further information you need.	Use brainstorming and outline hypotheses. **Note:** Individual teams could start this and then supplement when sharing with other team members in the school.
Ten to twenty minutes	**T**ake action.	Follow these three steps. 1. Establish SMART goals. 2. Generate and record possible solutions and criteria for success. Solutions should address areas identified and take concerns into consideration. 3. Generate specific action plan (time line, who is responsible, and so on).	Use brainstorming activities to plan specific actions. **Note:** The actions should target hypothesis areas. Actions may include: • Implementing a program to directly impact an area • Adjusting communications with families or other stakeholders • Participating in professional development • Building schoolwide commitment for implementing key instructional strategies

Note: You can vary and adjust the structure of this protocol to implement across more than one session.

Visit go.SolutionTree.com/PLCbooks for a free reproducible version of this figure.

Data area: _____

Team members: _____

Pose questions and any potential bias or predictions.

Purpose: Why Is This an Important Area?	Questions We Want to Answer	Possible Bias or Predictions About What We'll Find

Analyze the information.

Factual statements about the information (what do we see, notice?)

General:

Specific subgroup information:

Trends:

Infer from facts:

Hypothesis or Hunch	Questions to Answer	Sources of Information to Examine to Support or Dismiss Hypothesis

Take action using the following three steps.

1. Establish SMART goal or goals.

2. Generate possible solutions and criteria for success. Solutions should address areas identified and take concerns into consideration. Determine solutions as a team using criteria for acceptability.

3. Generate recommendations for a specific action plan (time line, who is responsible, and so on).

By When	Action	By Whom	Evidence of Implementation

4

Figure 1.8: Note page for PAVE IT protocol.

*Visit **go.SolutionTree.com/PLCbooks** for a free reproducible version of this figure.*

Once teams analyze data and identify specific areas of need, the next step is for each collaborative team to set its own SMART goals. Teams use SMART goals to develop collective responsibility for all their students and set specific targets to improve learning. Teams start writing these goals by identifying their current reality around specific areas. For example, they may look at achievement results and commit to improve student learning that test scores measure. They may look at failure rates and commit to improving student success in their classes. Quality SMART goals consist of two parts: (1) the goal itself and (2) the action plan.

1. **The goal itself:** This may start with the team's current reality and what the final desired outcome will be. The goal reflects the characteristics that come from the acronym: strategic and specific, measurable, attainable, results oriented, and time bound (Conzemius & O'Neill, 2014). To be strategic and specific, the team must align the goal to the district and school goals. To be measurable, there must be a way to determine whether the team is making progress on improving student learning. To be attainable, the goal must be possible to achieve but also require working together to make a difference. Results-oriented goals must have student learning as an outcome rather than the completion of a process or task. Finally, the goal must be time bound. This means there is an anticipated completion date.

2. **The action plan:** Some consider this the SMART goal's most important part—the action plan the team puts together to accomplish the goal. This plan must be specific and include actions the team can control.

Teams write SMART goals on multiple levels and generally align them to the school and district's global goals. Initially, a school might write long-term annual SMART goals based on core areas of learning, such as literacy and mathematics. Specific grade-level or course teams contribute to the development of annual goals. Additionally, teams can also establish SMART goals on a short-term basis, designed to create improvement targets as they teach instructional units. Whether to write long-term goals (usually for the entire school year) or short-term goals (often based on a unit of instruction) often depends on the team's experience in writing and using goals. We recommend that teams start with year-long goals when beginning the process, so they can learn together how best to write the goals and action plans. Once they are more comfortable with the process, they can shorten the time they need for planning and alignment. Table 1.1 reviews the criteria for planning SMART goals.

One common mistake we see teams make is to write a SMART goal that relies on the team completing a list of activities rather than accomplishing a goal they set for improving student achievement. For example, when a team sets the goal to implement a new reading program, they can check it off as accomplished at the end of the year. A results-oriented SMART goal would instead sound something like this: Reading achievement will increase from 78 percent of students proficient on the state test to 90 percent of students proficient on this test.

Help Teams Write SMART Goals and Action Plans

In many schools, it is the team leader's responsibility to facilitate the process of writing SMART goals and action plans for their teams. How the coach is involved in this process might depend on the context in which the

4

Table 1.1: Criteria for Planning SMART Goals

Criteria	Application
Strategic and specific	The team goal aligns to the district and school goals.
Measurable	Measurable goals allow the team to monitor the effectiveness of its action plan. We recommend a variety of measures, including test scores, graduation rates, grades, and attendance.
Attainable	Attainable goals have a likelihood of success but also expect the team to stretch itself beyond what it accomplished in the past. If team members look at the range of data over the last several years, they'll see that scores likely fluctuated due to a number of factors. The team should make sure its new goals increase in achievement over previous years.
Results oriented	Don't make the mistake of writing a process goal, one that just requires the team to check off as accomplished. For example: *Implement the new reading program* is a process goal, while *Improve reading scores from 72 percent of students proficient or beyond to 82 percent of students proficient or beyond* is a results-oriented goal.
Time bound	By determining a time period for a goal (year, unit, quarter), there is a sense of urgency for accomplishment. If there is no time constraint, completion could take several years.

*Visit **go.SolutionTree.com/PLCbooks** for a free reproducible version of this table.*

coach is working. For example, an elementary literacy coach may be more directive in writing team SMART goals in English language arts for each grade-level team. The coach may want to focus on a few specific strategies at each grade level so the school gathers data on the effectiveness of these strategies. On the other hand, an instructional coach at a middle school may be working with teams without specific content knowledge of certain courses. In this case, the coach might be able to see the connections across subject areas on which teams could capitalize.

Whether you are a team leader or an instructional coach, the activities in figure 1.9 (page 26) can help you develop team goals.

Following is a five-step protocol for writing an annual SMART goal.

1. Have teams examine the data that exist about the current reality at the school or grade level. Use the guiding question "What are the strengths and weaknesses you see in these

data?" (Note: You can use the PAVE IT protocol in figure 1.7 on pages 21–22 to engage faculty in an examination of their schoolwide data.) The conversation should focus on team practices they control, not students. Once they analyze the data, identify the greatest area of need. This serves as the basis for creating your SMART goal. Choose a goal that represents the greatest area of need and will have the greatest impact on student learning. Using the previous criteria, teams can write the goal in SMART format in section 1 (Goal) on the action-planning template. Figure 1.10 (page 27) shows an example of a completed template for third grade. (You can find a blank reproducible for teams to use on page 32.)

2. Then, have teams make a list of factors they can't control, such as: student poverty, parents who don't follow up, and so on. We've sometimes seen

4

The following are examples of goals a team might set. For each goal, determine if it includes all the criteria of a SMART goal.

Example	S	M	A	R	T
A middle school sees that writing is an area of weakness, so the seventh-grade science team sets the following goal: Last year, 54 percent of our students were proficient or beyond on the district's writing assessment. This year we will increase that to 64 percent of students being proficient or beyond.					
A high school world history team writes, "We will reduce the number of students failing world history by 10 percent."					
The elementary school-improvement teams write, "We will create a system of response for students who aren't learning at the same rate as expected."					
The algebra 1 team writes, "We will ensure that all students are proficient or above."					
The fifth-grade team writes, "We will increase the amount of cooperative learning activities by 25 percent."					

Take one of the following ideas and write a SMART goal your team could create with all the SMART criteria included.

Proposed Goals

The five goals:

1. Implement the new reading curriculum so all fifth graders become better readers.

2. Decrease the number of students failing one or more classes.

3. Increase the number of students who are successful in our most rigorous classes.

4. Help students do better on high-stakes tests.

5. Reduce the number of students who don't turn in their homework and assignments.

Figure 1.9: Activities to plan team goals.

*Visit **go.SolutionTree.com/PLCbooks** for a free reproducible version of this figure.*

the goal-setting process get derailed when teams focus on these issues. By acknowledging this right away, they can put these concerns aside. They can list these concerns in section 2 on the template (Factors We Can't Change).

3. Have teams list current practices they want to continue using because they are effective for improving student achievement in template section 3 (Current Strengths). Note: Include this step because it's important that teams don't feel as though they have to start completely over.

4. In the next step, ask teams to brainstorm the circumstances or conditions that are getting in the way of all students learning at high levels. They list these in section 4 (Obstacles) and may include items such as materials, time issues, or even lack of teacher training.

5. Finally, in the last section (Action Plan), teams describe the steps they will take in order to overcome the obstacles they've listed. Notice that these steps are directly tied to obstacles. Teams write these steps in section 5 (Action Plan).

Figure 1.11 (page 28), figure 1.12 (page 29), and figure 1.13 (page 30) show examples of completed SMART goals worksheets for elementary, middle, and high school.

Use the Coaching Reflection reproducible on page 33 to reflect on the information you explored in this chapter.

1. Goal:

Last year 67 percent of third-grade students were proficient or beyond on the end-of-year test. Our goal this year is for 77 percent of students to be proficient or beyond.

3. Current Strengths:

Strengths include:

- We use interim assessments to identify students who need support.
- We share students during our intervention time so each teacher has a more homogenous group.

4. Obstacles:

- Many students come to us with significant reading deficits.

- The reading program we have doesn't strongly align with the standards.

- We don't get frequent or targeted enough feedback to respond quickly.

5. Action Plan:

- Develop a strong Tier 3 program that provides support for different reading issues.
- Use benchmarking to become specific about student needs.

- Identify essential standards and create a pacing guide to make sure we have enough time to teach, assess, and provide corrective instruction.

- Start writing and using common formative assessments for our essential standards.

-

-

2. Factors We Can't Change:

- Many of our students live in poverty and don't have many resources at home.
- Some parents don't follow through with homework or reading expectations.

Source: Adapted from Dennis King, Solution Tree Associate. Used with permission.

Figure 1.10: Sample third-grade team SMART goal planning tool.

Visit go.SolutionTree.com/PLCbooks for a free reproducible version of this figure.

SMART Goals Worksheet				
School: Sunrise Elementary School — Team name: Third Grade — Team leader: Beth				
Team members: Beth, Jackie, Sara, Karen				
District goal: Ninety percent of all students will be reading at proficient or higher levels as measured by their performance on the state reading test.				
School goal: Ninety percent of all students will be reading at proficient or higher levels as measured by their performance on the state reading test.				
Team SMART Goal	**Strategies and Action Steps**	**Responsibility**	**Time Line**	**Evidence of Effectiveness**
Our reality: Last year 78 percent of students met or exceeded standards on the state reading test. Our goal: This year, 90 percent of our students will meet or exceed standards on the state reading test.	During the first quarter, our team will identify the essential standards for the third-grade reading curriculum and examine our pacing guides to make sure they reflect the importance of these standards.	All team members will be responsible for the final list of essential standards. Our instructional coach, Jackie, will be the facilitator.	Finished by the last day of the quarter, October 30	The outcome of this step will be a list of the essential standards for all the strands in the English language arts curriculum: reading, writing, speaking and listening, and language. We will have a copy of the pacing guide with these standards highlighted.
	In the second quarter, we will start writing common formative assessments in English language arts.	We will all participate in writing the assessments. As we get started, we'll look for appropriate text passages for the assessment tasks together during our meetings. But after the second quarter, each of us can take turns with that task.	We will write and use a common formative assessment every three weeks.	At the end of quarters 2 and 3, we will examine our benchmark reading scores to see if this is making a difference. We will be open to tweaking our work depending on what the results say.

Figure 1.11: Sample elementary school SMART goals worksheet.

4

SMART Goals Worksheet				
School: Woodlawn Middle School Team name: Eighth-Grade Social Studies Team leader: Sandra				
Team members: Sandra and Jacob				
District goal: All schools will improve student writing scores by at least 10 percent.				
School goal: Ninety percent of all students will be proficient or better writers as measured by their performance on the state writing test.				
Team SMART Goal	**Strategies and Action Steps**	**Responsibility**	**Time Line**	**Evidence of Effectiveness**
Our reality: Last year 85 percent of students were proficient or better on the writing test. Our goal: This year 90 percent of students will be proficient on the writing test.	During the first quarter, we will focus on using evidence as a means of supporting ideas in writing. We will work with document-based questions.	Team members will bring sample primary and secondary source documents to the meeting to develop the document-based questions for that unit.	During week 3 of the quarter we will do the first activity. Students will receive feedback within one week and will rewrite based on feedback. Same process during week 6.	We will administer a document-based question as a common assessment at the end of the quarter. We want at least 85 percent of students to meet expectations by the end of the first quarter writing test.
	During the second quarter, we will focus on using examples as a means of supporting ideas in writing. Students will be expected to use specific historical information in their writing.	Each unit of instruction will include at least one essay that requires students to use examples in their support. Questions will be developed at team meetings.	Four chapters or units are covered during quarter 2. There will be one essay for each one.	The end-of-quarter-2 assessment will include an essay question that requires students to use examples in their answers. At least 85 percent will be proficient.

Figure 1.12: Sample middle school SMART goals worksheet.

4

SMART Goals Worksheet				
School: Washington High School Team name: Algebra Team leader: Brian				
Team members: Mary, Brian, Heather, Cindy				
District goal: Eighty percent of students will demonstrate proficiency in mathematics as measured by their performance on the state mathematics test.				
School goals: Eighty percent of students will demonstrate proficiency in mathematics as measured by their performance on the state mathematics test.				
Team SMART Goal	**Strategies and Action Steps**	**Responsibility**	**Time Line**	**Evidence of Effectiveness**
Our reality: Last year, 69 percent of students met or exceeded standards on the state mathematics test. Our goal: This year, 80 percent of our students will meet standards on the state mathematics test.	We will examine our standards and choose the most essential (power) standards using the criteria endurance, leverage, and readiness. We will identify the essential standards in each unit of instruction.	We will participate fully in this step, making sure we build consensus around the final decision.	We will complete this process during the first four team meetings of the year.	We will create a document. As we move through the year, we'll make sure that any changes we need to make are recorded for the following year.
	Approximately every three weeks, we will administer a common assessment covering the key targets identified from the essential standards. We will give students who don't demonstrate proficiency additional instruction and reassess them to be sure they master the standards.	Team members will write the assessment together. They will administer it within the time line assigned. After giving the assessment, the team will use the data process to determine how to respond.	Our plan is to assess frequently, at least every three weeks, and meet as soon as possible after the assessment to create a response plan.	We will use our end-of-unit tests to make sure all students are mastering the essential standards.

Figure 1.13: Sample high school SMART goals worksheet.

4

Conclusion

This chapter focused on how to get started as an instructional coach, exploring topics such as expectations for the work, how schools support coaches, communication with teachers and administrators, school culture, working with collaborative teams, and more.

Focusing on the following four foundational ideas, a coach's work begins by:

▸ Reviewing the *why* of PLCs and the big ideas behind the model

▸ Clarifying the foundation of the work (mission and vision)

▸ Reviewing or developing collective commitments (values)

▸ Identifying current schoolwide and team goals

With these foundational pieces in place, coaches can begin focusing on working to support students and teachers within the framework of the four critical questions of PLCs. The next chapter explores the first question: What do we want students to know and be able to do? (In other words, what knowledge, skills, and dispositions should every student acquire as a result of this unit, this course, or this grade level?)

SMART Goal Planning Tool

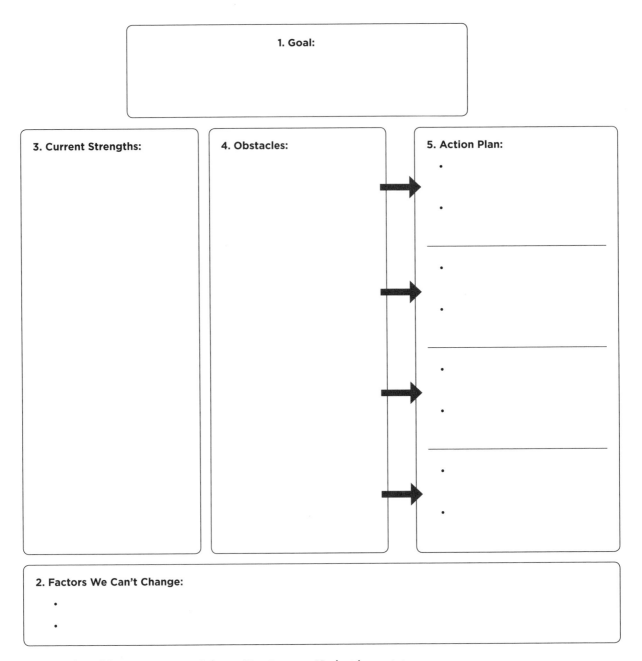

Source: Adapted from Dennis King, Solution Tree Associate. Used with permission.

Coaching Reflection

Use the questions in this chart to reflect on the information you explored in chapter 1.

What do I know about my role and the expectations for my work?	What did I learn about the culture of my school?
What is the current structure of the school and its collaborative time?	What background knowledge do teams have about PLCs and working collaboratively to support student learning?
What is the school's status regarding its mission, vision, commitments, and goals?	What might be my first area to focus on as an instructional coach?

Coaching focus for PLC critical question 1:
What do we want students to know and be able to do?

1

ACTION 1: Identify Essential Standards
▸ Establish the *why* behind essential standards.
▸ Identify draft grade-level or course essential standards.
▸ Engage in vertical alignment conversations.
▸ Support and monitor the use of essential standards.

2

ACTION 2: Clarify Proficiency
▸ Establish the importance of clarifying the end-of-year picture of proficiency.
▸ Use common language to characterize rigor and proficiency.
▸ Include singletons in the work.

3

ACTION 3: Establish Common Pacing
▸ Support teams' understanding of pacing.
▸ Collaboratively build a pacing guide.
▸ Include singletons in the process.
▸ Monitor the work.

4

ACTION 4: Unwrap the Standards
▸ Establish the purpose for unwrapping.
▸ Engage teams using an unwrapping protocol.
▸ Examine the rigor of learning targets.

What Do We Want Students to Know and Be Able to Do?

If a school's mission is to ensure all students learn at high levels, the natural question that comes to mind is: *Learn what?* The answer is driven by digging into the first critical question teams address in the cycle of improvement: What do we want students to know and be able to do? (DuFour et al., 2016). In order to effectively answer this question, team members must build consensus about four key actions.

1. Identifying the most important or *essential standards* they will ensure students learn and therefore prioritize in their teaching

2. Discussing and clarifying what the standards mean and what *proficiency* looks like

3. Developing a *common pacing guide* that ensures adequate and specific instructional periods during which the essential standards are taught for implementation

4. Unwrapping the standards to identify the *learning targets* necessary for students to learn in order to master these standards

Collaborating around these four actions is critical and foundational to teamwork within a PLC and is often one of the first major decisions collaborative teams make. By engaging in processes designed to address these actions, teams build shared knowledge and collaborative clarity and focus. And rather than working in isolation, team members are doing the important work by learning together and engaging in a process that impacts their collective practice and ultimately, student learning.

Before we begin working with a school, we must explore the context of that school, including the background, culture, and curriculum.

Explore Your Context

Whenever we work with schools that want us to coach them in the PLC process, we start by getting a sense of what they are already doing related to the work and the successes they've had. We also identify the problems they've encountered. We encourage coaches to take this same approach in identifying the context of their school and its teams in terms of the work they're going to be doing. Knowing what schools and teams have done in the past about answering the four critical questions will help coaches decide what teams really need from them, as well as any successes and prior work they can ultimately build on. Teams and coaches can then decide on next steps together.

Coaches or other instructional leaders must be aware of who has decision-making power around curriculum and pacing in the school and district and any parameters or guidelines that have been established. Usually when districts are striving for uniformity across schools in their guaranteed curriculum for students, they may be concerned or resist the idea of a coach or a single site making changes to a set of essential standards or pacing. There may be benchmark assessments that align to pacing guides or other implications that the coach must consider. However, there may be opportunities for input and flexibility when it comes to these items. In these situations, we suggest sharing information and making recommendations to the decision makers in the school.

We recommend that coaches reflect on the following questions to examine the current context of their work when thinking about this first critical question.

▸ **Is a curriculum already in place? Do the teachers follow the curriculum exactly as it's written, or does each teacher interpret it for him- or herself?** Schools that have a curriculum might find the idea of identifying essential standards a bit threatening because the curriculum probably wasn't written to emphasize what will become of their essential standards. Having teams go back and highlight the essential standards (once they're identified) in their curriculum documents helps them see how they might modify what they're doing to

align with the standards. However, if identifying the essential standards doesn't lead to action, teams will likely see little improvement in student achievement.

▸ **Is there a pacing guide and, if so, how detailed is it?** Some pacing guides are written by the quarter, some by the week, some by the day. Does the district expect teachers to follow the pacing guide exactly, or is it just a suggestion? We've worked in schools where teachers are expected to follow a pacing guide that lays out, almost daily, the activities that teachers need to use in their classrooms. Coaches may need to work with the team as well as with the administration if expectations around pacing get in the way of responding effectively to student learning issues. On the other hand, we've also encountered situations where the pacing guide is open-ended and individual teachers may teach the same standards at very different times and rates. Coaches should make sure they know what the current reality is about pacing so that they can lay out a plan for getting teams on the same page.

▸ **What is the expectation for teachers teaching content at the same time?** Sometimes we encounter teachers who are reluctant to embrace this process because they are afraid to give up their autonomy. When we encounter teachers in our work who hold this perspective, we generally go back to the idea that teachers have autonomy about instructional strategies, but they must give their common formative assessments at the same time as the rest of the team so there is equity in student learning.

▸ **Has the school or district done any work with unwrapping the standards?** We frequently encounter teams who unwrapped the standards at some point but haven't really used the unwrapped standards in their day-to-day work. The process of unwrapping is the step collaborative teams take to discuss what they mean for student learning both in content and in expectations about rigor. When the Common Core standards were released, many schools and districts we worked with had teams of teachers unwrap them. Teachers who were involved in this process may not have understood the *why* behind it. Coaches want to make sure teachers understand the *why* behind unwrapping standards and how the process affects both their pacing and their assessments.

▸ **Has the school or district done any work to identify essential standards?** Some districts expect each school to carry out this process for themselves.

The advantage of this is that every teacher has input into the process and ownership in the final product. Other districts want all schools to have the same essential standards and, therefore, want a representative group of teachers to identify the essentials and then share them back to their schools. The advantage of using this process is that districts will have the same expectations for proficiency at each school. Students who move between schools in the district will have an easier transition, and the district can write benchmark assessments that all students can use. We've worked in many different settings and have seen both of these approaches work successfully. Coaches must understand the district's expectations for essential standards.

The following four actions support the work of PLC critical question 1: What do we want students to know and be able to do?

Action 1: Identify Essential Standards

When teachers don't collaborate to answer this first critical question of a PLC, each teacher will, perhaps unknowingly, choose to spend more time on standards he or she believes are most important and skim through those they don't. When this happens in schools with multiple sections at a grade level or course, students will be prepared differently for the next grade or course because they will have learned different content. Likewise, if teachers have different perceptions about what proficiency looks like for a particular standard, there will be different expectations and results in student learning across a system. Even schools with singletons (one teacher per grade level or course) will see

uneven implementation without a focus on vertical alignment.

Instead, a collaborative team in a PLC answers this first critical question by:

▸ Discussing what standards mean

▸ Defining each standard's relative importance to students learning the content and concepts of the grade or course

▸ Investigating and agreeing on what proficiency looks like for these standards

▶ Identifying what underlying learning targets a student must learn to be able to master these standards

Teams then engage in a vertical-alignment process to ensure there is coherence from grade to grade or from course to course.

Identifying essential standards, building consensus about proficiency, and developing common pacing are all the foundational pieces a team needs to have in place to ensure a guaranteed and viable curriculum. Yet, we have seen teams engage in this work because an administrator or coach asks them to do it without really understanding why this work is meaningful.

These steps describe the process that includes four major actions, which we address throughout this chapter. As an instructional coach, you will facilitate this process by taking team members through a defined process or protocol to engage in each action. Every protocol is intended to help build trust among team members and engage them in a structured conversation as they share their understanding about the meaning of the standards and our expectations about student proficiency. Teams who use protocols find it easier to keep to their agenda and avoid getting off topic. They design them to ensure that all team members have a voice in the process and some investment in the outcome.

In order to identify the essential standards, coaches must work with teams to:

▶ Establish the *why* behind essential standards

▶ Identify draft grade-level or course essential standards

▶ Engage in vertical alignment conversations

▶ Support and monitor the use of essential standards

Establish the *Why* Behind Essential Standards

Essential standards are "a carefully selected subset of the total list of the grade-specific and course-specific standards within each content area that students must know and be able to do by the end of each school year in order to be prepared to enter the next grade level or course" (Ainsworth, 2010, p. 323).

Educational researcher Robert J. Marzano (2003) researches the significant impact to student learning when schools build a guaranteed and viable curriculum. He finds that the number-one factor impacting highly effective schools is a curriculum that is guaranteed no matter which teacher is teaching it and that is viable—meaning the teachers have enough time to effectively teach it. Since the time of this research, much work has been done around the idea that the guaranteed and viable curriculum must be rigorous, and teachers must hold the expectation that all students can learn at high levels. For example, in 2008, Gary L. Williamson found a 350-Lexile point gap between the end-of-high school and college texts leading to the change in expected text complexity for the K–12 Common Core standards. Additionally, Daggett's Rigor and Relevance Framework (2012) is often cited as a tool for ensuring that curriculum, instruction, and assessments meet more complex expectations established with these standards.

Instructional coaches can be instrumental in helping teams understand the importance of answering the first critical question. They'll find that some collaborative teams are reluctant to answer the question because they believe *everything* they teach is important. Other teams might feel they're losing their autonomy when they have to agree to priorities and anticipated pacing. In both situations, the coach should make sure they answer the "Why would we do this?" question at the beginning of the work. Additionally, for teachers who think everything is important, we often hear "It might be covered on the test" as the reason not to place less emphasis on some standards. We make sure these teachers know that one step in the process is to examine the documents supporting the state (or province) test to see what it emphasizes.

For the teachers afraid to lose their autonomy, we remind them that in a PLC, teachers maintain the autonomy to use the instructional strategies they believe will work best for them and their students. They just have to make sure their students reach the same endpoint of proficiency as the other teachers on the team.

When teams engage in answering this first question, the result is a better understanding of the standards they teach. In 2010, for example, the National Governors Association Center for Best Practices and the Council of Chief State School Officers (NGA & CCSSO, 2010a, 2010b) published the Common Core State Standards, and almost every state immediately adopted them. Teachers across the United States were tasked to understand the meaning of these new standards as well as change their instructional strategies to ensure more rigorous instruction. Finding curriculum materials that aligned to these standards (and not just crosswalked to them) proved difficult for many teachers. For example, some reading series used materials that had previously been developed for older state standards and then linked, or crosswalked, them to the new standards without increasing the complexity level of those materials. Thus, on the surface, the content might have appeared to align to the new standards but, upon closer inspection, the rigor wasn't truly aligned to the new standards.

Teachers also often found that some new standards didn't have appropriate text in these materials because of the change of emphasis from literature to informational text. For example, a seventh-grade standard in English language arts (ELA) expected students to "trace and evaluate the argument and specific claims in a text, assessing whether the reasoning is sound and the evidence is relevant and sufficient to support the claims" (RI.7, NGA & CCSSO, 2010a). Teams struggled to find an argumentative text written at the appropriate grade level to teach, another to assess, and possibly a third to use for intervention. Many schools we worked with found that by engaging in the processes of identifying essential standards, unwrapping them, and developing common pacing, teams were better able to understand both the complexity and content students must learn.

Identify Draft Grade-Level or Course Essential Standards

At the beginning of the chapter, we discussed that coaches should investigate the context around curriculum expectations for their school noting how much autonomy teams have. Coaches should also become familiar with how different teams have embraced these expectations. For example, it's not uncommon for elementary teams to use a basal text and follow it unit by unit in reading.

When working with teams who are required to follow the text with fidelity, coaches will want to help them recognize places where the materials aren't aligned to the standards. At the same time, a coach may help teams who are faced with teaching fifteen different ELA standards in a seven-to-ten-day unit—which I think we can all agree is impossible. Facilitating the discussion with teachers about which standards are essential in the unit and what materials they might need to supplement the textbook is an important first step.

Other schools teach instructional units by topic. For example, a history teacher may have units such as ancient Greece, Imperial Rome, early religions, and so on. Depending on the state's (or province's) social studies standards, these units might be designed around specific standards, or the curriculum may be designed to cover these topics but not necessarily the expected standards. The role of the coach here is to make sure the team has the capacity to design a standards-based curriculum. If this is the case with a team you are coaching, you will likely need to take a more directive role to make sure team members understand how to design and use a standards-based curriculum. You may need to teach and facilitate all the actions in this chapter.

Many teachers believe if the content of their units matches the content of the standards, they're teaching the standards. Consider this Reading standard for fourth grade: "Compare and contrast a firsthand and secondhand account of the same event or topic; describe the differences in focus and the information provided" (RI.4, NGA & CCSSO, 2010a). Some teams might believe they should teach students how to compare and contrast two texts, but not necessarily a firsthand and sec- ondhand account. Other teams might focus only on point of view rather than how point of view affects the way the article is written and the content it includes.

Coaches can help teams choose essential standards by learning about their current cur- riculum reality, making sure they are familiar with the expectations for rigor from the stan- dards, and analyzing how these two align. If a team has been teaching topics rather than standards, the coach can help it see which standards are currently being met and which require teachers to write new curricula to ensure student mastery.

The following sections describe how teams can determine and prepare for implementing essential standards in the classroom.

How Collaborative Teams Determine Essential Standards

Coaches can help teachers by taking them through the seven steps for determining essen- tial standards.

1. **The coach explains the criteria for choosing essential standards and what these criteria mean:** The criteria include (1) endurance, (2) leverage, (3) readiness, and (4) prioritized for high- stakes assessments.

   ▸ A standard should have *endurance*, which is when it is something students must know for the long haul and will likely need years after they learn it.

   ▸ A standard should have *leverage*, which is when it crosses into more than one subject area.

   ▸ A standard should have *readiness*, which is when it is a prerequisite skill for something taught later that unit or that year (Ainsworth, 2004, 2010).

   ▸ Finally, a standard should be *prioritized for high-stakes assessments* (Ainsworth, 2013). (Note: Step 6 in this process also supports the use of this criterion in the decision-making process.)

2. **The coach decides how to chunk the standards, if appropriate:** For exam- ple, middle school science teams may want to work through life science first and then physical science; elementary English language arts teams may want to work through reading, writing,

and then speaking and listening and language.

3. **The coach provides an opportunity for individual team members to reflect on their own beliefs about what's important:** This is a short period of quiet time during which each team member reviews a set of standards and applies the four criteria for choosing essential standards (endurance, leverage, readiness, and prioritized for high-stakes assessments). This is an important step in the process because if teams jump right into making decisions about which standards are essential, some teachers will be left out of the process and others might take over the conversation. Team members should complete this step together in the same space. Coaches might think it's more convenient to ask each teacher to do this step prior to the meeting, but some teachers might take ten minutes to make these decisions, while others will labor over each standard for a longer period of time. Surprisingly, when someone takes a long time thinking through the process, it often becomes much harder to differentiate between essential and nonessential standards.

When teams agree to work together collaboratively, they begin to see that making decisions through consensus is often more effective than simply voting on the outcome. In a PLC environment, consensus occurs when teams meet two conditions: (1) everyone's voice is heard, and (2) the group's will is obvious even to those who most oppose it (DuFour et al., 2016). When teachers have input on decisions, they are more likely to understand the outcome and will be more likely to support it. Groups generally use consensus when the decision involves several different ideas or parameters that might impact each teacher differently. In these cases, it's important that teams consider all points of view.

4. **With the coach facilitating the process, team members begin building consensus on which standards will be on their draft list of essentials:** Teams can use specific ways to build consensus. The first is to work through any standards where there is already agreement. Some standards are so important that every team member identifies them as essential. On the other hand, all team members will likely view some standards as nonessential. Identifying these right away helps teams see where there is consensus already. Teams then work through each standard discussing which team members mark the standard as essential and why. We recommend using the same terms teams used when identifying essential standards, such as *endurance, leverage, readiness for the next level of learning,* and *prioritized for high-stakes assessments* because it gives team members specific ways to explain their thinking about the importance of a standard.

In his book *Rigorous Curriculum Design,* Larry Ainsworth (2010) suggests teams choose approximately one-third of the standards as essential. This means that courses or grade levels that have a large number of standards (such as ninety in third-grade Common Core ELA) will have more essential standards than those that start with a smaller number of standards. Coaches

1

Ways to Build Consensus on Essential Standards

The following are ways to build consensus on essential standards. The decision is easy if everyone believes the standard is essential or nonessential.

- Have members clarify why they chose a standard using the criteria *endurance, leverage, readiness,* or *prioritization on high-stakes assessments.*

- Read the standard from the course or grade level before and after yours.

- Consider other standards that might be similar (for example, you can find vocabulary standards in reading and language in the Common Core).

- Allow members to share their thinking about whether the purpose of the standard might be to introduce a new concept or to expect mastery of that concept.

- Use the *fist to five* strategy (DuFour et al., 2016) to gauge how receptive members are. The value system:

    - **Five fingers—**I love this proposal. I will champion it.

    - **Four fingers—**I strongly agree with the proposal.

    - **Three fingers—**The proposal is okay with me. I am willing to go along.

    - **Two fingers—**I have reservations and am not yet ready to support this proposal.

    - **One finger—**I oppose this proposal.

    - **Fist—**If I had the authority, I would veto this proposal, regardless of the will of the group.

---

can facilitate this process with or without having taught a course or grade level because teachers with expertise in their grade level or content area will ensure that they choose the most important standards.

5. **Once the team creates its first draft list of essential standards, the coach helps the team with several other activities to either confirm it chooses the right standards or to consider adjusting the list:** The next step is for the team to examine its current data about student learning. Are there any areas with which students seem to have more difficulty or where larger numbers of students are not reaching proficiency? In this

case, the team may want to make sure it represents these concepts more fully in its essential standards. For example, a fourth-grade team may see that vocabulary is an area of difficulty for its students. In this case, the team should identify a vocabulary standard as essential in both reading and language.

6. **With the coach facilitating, the team examines released documents to build shared knowledge about end-of-year tests to become familiar with the expectations students must meet to be proficient:** Released documents might include blueprints or proficiency documents from standardized tests used by the district or state

that explain expectations for students in that content area. For example, at the beginning of each grade level through eighth grade mathematics standards, NGA and CCSSO (2010b) discuss the most important concepts taught in that grade. When NGA and CCSSO released their Common Core mathematics standards, the two major assessment systems, the Partnership for Assessment of Readiness for College and Careers (PARCC, 2014, 2017) and the Smarter Balanced Assessment Consortium (SBAC, 2015a), published what they call mathematics content specifications. These specifications identify the major supporting and additional clusters in mathematics (PARCC, 2014, 2017; SBAC, 2015a).

Sometimes teachers fear that they are "teaching to the test" when they investigate these documents. We contend that this is just making sure everyone knows what the goal looks like. By securing copies of these documents for the team, the coach can save time by making sure teachers are using the best available information.

7. **Guided by the coach, the team works vertically with other collaborative teams in the school to make sure essential standards are aligned throughout the courses or grade levels:** Coaches may want to use the protocol for vertical alignment to facilitate this discussion (presented later in this chapter). The purpose of this step is to ensure no gaps or redundancies in learning exist for students who might only learn the essential standards. For example, the kindergarten and first-grade phonemic awareness and phonics standards lay the foundation for reading, so it's important that these standards are highly represented in the essential standards for those grade levels. On the other hand, instead of all three middle school grades (sixth, seventh, and eighth) teaching the standard of determining the central idea of a text, we recommend one grade take responsibility to teach and make sure all students know how to do this, and then the other teams can build on the skill with more complex texts.

Coaching the Issue

A first-grade team is composed of three team members. Having recently returned from a PLC institute, team members know that choosing essential standards will help them lay a solid foundation of their work for this first year of implementation. Because they don't have instructional coaches in their school, the team leaders recently received training in which they learned a protocol for answering the first PLC critical question—What do we want students to know and be able to do? Carlos, the team leader, is responsible for taking his team through the process.

- **Coach's role:** Because Carlos recently underwent some training about the process for identifying and using essential standards, he knows that he will have to take on a presenter role, especially as the team begins its work.

continued ➝

1

- **Team meeting:** The principal offered grade-level teams release time to identify their English language arts essential standards knowing that they wouldn't be able to get their draft list of standards complete in a typical forty-five-minute planning session. To do this, the principal agreed to hire substitute teachers to cover their classes. Carlos starts the meeting by sharing the research behind the work, offering an overview of the process with his team, and discussing the four criteria his team will use to choose essential standards. He gives team members the list of reading standards, including those from informational text and literature and reading foundation standards. He then asks team members to individually apply the criteria to these standards, choosing what he or she believes are essential for all students to learn. The team takes about ten minutes to engage in this step, and Carlos reminds team members that they do this individually before they begin working together.

  As they get ready to build consensus about their decisions, one team member asks an important question: "As I was making my choices, it seemed to me that for first graders, the foundational skills, especially phonics and word recognition, seem to have a higher priority to me than even the reading standards themselves. Shouldn't its essential standards, then, include more of these standards?" A discussion follows with all the team members contributing thoughts and ideas. Finally, after much debate, the team agrees to include in their essential reading standards a larger proportion of foundational skills standards to show the greater emphasis for their grade level.

- **Next steps:** The team successfully completes the process to identify its draft list of essential standards in English language arts. At the next leadership team meeting, Carlos raises the issue with other teacher leaders about their discussion of foundational standards and is pleased to hear that a similar discussion occurred with the kindergarten team.

Coaching Tips

When working with teams to identify essential standards, coaches often encounter some of the following challenges. The following are four ways to facilitate team reflective conversations and decision making through the use of questions.

1. **The team deems everything as essential:** The coach should ask, "What standards do you feel must be guaranteed?" In other words, the coach is helping teams identify what skills would prevent students from being ready for the next grade level or course.

2. **It's not a grade-level standard, or it's only a portion of the standard:** The coach should ask, "Is this truly a standard for this grade level? Is the entire standard represented or only a portion of the standard?" For example, a team might include a standard that is an expectation for a previous or future grade level. A team may write down a portion of the standard rather than the entire standard, which represents the full expectation for learning.

3. **The rigor isn't represented:** The coach should ask, "Have you identified highly prioritized standards that we know are on high-stakes assessments? Will the identified essential standards contribute to the staircase of proficiency from grade to grade within the school?"

4. **The list doesn't address content-relevant literacy standards:** This challenge applies primarily to secondary-content teams other than English. When it appears, the coach should ask, "What type of literacy skills are necessary for your students to demonstrate their knowledge of the content? Will you require them to read key documents, research information, or write to communicate their understanding of concepts and ideas?"

Coaching Preparations for Team Identification of Essential Standards

High-performing teams often build shared knowledge when they are making decisions. This means that rather than relying simply on their opinions, team members actively learn together about the topic they are considering. When team members take time to learn together, they often find that making the final decision is much easier and that teachers are more likely to confidently support it. Coaches can help teams work together to identify essential standards by doing the following six steps.

1. Help facilitate the decision about whether all teachers will be involved in the process and each school will complete the work individually or whether the district will ask representatives from each school to go through the process so all the schools in the district will have the same essential standards. When everyone participates, there is greater understanding of the process and the final outcome; when representatives participate, essential standards are the same for all schools in the district.

2. Inform teams that the process will take approximately a full six-hour day if done all at once. Teams can use their common planning time to choose draft standards and then come to the vertical alignment step prepared. It's important that all participants are available for the vertical alignment step.

3. Make sure all team members have a copy of the standards they will be working with and some highlighters to use during individual reflection time.

4. Provide a sheet with the definitions of *endurance*, *leverage*, *readiness for the next level of learning*, and *prioritized for high-stakes assessments* so team members can easily refer back to them.

5. Provide chart paper and markers for teams to use to copy their draft standards so they can edit them during the vertical-alignment process.

6. Reproduce any documents that will help teams know the ultimate expectations for students on high-stakes assessments. These might include assessment blueprints, sample questions, proficiency expectations, and rubrics for anticipated constructed responses.

Figure 2.1 (pages 46–47) outlines the protocol for choosing essential standards.

1

Step	Description	Expected Product	Coaching Role
1	The team discusses the three criteria it will use to choose its essential standards: endurance, leverage, readiness for the next level of learning, and prioritized for high-stakes assessments.	Team members will have a common understanding of how to determine which standards will be on their list and which ones will not be on their list.	The coach prepares some examples of standards that the team will be working with that might meet the criteria and those that likely will not.
2	The team considers how to chunk the standards if necessary. For example, in English language arts the first chunk can be the reading and reading foundations standards, the second chunk the writing standards, and the third chunk the language and speaking and listening standards.	For each chunk, the team will have a draft list of those standards it finds most important.	The coach prepares the materials the team needs, determines when this will happen, and facilitates conversations if possible.
3	Each team member independently works through a chunk of standards and chooses those that he or she believes fit one or more criteria.	Each team member marks his or her copy of the standards with those he or she believes are essential. Team members should complete this step while they are together, so one person doesn't spend a long time on this step. The more time a teacher takes, the harder it is to narrow the standards to the essentials.	This is a time for personal reflection. In order for each member to have a voice in the process, it's important that he or she takes time to consider which are the most important standards. Encourage team members to avoid conversation until everyone has had a chance to go through all the standards.
4	The team builds consensus on the standards, making sure all team members participate in the process. Some standards will start with total agreement (everyone believes it is or is not essential), but the majority involves discussion.	The team develops a rough draft list of essential standards, which represents the collective thinking of the team after discussion.	While team leaders should take a leadership role in this process, the coach can provide support and help teams when they get stuck. The coach can observe the process across the school and ensure teams effectively use it.
5	The team examines data about student performance. Are there areas of particular strength or weakness? If so, the team ensures their essential standards list reflects this by adding additional standards to shore up the weaknesses.	Team members make changes to the draft list that reflect strengths and weaknesses.	Looking at data can be intimidating for teams that don't do this on a regular basis. The coach should have a conversation with the team about the facts first. He or she allows team members to talk about their inferences after they acknowledge the facts. This makes the process less threatening.

| 6 | The team uses documents released by the district or state to ensure that the expectations drafted align to the expectations for students. These might include test specifications, blueprints, or documents developed by the standards writers. For example, if assessment blueprints show an emphasis on text-dependent questions, it's important that the team reflects this emphasis in the draft list. | The team can change or add to the rough draft list it puts together in order to effectively reflect what students must be able to do on high-stakes tests. | Sometimes teachers are reluctant to spend too much time on these released documents thinking they might be "teaching to the test." Coaches can explain the difference. Teachers also may feel inadequate in interpreting the blueprints and proficiency expectation documents. Coaches should be prepared to help interpret and explain these documents. |
| 7 | Team members work with the other teams in their school to vertically align their essential standards. | Coaches create a final draft list of essential standards for each team in the building, which reflects the outcomes of each of the previous steps. | Coaches can facilitate this step in order to make sure everyone's voice is heard. |

Source: Adapted from Ainsworth, 2004, pp. 103–104.

Figure 2.1: Protocol for choosing essential standards.

Engage in Vertical Alignment Conversations

The purpose of engaging in vertical alignment is to examine the essential standards from grade level to grade level or from course to course to make sure there are no gaps in student learning or unnecessary repetition. One way teams can accomplish vertical alignment is to consider learning progressions. We like W. James Popham's (2007) definition for a learning progression. Popham (2007), an expert on educational testing, defines it as "a carefully sequenced set of building blocks students must master en route to mastering a more distant curricular aim" (p. 83). Some standards are written with these progressions in mind.

For example, educators and other officials developed the Common Core ELA (NGA & CCSSO, 2010a) and identified a final outcome (called an *anchor standard*) and backward mapping for how a student can get there beginning in kindergarten. High-performing teams understand the importance of students learning prerequisite skills in each grade level in English language arts so they are able to reach mastery of the anchor standards by graduation. In their work identifying essential standards, teams will want to consider these progressions, looking for when there is a major jump in rigor from one grade level to another or when they add a new concept.

We recommend that schools and districts use a protocol for their vertical alignment of standards. In many cases, a coach may effectively facilitate this process because he or she comes to the process with little bias and often experience working with lots of different teams. If the school doesn't have a coach, the facilitator might be an administrator, a curriculum coordinator, or another person who understands the process. Figure 2.2 (page 48) shows a protocol for vertical alignment of essential standards we have found to be effective.

1

Step	Action	Anticipated Time of Completion
1	All teams write their draft list of essential standards on chart paper and post it in a location accessible to everyone. The best way to do this is to cluster all grade levels or courses in one area of the room. For example, in an elementary school aligning its ELA standards, teams post all these standards, from kindergarten through fifth grade, by cluster: reading, writing, speaking and listening, and language.	Fifteen minutes
2	One representative from each team gives an elevator speech (two minutes) sharing any important considerations his or her team makes in choosing essential standards. For example, a kindergarten representative may explain that the team chooses many more phonemic awareness or phonics standards than any other cluster because it believes these are the most important standards for all students to learn at their grade level.	Fifteen minutes
3	The coach or facilitator asks all participants to "walk the wall," paying particular attention to the standards before their grade level or course and those after their grade level or course. Notice any gaps or redundancies.	Fifteen to thirty minutes, depending on how much the teams talked about this work before the meeting
4	The coach or facilitator should take some time with the entire group looking at each cluster and responding to any noted gaps or redundancies. If teams agree, they can make changes.	Thirty to forty minutes
5	The coach or facilitator asks teams to pair up by having two grades or courses work together. The coach or facilitator asks the team to consider questions (see figure 2.3) that apply to their standards. Encourage participants to add or delete standards as they make decisions. You might provide participants with the following sentence stems. • We wondered . . . • We noticed . . . • We wish . . .	Twenty minutes
6	The coach or facilitator then asks the group to change which team they've paired up with, giving them a chance to talk with teachers in the grade level or course before and after theirs. For example, if a second-grade team worked with first grade in step 5, they will work with third grade in step 6. Discuss the same alignment questions (see figure 2.3).	Twenty minutes
7	The coach or facilitator asks the following question, "If a student attends our school or district and only learns these standards, would the student be prepared for the next level?"	Ten minutes

Figure 2.2: Protocol for vertical alignment of essential standards.

Figure 2.3 provides example discussion questions for vertical alignment of different content areas. In working with schools as they engage in this process, we have found that having some general questions for teams to consider before they finalize their list of essential standards helps participants feel confident that they've chosen the right standards.

Subject	Questions
English language arts	Six English language arts questions: 1. Do we have a balance of literature and informational text? 2. Will students have the phonics skills they need by the end of fifth grade? 3. Will students be able to answer text-dependent questions? 4. Do we have at least one vocabulary standard at each grade? 5. Do we cover all types of writing (explanatory, opinion, argument, narrative, research)? 6. Do we represent the intended rigor of our standards?
Mathematics	Five mathematics questions: 1. Do our essential standards align with the major work of the grade? 2. Can we embed the mathematical practices into these standards? 3. Will our students have sufficient number sense by the end of fifth grade? 4. Will students be proficient with fractions by the end of fifth grade? 5. Do we represent the intended rigor of our standards?
Science	Five science questions: 1. Do we represent the scientific process at each grade? 2. Do we balance content with process? 3. Do we include engineering standards at each grade? 4. Do we make sure to include the ELA standards for science and technical subjects? 5. Do we represent the intended rigor of our standards?
Generic	Three generic questions: 1. Do we have a balance of content and process? 2. Do we represent the intended rigor of our standards? 3. Do we include the ELA standards appropriate to content?

Figure 2.3: Discussion questions for vertical alignment.

*Visit **go.SolutionTree.com/PLCbooks** for a free reproducible version of this figure.*

Support and Monitor the Use of Essential Standards

So, what takes place now that teams have identified the essential standards? Through experience, we know that the essential standards that collaborative teams identify will change over time. This makes sense because as students move through grade levels or courses similarly prepared, teachers are able to dig more deeply into their own essential standards. After a few years, teachers see that they can guarantee more rigorous standards than they have in the past. We ask teams to reflect on their essential standards every few months and make notes of anything they think should change. This also means that schools and districts should plan to come together every few years to review their essential standards.

The process of identifying essential standards isn't simply about creating a product. It's about forming a core focus for team work. In the

1

coaching role, it's important to check on that focus as teams move through the PDSA cycle.

Some questions to consider include:

▸ Is the instructional focus within this unit or cycle of instruction placed on one or more essential standards?

▸ Are team members clarifying how they will address an essential standard within the unit?

▸ Have team members determined how they will intentionally assess it at the

end of the unit as well as formatively during unit instruction?

Identifying essential standards lays the groundwork for impacting student learning. But simply identifying them isn't enough. The next section of this chapter explores how teams can build common clarity by defining what it looks like when students are proficient.

Use the Coaching Reflection on page 72 to reflect on the information you explored for Action 1.

Coaching the Issue

A high school algebra 1 team recently returned from a PLC institute excited about the possibilities for closing the gap for its students most in need. The team includes three teachers: Mary has been teaching mathematics for fourteen years, Kasie is in her second year of teaching, and Matt has taught all levels of mathematics at this school and is retiring at the end of the school year. They understand that their work needs to revolve around the four critical questions of a PLC and feel pretty confident they are already doing many of the activities that will make a difference for their students. The one activity that worries them the most is identifying their essential standards because they worry that all their standards are important and they can't imagine eliminating any of them.

- **Coach's role:** Mike is their instructional coach, and his background is in science. After learning about what the team hopes he can help it do, Mike realizes that this team will benefit from him using the facilitating coach approach. Mike agrees to facilitate the process and reminds the team members that they are the mathematics experts. His role is to make sure they all have a voice in the process, and they stay on topic using a protocol to make sure that their final product will be effective.

- **Team meeting:** As the meeting gets started, Mike acknowledges that he has heard their concerns about all the standards being important for algebra students. He shares a copy of the protocol with team members (see figure 2.1, pages 46–47) as well as the documents he has gathered for step 6 (assessment blueprints, sample questions from the end-of-year test, and information about cluster emphases suggesting relative priorities for the high school standards). Mike also emphasizes that the team will still teach all the standards but will spend more time on those that are essential.

Feeling more confident about both the purpose and the process, team members dig in. This confidence builds as they complete the first several steps of the protocol, although they do see that they are not in total agreement as they build consensus on their draft list. Occasionally, members ask Mike to take a position about whether a standard belongs on the list.

He asks, "Is this concept really important enough to spend class time assessing and reteaching?"

Mike finds that he doesn't have to offer an opinion because this question helps them build their own priorities. After team members work through the six steps and look at both their own data and the assessment blueprints and sample questions, they are more confident that they are on the right track.

- **Next steps:** The team looks forward to working with other mathematics colleagues in completing the vertical alignment. Members value the insights gained throughout the process.

Action 2: Clarify Proficiency

When teams engage in the first action (identifying essential standards), they begin to develop a common understanding of what each standard means. During this next action step, clarifying proficiency, teams will dig deeper into understanding standards by discussing what it looks like for students to be proficient. Without these conversations, teachers may have different interpretations than their teammates about what students must be able to do to show mastery of the standard.

In order to clarify proficiency, coaches must work with teams to do the following.

▸ Establish the importance of clarifying the end-of-year picture of proficiency.

▸ Use common language to characterize rigor and proficiency.

▸ Include singletons in the work.

Establish the Importance of Clarifying the End-of-Year Picture of Proficiency

When teachers and students are clear on where they're headed, they're more likely to hit the target (Marzano, 2003). This finding makes the case for the next step in the process. While teams may have reached consensus on which standards they will guarantee across their classrooms and reached agreement in vertical fashion across their school, it doesn't necessarily mean they're all visualizing the same outcome. If we believe that every student needs to learn what is most essential, regardless of the teacher he or she has, we need to ensure that all team members agree about exactly what each standard means in terms of the level of rigor, complexity, or quality of performance that would be evidenced by student mastery.

Some guiding questions teams ask themselves as they address this action are: "What would it

2

look like by the end of our course or grade if students were proficient in this standard? What type of problem would they be able to solve? What type of product would they be able to produce and with what quality?"

In this process, the goal is that it is abundantly clear what each student will learn and what it looks like when they're successful. As part of the conversation, teams may identify sample problems in mathematics, define their qualitative rubrics for writing, and identify benchmark texts and questions students would be able to address after reading the text.

Figure 2.4 shows an example of the Putnam County Schools in Winfield, West Virginia, middle school social studies team efforts to

define proficiency for essential standards they identified in middle school social studies.

The seventh-grade social studies team has built consensus around its expectations for students' end-of-year achievement in each essential standard. It came about with discussion and even some healthy debate, but team members now have a guiding document to assist them as they design their units, including their instructional focus, strategies, and assessments.

When teams get clarity about their end-of-year targets, the process of designing the end-of-unit and formative assessments becomes more fluid. When teams are clear on their end-of-year targets for students, their instructional design becomes more focused and intentional.

	Essential Standards Domain	Evidence of Mastery
Civics	Classify and compare forms of government (SS.7.1).	Students will be able to do the following. • Research: Students will research eight types of government. They will be able to identify the major characteristics of each type of government. They will need to research the pros and cons of each government. • Informative and argumentative writing: Students will be able to write a five-paragraph argumentative essay on one type of government where they identify three reasons as to why their government is best. • Debate: Students will be able to compare and contrast various forms of government according to a common rubric.
	Recognize and examine patriotism and nationalism (SS.7.2).	Correctly label examples of patriotism and nationalism.
	Compare and contrast the roles, rights, and responsibilities of all people (SS.7.3).	Students will write a play where they pretend to travel back in time and meet at least four individuals from a particular time period. The individuals must come from different social classes. Students will research the roles and use historical facts to write characters into a script. Every script must include a town crier (narrator) who will detail the specific jobs, including the rights and responsibilities each role had in the society at the time (for example, noble, peasant, serf, vassal). The teacher will use a rubric to assess students.
	Examine current events (SS.7.4).	Students choose a current world event. They research and present the topic to the class. At the end of all presentations, students will choose their three favorite events and write at least five sentences about each event and how it has impacted the world on a local, national, or global scale.

Economics	Summarize and give examples of basic economic terms (SS.7.7).	Students will receive cards that represent various economic terms. They will simulate an economic system by bartering and trading for resources. Students will summarize the activity by writing how they obtained the essentials.
	Examine and draw conclusions about how the effects of natural and human events influence an economy (SS.7.11).	Students will write five sentences on the cause of the event and then draw conclusions by writing five sentences on the effects on the economy.
	Research and investigate how natural resources impact the economy (SS.7.12).	Students will create a flip chart using pictographs of various resources. The flip chart will show each stage of the resource and how the economy is impacted as a result.
Geography	Use correct geographic terminology to draw conclusions about information on maps, charts, and graphs (SS.7.13).	Students define various geographical features, draw pictures, and provide examples.
	Identify, locate, and draw conclusions about information on a variety of maps (SS.7.14).	Students identify and locate places on maps. Students will explain where and why transportation routes began and the role that natural resources play.
History	Demonstrate an understanding of the ancient civilizations (SS.7.19).	Students will create a chart identifying the leaders and basic principles and philosophies of five major world religions.

Students will create a slideshow that identifies the contributions of at least three ancient civilizations. Students will also identify the factors that led to the demise of the civilization. |

Source: © 2018 by Putnam County Schools, West Virginia. Used with permission.

Figure 2.4: Putnam County Schools essential standards—Grade 7 social studies.

Use Common Language to Characterize Rigor and Proficiency

One tool for clarifying the level of rigor we're seeking in students' learning outcomes is the use of a common language. A large majority of schools is now working with the language from Norman Webb's Depth of Knowledge (DOK). The following sections summarize the four levels of cognitive rigor described within the DOK framework (Webb, 2002).

Level 1: Recall and Reproduction

Tasks at this level require recalling facts or using simple skills and procedures. For example, it includes basic reading and comprehending text (for example, explicitly stated ideas and details), writing or reciting simple facts, or recalling definitions and terms. In mathematics, we can see level 1 in the use of one-step algorithmic procedures.

Level 2: Skills and Concepts

DOK 2 includes tasks that require more than one mental step that goes beyond basic recall and reproduction. Students go beyond the basic application to process information such as comparing, classifying, organizing, summarizing, predicting, and estimating. For example, students might identify and summarize major factors leading to an historical event or make inferences after reading literature passages. In mathematics, they would need to decide how to approach a problem rather than simply follow a procedure provided to them.

Level 3: Strategic Thinking

DOK 3 refers to strategic thinking tasks in which students must use a plan based on evidence and justify their thinking choices. In literacy, students are going beyond the text to make deeper inferences and connections to related ideas. In mathematics, DOK 3 tasks require more demanding reasoning and explanations for a concept.

Level 4: Extended Thinking

Level 4 tasks require the most complex cognitive effort. Students synthesize information from multiple sources, often over an extended period of time, or transfer knowledge from one domain to solve problems in another. Designing a survey and interpreting the results, analyzing multiple texts to extract themes, or designing a solution to a problem using information from multiple sources would be an example of level 4.

When learning this language of rigor, it's helpful to visualize the different levels as nesting cups. Generally speaking, students would need to have certain basic information or knowledge (DOK 1) before being able to perform tasks requiring basic reasoning (DOK 2). They would need to demonstrate basic reasoning before they would be able to move into DOK 3, and so on. When teams unwrap the standards to identify learning targets, the process often reveals learning targets that represent multiple levels of rigor. Some learning targets will be at DOK 1-level targets, some will be DOK 2, and so on. We'll see more examples of this as we examine the unwrapping process later in this chapter.

Many resources exist to support teams in the use of DOK when examining their standards and developing their assessments. Some resources are embedded in specific textbook adoptions. Others are available online. Karin Hess is a tremendous resource for translating the concepts of DOK to a level of practical

application, and you can access many tools on her website (www.karin-hess.com/free-resources). (Visit **go.SolutionTree.com/PLCbooks** to access live links to the websites mentioned in this book.) Hess (2013) discusses the "ceiling" of a standard as the highest DOK level or the most rigorous element of the standard. When teams are defining end-of-year proficiency for their essential standards, they should reference the ceiling level. For example, consider this standard (NGA & CCSSO, 2010a):

> Write arguments to support claims in an analysis of substantive topics or texts, using valid reasoning and relevant and sufficient evidence. (W.9–10.1)

To accomplish this standard, students must have the specific knowledge that a claim is the writer's position on a particular topic or text based on analysis of a topic or text, which reflects DOK 1. However, they would ultimately need to structure an argument that effectively clarifies the relationship between their claims, evidence, and reasons, which would reflect DOK 3. Therefore, the ceiling of this standard would be considered DOK 3.

When teams discuss their proficiency expectations for the learning targets and the standard, they are setting themselves up for creating a valid and reliable assessment. While we will discuss this in greater depth in chapter 3 (page 79), it's important for teams to reach clarity on their expectations during this step of the process, or they will struggle to write quality assessments during the next step.

Include Singletons in the Work

As a coach, you will likely encounter some teachers whom we call singletons, as they are the only teachers who teach their grade level or course. Most small schools have singletons in one or more configurations: small elementary schools may only have one first-grade teacher, one second-grade teacher, and so on. Small secondary schools might have only one sixth-grade science teacher, one biology teacher, or even one science teacher for a whole high school. In some secondary schools, a teacher might be a member of the algebra 1 team with other colleagues, but he or she might be the only teacher in the school teaching honors algebra 1. In all these cases, the way that these teachers collaborate is important to their success. Therefore, choosing the best configuration is the first step in the process to support collaborative singleton teams.

We generally see four structures that effectively support singleton teams: (1) vertical teams, (2) horizontal teams, (3) cross-school and district teams, and (4) electronic teams (DuFour et al., 2016). *Vertical teams* include members who teach a similar curriculum such as high school science or elementary school reading. These teams may be structured as the grades K–2 team or the science team. *Horizontal teams* share a common group of students but teach different content. They are also sometimes called interdisciplinary teams. Middle schools often organize this way to ensure teams can support individual students. Schools often form *cross-school and district teams* when there is only one person (a singleton) in a school or one person in a district who teaches a course or grade level. For example, there may be one music teacher in an elementary school, but the district has multiple elementary schools. Another example includes a district with one high school that has one physics teacher who may work with a physics teacher in another district. *Electronic teams* often include cross-school or district teams but also include any team configuration in which teams meet using computer-sharing software such as Skype (www.skype.com), Google Hangouts (https://

hangouts.google.com), Zoom (https://zoom.us), and so on.

Whichever structure the school or district chooses to use, it's important that team members are able to answer the four critical questions of a PLC in their work. We've occasionally seen schools who put disparate members onto a team (consider a fourth-grade team in which the music teacher is a member) or put all their singletons onto a team together. While someone might argue that the music teacher can find ways to integrate his or her standards in the reading and mathematics curriculum, it makes little sense for this teacher to meet consistently with a team that is doing work that doesn't involve music. Wouldn't it be better to create a districtwide team of music teachers who can actually answer the four questions around their standards?

Teachers frequently ask whether singletons should be allowed to pick which team they join. When teachers genuinely want to work in a collaborative culture, they generally choose a team structure that allows them to be an active and involved member. However, we sometimes see teachers who don't really want to work collaboratively choose a team that requires him or her to do little to help the team move forward. As a coach, you'll need to listen carefully to singletons to make sure they are working in the most effective way.

When singletons answer this first critical question, real collaboration happens most often after they choose the essential standards and begin the vertical-alignment process. Consider, for example, an elementary team working on ELA standards. In a larger collaborative team, the teachers are going to discuss what their standards mean and what proficiency looks like as they build consensus on what to put on their draft list. In a small school with a K–2 team, this discussion happens, instead, during the vertical-alignment process. Teachers discuss what it means to identify a main topic with guidance and support (grade K) versus identify a main topic of a text (grade 1) versus identify the main topic of a multi-paragraph text (grade 2). The final outcome of both larger collaborative teams and vertical singleton teams will likely be comparable.

Once teams identify essential standards and expectations for end-of-year proficiency, the next action step comes to the forefront: When will educators teach these standards? How much time will they spend making sure students learn the essential standards? The next action, establishing common pacing, will focus on answering those questions.

Use the Coaching Reflection on page 73 to reflect on the information you explored for Action 2.

Action 3: Establish Common Pacing

Educators use pacing guides and curriculum maps in many different formats and with different expectations across North America. As we discussed in the chapter opening, we've seen schools or districts where teachers use a day-by-day plan laid out for instruction. We've also worked with schools or districts that simply ask teacher teams to turn in lesson plans with little expectation for unity of pacing among team members.

Schools or districts might have certain expectations but also ask coaches to advocate for a process that should result in greater student achievement. After teams choose their essential standards, it becomes important for them to work collaboratively to determine anticipated timelines for effectively teaching, assessing, and providing corrective response for these standards. We use the term *corrective response* to distinguish how a team responds during regular Tier 1 instruction when a student needs extra time and support to learn an essential standard currently being taught. We use the term *intervention* to refer to the practice of giving extra time and support to students who need more help than occurs in the normal instructional process or help with the prior year's essential standards (Tier 2 and Tier 3 support).

Support Teams' Understanding of Pacing

As coaches consider their role in helping teachers pace their curriculum, they may find that they can facilitate this process more easily than someone who has a personal stake in the outcome, such as a team member. For example, some teachers want to make sure topics and activities that they've previously used and have enjoyed teaching are included in the pacing guide whether or not they are needed to ensure mastery of standards. Colleagues might be uncomfortable pointing out that the activities don't align to the standards, but a coach can more easily point out the problem.

Coaches can share the direct benefits of eliminating unnecessary curricula with teams they are working with. For example, most teachers agree that they have too much to teach even without expectations to include formative assessment and time to respond. Our goal in this work is to be sure we have enough instructional time to guarantee all students learn the essential standards. We generally remind teachers that all students must learn the essential standards; some students may learn a bit more than those standards and some students may learn much more. Pacing guides provide the guidance teams need to make this happen.

Collaboratively Build a Pacing Guide

Many districts bring teachers together whenever they are developing a new curriculum to collaboratively determine when to teach standards (through curriculum maps or pacing guides), determine what assessments to use to monitor student learning, and choose curriculum materials and resources teachers need to effectively implement this new curriculum. The entire process may take a year or more and may occur every five to six years, and districts may establish their curriculum development cycle so it aligns to the times their state rewrites or adjusts the standards.

Collaborative teams working in a PLC must also pay attention to their pacing whether or not they are developing a new curriculum as they engage in discussion around the first critical question. In these situations, a team will want to use its current curriculum map or pacing guide as the framework to start the process.

In either case, the process begins as teams are identifying and unwrapping their essential standards. Teachers often ask whether the pacing guide should reflect only essential standards or if it should include all the standards. The guide should include all the standards, giving special attention to the essential standards to ensure there is enough time for teachers to teach, assess, and reteach as they need to.

If a team already has a pacing guide or curriculum map, members highlight their essential standards right on the document so they can check the balance within each unit. Are there units with no essential standards, only supporting standards? They might shorten those units to allow more time for units with more essential standards. Are there units with numerous essential standards? The team may need

to add more time for assessment and response for those units. As noted earlier in this chapter, little or no improvement in student achievement will result if all a team does is highlight the essential standards in their pacing guide without making adjustments reflecting their importance.

Educators also ask whether the pacing guide should reflect standards or learning targets. The answer to this question might vary depending on the standards the team is using. Consider, for example, the Next Generation Science Standards (NGSS Lead States, 2013). Typically, with these standards, a teacher will teach the entire standard in one unit. Consider, for example, this high school life science standard: "Ask questions to clarify relationships about the role of DNA and chromosomes in coding the instructions for character traits passing from parents to offspring" (NGSS Lead States, 2013). While it's still important for teachers to unwrap these standards and consider all three dimensions (disciplinary core ideas, cross-cutting concepts, and science and engineering practices), which will lead to identifying the learning targets, they will likely teach all these targets during the same unit on heredity. On the other hand, consider the following second-grade mathematics standard (NGA & CCSSO, 2010b):

> Use addition and subtraction within 100 to solve one- and two-step word problems involving situations of adding to, taking from, putting together, taking apart, and comparing, with unknowns in all positions, e.g., by using drawings and equations with a symbol for the unknown number to represent the problem. (2.OA.A.1)

Educators will likely teach from this standard in several different units so the team will want to work with learning targets as they pace.

Educators might also ask how to approach a subject when standards or learning targets are

3

intentionally taught multiple times before they expect students to master them. The pacing guide should reflect this by listing the target each time it is to be taught and differentiating the guide to indicate when educators will assess the target. If the curriculum hasn't set a time for mastery, the team should make this decision collaboratively.

The work of pacing often feels like putting a jigsaw puzzle together. Teams may want to work collaboratively using an enlarged copy of a pacing guide template (see figures 2.5–2.8, pages 58–60, for examples). The coach may start by asking the team to name its instructional units. The coach then gives the team labels with the learning targets printed on them. If that target is taught in the unit, the team posts a label to show that. Team members work together to make sure every label has at least one place on the pacing guide. Some learning targets will require multiple copies of the label. For example, an elementary reading team starts by putting the reading foundations learning targets on the guide first and then follows with the reading literature targets, reading informational text targets, writing targets, speaking and listening targets, and finally, language targets.

Essential Standards	Unit 1	Unit 2	Unit 3	Unit 4	Unit 5	Unit 6
Reading Foundations						
Evidence of Mastery						
Reading Comprehension (Literature and Informational Text)						
Evidence of Mastery						
Writing						
Evidence of Mastery						
Language						
Evidence of Mastery						

Figure 2.5: Essential standards pacing guide template—English language arts (elementary).

*Visit **go.SolutionTree.com/PLCbooks** for a free reproducible version of this figure.*

Essential Standards	Unit 1	Unit 2	Unit 3	Unit 4	Unit 5	Unit 6
Reading Literature						
Evidence of Mastery						
Reading Informational Text						
Evidence of Mastery						
Writing						
Evidence of Mastery						
Language						
Evidence of Mastery						

Figure 2.6: Essential standards pacing guide—English language arts by strand (secondary).

*Visit **go.SolutionTree.com/PLCbooks** for a free reproducible version of this figure.*

3

Essential Standards Domain	Evidence of Mastery
Operations and Algebraic Thinking	
Number and Operations in Base Ten	
Number and Operations: Fractions	
Measurement and Data	
Geometry	

Figure 2.7: Essential standards pacing guide for mathematics.

*Visit **go.SolutionTree.com/PLCbooks** for a free reproducible version of this figure.*

	Unit 1	Unit 2	Unit 3	Unit 4	Unit 5	Unit 6
Essential Standards						
Evidence of mastery						

Figure 2.8: Generic essential standards pacing guide.

*Visit **go.SolutionTree.com/PLCbooks** for a free reproducible version of this figure.*

Include Singletons in the Process

Typically, teachers who are most familiar with the content they are pacing develop the pacing guides. Therefore, in the case of a team made up of singletons, it's likely that each team member will develop his or her own pacing guide for the grade or course he or she teaches. However, in the case of many teams composed of singletons, there are powerful opportunities for them to identify their common threads of learning around which they could write common formative assessments and work collaboratively in response to these data.

Once teachers identify those common threads, the team could align its pacing to build a common time frame for teaching similar standards. For example, a social studies team from a small middle school with one sixth-, one seventh-, and one eighth-grade teacher may decide that it wants to develop a common formative assessment on the learning target: Cite textual evidence to support analysis of primary source documents. The team decides to focus on teaching students about how to investigate the issue of time and the time period when looking at these documents. All team members choose primary-source documents that link to their own curriculum but will want to teach these concepts together so they can learn from each other. Therefore, they may need to change their pacing to make sure they have time for this.

Monitor the Work

One characteristic of high-performing teams is that they are always looking for continuous improvement. With a focus on student learning and pacing guides, this means teams must be flexible as they implement units of instruction. As a school works on this from year to year, students move through the system more commonly prepared from one year to the next. This allows teachers to more effectively teach their standards, and they must update their pacing guides regularly to take advantage of this.

Use the Coaching Reflection on page 74 to reflect on the information you explored for Action 3.

Coaching the Issue

Three sixth-grade science teachers are meeting to discuss an upcoming unit in life science. Andrea has taught sixth-grade science for a number of years but in a different school, and Mateo is new to sixth grade but not to this school. Ana has been teaching sixth grade for two years in this school but with the old standards. They are completing the cell unit and are moving into the next unit on body systems. They've given a common formative assessment on cells, assessing the difference between unicellular organisms and multicellular organisms.

Their district recently adopted the Next Generation Science Standards, but teams received their standards lists without the supporting information about the three dimensions the science standards were built on. Their coach, who is not a science teacher, is attending the meeting and brings the documents for NGSS along in case of questions or concerns. She knows this team is trying to teach the new standards without having had time to dig into the nuances of how it should change instruction for its students.

- **Coach's role:** Their coach, Sue, who is not a science teacher, takes on the role of facilitator.

- **Team meeting:** Even though this meeting is for the team to look at its upcoming standards and determine the pacing of the unit, the meeting quickly gets derailed as the teachers discuss a new, emerging problem. Because they are moving into a new set of standards, their students don't necessarily have the prerequisites they need for these standards. Sue encourages members to look at the clarification statements and assessment boundaries in the NGSS documents. Team members are pleased to see that they interpreted the standard about cells accurately. However, as they look at their older pacing guides, they realize that they need to do some additional work—build the concepts of tissue, organ, and system prior to engaging students in the body systems unit.

  Sue reminds the team that they are trying to rewrite their pacing guide to fit the new standards "on the fly." She releases the team for a full day of professional development in order for them to develop more aligned pacing guides. Because the team identifies this need as well, they easily agree to Sue's suggestion of doing this work.

- **Next steps:** Sue makes copies of the NGSS documents for the team and prepares large copies of the pacing guide template she recommends they use. She also adds the unwrapping template to their shared drive because she knows it will be important for them to unwrap their new standards to become familiar with everything students need to know to be proficient. She recognizes that they will also need to do this to get clarity around pacing.

Action 4: Unwrap the Standards

4

A number of terms are synonymous with *unwrapping*, including *deconstructing* and *unpacking*. They all refer to the process of closely examining a standard in order to identify the small subset concepts (knows) and skills (dos) that lead to their accomplishment. These subsets are called *learning targets*. Teachers can view each learning target as a step toward accomplishing the standard.

As teams work collaboratively to unwrap a standard, they build collective clarity about what it really takes for a student to accomplish a standard. They also get clear about the big ideas and essential questions that drive learning the standard.

Learning targets can each have different levels of rigor. Teams can organize their learning targets according to the sequence of how they will teach concepts or by level of rigor (for example, using DOK terminology). Once identified, learning targets set the stage for teams to more effectively design their formative assessments and build their instructional sequence.

In order to unwrap the standards, coaches must work with teams to do the following.

▸ Establish a purpose for unwrapping.

▸ Engage teams using an unwrapping protocol.

▸ Examine the rigor of learning targets.

Establish the Purpose for Unwrapping

Standards are often complex. They may contain ambiguous language or be written to address multiple or complex skills. Each team member could potentially interpret the standard differently, which would ultimately lead to students in each classroom learning a different set of skills and concepts. Take the following example (NGA & CCSSO, 2010a):

> Explain the relationships or interactions between two or more individuals, events, ideas, or concepts in a historical, scientific, or technical text based on specific information in the text. (RI.5.3)

The language in this particular standard is definitely open to interpretation and clearly implies multiple learning targets. A team focusing on this standard might need to build

shared understanding about what *relationships or interactions* means and how students would specifically be referencing this information in the text. The team might need to define *how* a student would explain the relationship or interaction.

The need for a team to get to common clarity about the standard's intent and the steps to getting there (or learning targets) is the rationale behind unwrapping. The unwrapping process is a strategy that enables collaborative teams to achieve collective clarity and agreement regarding the intent of the standard and specific learning targets within the standard. Learning targets are the smaller increments of learning, in other words the steps of knowledge, concepts, or skills that lead to the standard's attainment (Bailey, Jakicic, & Spiller, 2014). If you picture the top of a stepladder as the complete standard, each rung in the ladder leading upward represents a skill or concept that students need in order to accomplish that standard.

When teams understand the *why* of the unwrapping process and experience the power of an unwrapping conversation, they will be more willing to engage in the process. Ironically, one of the most convincing ways to explain the why behind unwrapping the standards is to actually engage teams in the process. In other words, the experience of unwrapping standards deepens team members' understanding of the why behind the process.

Engage Teams Using an Unwrapping Protocol

Determine the timing of engaging in the unwrapping process based on the context and nature of the standards. As stated in the previous section on pacing the essential standards, some teams, particularly those working with literacy standards, benefit from unwrapping the standards so they can pace them by learning target. However, this can be a time-consuming, even overwhelming process for teams to complete. Alternatively, teams could choose to unwrap their essential standards as they encounter them unit by unit. Once educators teach all the units throughout the year, teams will have identified the learning targets for each essential standard. Regardless of the approach, all unwrapping efforts should reference the identified essential standards, including their examples of proficiency. This enhances learning target alignment as they build toward accomplishing the standard.

In *Simplifying Common Assessment: A Guide for Professional Learning Communities at Work* (Bailey & Jakicic, 2017), we outline the following four-step process for effectively unwrapping the standards.

1. Individually or collectively, annotate the standard using the following three-part notation.

    a. Put brackets, [ ], around any information in the standard that tells about the context. Context may refer to the type of text students will be reading, the type of problem students will be solving, or any other situational information about the nature of the challenge or task students will encounter as they demonstrate their understanding of key concepts and skills.

    Review this example of a literacy standard for ninth grade: "Analyze how an author's choices concerning how to structure a text, order events within it (e.g., parallel plots), and manipulate time (e.g., pacing, flashbacks) create such effects as [mystery, tension, or surprise]" (RL.9–10.5).

    We have placed brackets around information that clarifies students will be working with literature which contains an element of mystery, tension, or surprise.

    b. Circle the verbs. Doing so points to the main skills students are expected to do or demonstrate. In this standard, the word *analyze* is the major verb.

    "(Analyze) how an author's choices concerning how to structure a text, order events within it (e.g., parallel plots), and manipulate time (e.g., pacing, flashbacks) create such effects as [mystery, tension, or surprise]" (RL.9–10.5).

    c. Underline the significant nouns or noun phrases. These words help point to the concepts, definitions, facts, or ideas students will need to know or understand. In this example, the underlined words highlight concepts around an author's choices, text structures, and the topic or order of events, including parallel plots, time manipulation (including pacing and flashbacks), and the cause-and-effect relationship between these structures and the impact on a reader.

    "(Analyze) how an <u>author's choices</u> concerning how to <u>structure a text</u>, <u>order events</u> within it (e.g., <u>parallel plots</u>), and <u>manipulate time</u> (e.g., <u>pacing, flashbacks</u>) create such effects as [<u>mystery, tension, or surprise</u>]" (RL.9–10.5).

2. Using a graphic organizer or template (such as the example in figure 2.9, page 64), reference the annotated

Essential standard to address: (Analyze) how an author's choices concerning how to structure a text, order events within it (such as, parallel plots), and manipulate time (such as, pacing, flashbacks) create such effects as mystery, tension, or surprise (RL.9–10.5).		
Learning Targets		**Level of Rigor**
Students Will Know or Understand	• Literary text structures and their forms	DOK 1
	• What a parallel plot is	DOK 1
	• What a flashback is	DOK 1
	• Big idea: Authors use intentional strategies to engage their readers.	DOK 1
Students Will Do or Demonstrate	• Recognize and describe how an author chooses to structure a text and order events within it.	DOK 2
	• Recognize and describe parallel plots.	DOK 2
	• Recognize and describe time manipulation techniques.	DOK 2
	• Distinguish between literary effects (for example, mystery, tension, surprise).	DOK 2
	• Analyze how the text structure contributes to the meaning of a text.	DOK 3
	• Describe the cause-and-effect relationship between an author's choices and impact on the reader.	DOK 3
Students Will Use Academic Language or Vocabulary	Parallel plot, tension, manipulation of time, flashback, pacing, text structure	

Source for standard: Adapted from NGA & CCSSO, 2010a.

Figure 2.9: Sample graphic organizer for unwrapping a high school standard.

standard to collectively identify the specific learning targets that reflect what students will know and do.

▸ Use the circled and underlined words highlighted in step 1 to jumpstart the process of answering the question, "What would our students need to know and do in order to accomplish this standard?"

▸ During this process, teams should not only use these highlighted words but also "read between the lines" and add any concepts or skills implied but not explicitly stated. In our example, we identified several learning targets that weren't explicitly stated in the standard but are crucial *knows* and *dos* when students successfully complete the task. For instance, the standard didn't explicitly state anything about students demonstrating these in-between steps, but when teams fill in the blanks, they ensure the appropriate design of instruction and assessments that lead to high levels of student learning.

▸ When identifying the *knows*, be sure to include any concepts that support the big idea or *why* of the standard. Some teams put a specific location in their template for the main idea.

3. Identify any academic language or vocabulary students should master. Teams can reference not only the words they underlined when they highlighted the standard but can examine their list of learning targets to determine any other terms that they should intentionally teach and assess. Teams should see redundancy between this list of words and their learning targets.

4. Examine the rigor of the learning targets. Using a common language (we recommend Webb's DOK), examine the learning targets (the *knows* and *dos*) to determine the level of rigor and complexity being addressed. While teams can examine the verbs in the learning targets, we caution that if teams use verbs alone, there may be a misunderstanding about the actual rigor intended in the learning target. Teams should examine what comes after the verb, as well as the context (bracketed in step 1), to fully understand the expected level of knowledge processing. Examining the rigor of learning targets leads to more aligned assessment items.

Figure 2.10 is another example using an elementary standard. Again, we begin by annotating the standard, circling the verbs, and underlining key nouns and noun phrases. In this standard, we also circle the verb *applying* because it brings further clarity to the intent of the standard.

As a result of the unwrapping process, team members gain greater clarity about the why and how of the standard, including its focus for student learning and the necessary steps along the instructional journey to reach that destination. Through this structured analysis, they can clarify any ambiguity and identified specific learning targets, setting the stage for more effective instruction and assessment.

Essential standard to address: Recognize that in a multidigit whole number, a digit in one place represents ten times what it represents in the place to its right. For example, recognize that 700 ÷ 70 = 10 by applying concepts of place value and division (4.NBT.A.1).

Learning Targets		Level of Rigor
Students Will Know or Understand	• Place values of whole numbers in positions from ones to one million	DOK 1
	• When multiplying a number by ten, it shifts its position one place to the left.	DOK 1
	• The relationship between positions of differing place values from one to one million	DOK 2
Students Will Do or Demonstrate	• Identify the value of a digit in positions from one to one million.	DOK 1
	• Compare quantities using concepts of place value and the powers of ten.	DOK 3
	• Explain reasoning in real-world problems that incorporate the concept of values related to position.	DOK 3
Students Will Use Academic Language or Vocabulary	Digit; place value; power of ten / base-ten system; ones, tens, hundreds, thousands, ten thousands, millions	

Source for standard: NGA & CCSSO, 2010b.

Figure 2.10: Sample graphic organizer for unwrapping an elementary standard.

4

Coaching Tips

As you work with teams in the unwrapping process, you may encounter some challenges. The following are five common challenges and ideas for how to facilitate conversations around these concerns.

1. **Oversimplification:** At times, teams simply reorganize the standard and put it into the template rather than really thinking about what it would take for a student to successfully demonstrate the standard in action. The coach should ask, "What is the end in mind for this standard?" He or she should reference the essential standards documents that describe end-of-year proficiency. The coach should go on to ask, "What would it really take for students to get there? What would they have to learn about? What would they need to specifically achieve that final product?"

2. **Leaping:** The progression of learning isn't represented because several learning targets weren't included or team members weren't reading between the lines. The coach should ask, "What smaller skills or concepts would be necessary to accomplish this larger task?"

3. **Partial thinking:** The targets that the unwrapping process identifies don't get to the standard ceiling. In other words, team members focus on the simpler skills or concepts and don't include all aspects of the standard. The coach should ask, "Does this set of learning targets seem to reach the most rigorous parts of this standard? Does it align to the end-of-year picture of proficiency created in the essential standards document?"

4. **A focus on the activity or teaching strategy instead of the learning:** Teams often stray in their focus toward lesson planning ideas or activities instead of the purpose of unwrapping—clarifying the intent of the standard and the smaller pieces of learning (learning targets) students must attain to achieve that standard. The coach should ask, "When you look at the end in mind for this unit of study, what smaller skills will students need to have? What concepts do they need to learn? Before we move into *how* we will teach those things, let's decide what those things are so we're designing our instruction and assessment accurately."

5. **Pushback:** A coach may encounter situations in which teachers have already engaged in some type of unwrapping, possibly not connected to other parts of the process (such as designing instruction or assessment). They may see it as busywork disconnected from other parts of the process and may be reluctant to engage in the process. The coach should ask, "What was the value of unwrapping this standard? How did it help you become clearer regarding the intent of the standard and the smaller pieces? How might this help as you design your instruction and assessment? How might this help students?" The coach should ask the last question following the experience of collaborative unwrapping of a standard. Teams should unwrap a standard that teachers will emphasize in an upcoming unit of study so there is immediate value and relevance.

4

As we move into the actions necessary to answer the second PLC critical question (How will we know if they have learned it?), we will highlight the powerful connection between the unwrapping process and the design of accurate and effective assessments.

Figures 2.11–2.12 (pages 68–69) show additional samples of templates teams can use for identifying learning targets and discussing proficiency. These templates help teams focus on key words written in the standards. The verbs listed in the first column (What will students do?) are important, as they indicate what a student must be able to do as well as the rigor implied in the learning target. Consider the difference between a target that asks students to identify the types of figurative language an author uses versus a target asking students to interpret an item using figurative language. Other key words in standards are the nouns or noun phrases that indicate the content students must learn, as shown in the second column. If context is included in the standard, that information goes in the third column. Each row of the template, then, becomes a learning target.

Figure 2.11 (page 68) shows an example of what unwrapped standard RI.9–10.8 (NGA & CCSSO, 2010a) might look like. The team has identified six learning targets in this standard, including: delineate the argument and claims in a text; evaluate the argument and claims in a text; assess valid reasoning in a text; and so on. Figure 2.12 (page 69) shows an example of what unwrapped standard RI.4.6 might look like.

These templates also include a discussion about the summative assessments at the bottom. The team discusses what the summative assessment might look like at the end of the learning. Will it be a project, a piece of writing, or traditional test questions? Note that not all the learning targets have something listed in the final column for common formative assessment. This is because not every learning

target must be assessed, even if it comes from an essential standard. We will discuss this in more depth in chapter 3 (page 79).

There are six explicit learning targets from this standard.

1. Delineate the argument and specific claims in an informational text.

2. Evaluate the argument and specific claims in an informational text.

3. Assess valid reasoning in the text.

4. Assess relevant and sufficient evidence in the text.

5. Identify false statements in the text.

6. Identify fallacious reasoning in the text.

If a fourth-grade team uses this same template, it might look like figure 2.12 (page 69) when unwrapping RI.4.6.

There are five explicit learning targets from this standard.

1. Compare and contrast a firsthand and secondhand account of the same event or topic.

2. Know the definitions of *firsthand account* and *secondhand account*.

3. Identify whether a text is written as a firsthand account or a second-hand account.

4. Describe the difference in focus between the two accounts.

5. Describe the difference in information provided between the two accounts.

The reproducibles on pages 75–76 provide sample unwrapping templates teachers can use to unwrap standards using key words.

Finally, the unwrapping template in figure 2.13 (page 70) allows teams to discuss the rigor of the targets in a particular unit to see both the end point as well as how they might scaffold the learning to get there.

4

		Unwrapping Template		

Essential standard: Delineate and evaluate the argument and specific claims [in a text], in assessing whether the reasoning is valid and the evidence is relevant and sufficient; identify false statements and fallacious reasoning (RI.9–10.8).

What Will Students Do? (Skills or Verbs)	With What Knowledge or Concept? (Nouns or Direct Instruction)	In What Context?	What Is the Level of Thinking?	What Common Formative Assessment Will Students Have?
Delineate	The argument and specific claims	In a piece of informational text	DOK 2	Students complete a graphic organizer listing claims and supporting evidence.
Evaluate	The argument and specific claims	In a piece of informational text	DOK 3	
Assess	Valid reasoning	In the text	DOK 3	Students analyze the reasoning in a text by showing how the evidence links to each claim.
Assess	Relevant and sufficient information	In the text	DOK 3	
Identify	False statements	In the text	DOK 3	
Identify	Fallacious reasoning	In the text	DOK 3	Students identify if any evidence doesn't link to a claim.

Summative assessment: Students will use a new argumentative text as a stimulus. Students must read the text and complete a graphic organizer to evaluate the quality of the evidence used to support each claim, making note of poor support or incorrectly supported conclusions or evidence not connected to a claim.

Source for standard: NGA & CCSSO, 2010a.

Figure 2.11: Sample unwrapping for standard RI.9–10.8.

4

Unwrapping Template				
Essential standard: Compare and contrast a firsthand and secondhand account of the [same event or topic]; describe the differences in focus and the information provided (RI.4.6).				
What Will Students Do? (Skills or Verbs)	With What Knowledge or Concept? (Nouns or Direct Instruction)	In What Context?	What Is the Level of Thinking?	What Common Formative Assessment Will Students Have?
Compare and contrast	A firsthand and secondhand account	Of the same event or topic	DOK 2	Students complete a Venn diagram asking for three comparisons and three differences.
Know	The definitions of *firsthand* and *secondhand*	N/A	DOK 1	
Identify	Whether a text is written as a firsthand or secondhand account	In informational text	DOK 2	Students receive two pieces of text and identify which is a firsthand account and which is a secondhand account.
Describe	The difference in focus between a firsthand account and a secondhand account	Of the same event or topic	DOK 3	
Describe the difference in information provided	Between a firsthand account and a secondhand account	Of the same event or topic	DOK 3	
Summative assessment: Students receive two accounts of the same event or topic written from different points of view. They receive constructed-response questions asking them to explain the difference in focus between the accounts and explain the difference in information provided.				

Source for standard: NGA & CCSSO, 2010a.

Figure 2.12: Sample unwrapping for standard RI.4.6.

Examine the Rigor of Learning Targets

As described previously in this chapter, it is important for team members to agree on the level of complexity and rigor targeted for student learning. In the final part of the unwrapping process, teams examine the learning targets to collectively determine the level of rigor. Figure 2.13 (page 70) illustrates how the team records the level of rigor of each learning target by referencing the DOK level. This is also an opportunity for teams to clarify the ceiling of the standard. By ensuring common clarity of the rigor, teams set the stage for designing aligned assessments and instruction.

Use the Coaching Reflection on page 77 to reflect on the information you explored for Action 4.

4

Depth of Knowledge	Specific Learning Targets	Aligned Assessment Items
DOK 1: Recall What information, facts, simple procedures, properties, or definitions do we want students to know or recall?		
DOK 2: Basic Reasoning What basic reasoning and application of knowledge do we want students to demonstrate? May involve: • Compare/contrast • Classification • Conversion of information • Solve with formula		
DOK 3: Strategic Thinking/ Complex Reasoning What higher order/non-routine/ complex thinking and analysis do we want students to execute? May involve: • Critique • Opinion/judgment		
DOK 4: Extended Thinking What complicated task or problem involving multiple higher-order thinking processes would students resolve? May involve: • Synthesis • Innovation • Reflection and adjustment to solve real-world problems		

Figure 2.13: Unwrapping learning targets through DOK analysis.

*Visit **go.SolutionTree.com/PLCbooks** for a free reproducible version of this figure.*

4

Conclusion

This chapter focused on how coaches support teams as they answer critical question 1 (What do we want students to know and be able to do?), which serves as a foundation for the remaining questions collaborative teams must address. By implementing the four actions in this chapter, teams accomplish the following.

- Become empowered with a prioritized set of standards for students (essential standards).

- Have a visible example of what it looks like when students are proficient with those standards (evidence of proficiency).

- Create a guide that organizes when and where those standards will be taught during the year (pacing guide).

- Possess greater insight about the intent of the standards and the smaller pieces of learning that lead to accomplishing them (unwrapping the standards).

We guarantee that this work is worth doing. As you'll see, when teams get crystal clear about what students need to learn, it bridges teams to a more accurate and aligned response to question 2 (How will we know if they have learned it?). Chapter 3 explores considerations for coaches as they support teams in answering this question.

Coaching Reflection for Action 1: Identify Essential Standards

Use the questions in this chart to reflect on the information you explored in Action 1.

What curriculum documents are teams already using? Do they follow these documents closely?	What role (facilitator, consultant, coach) should I play with each team?
Does each team understand why choosing essential standards is an important step?	What issues do I need to anticipate and plan for?
What materials and resources can I find for teams as they do this work?	What is a reasonable time line for completing this step?

Coaching Reflection for Action 2: Clarify Proficiency

Use the questions in this chart to reflect on the information you explored in Action 2.

Have the teachers discussed and defined proficiency in any way?	What role (facilitator, consultant, coach) should I play with each team?
Will my teams understand *why* it's important to agree about what proficiency looks like for each standard?	What issues do I need to anticipate and plan for?
Should we all use a common language (for example, DOK) and, if so, which one?	What is a reasonable time line for completing this step?

Coaching Reflection for Action 3:
Establish Common Pacing

Use the questions in this chart to reflect on the information you explored in Action 3.

What are the current expectations for common pacing? What will I need to do to help teams move forward?	What role (facilitator, consultant, coach) should I play with each team?
Do I need to build an understanding about *why* this is important for my teams?	What issues do I need to anticipate and plan for?
How can I help teams organize their work around pacing?	What is a reasonable time line for completing this step?

Unwrapping Template Using Key Words, Example 1

Teams can use this basic unwrapping template to unwrap standards, as defined in this chapter. After annotating the standard, teams use the key words to identify specific learning targets (for example, the smaller subsets within the standard that students will need to know and do) and specific academic language or vocabulary that lead to achieving the standard. This template also includes columns that indicate the level of rigor (DOK) and aligned formative assessment items identified by the team.

Standard or standards to address:			
Context or Conditions (Explain what text, problem type, or situation students will encounter.)			

Learning Targets		DOK	Assessment
Students Will Know or Understand Concepts or Information	Big idea:		
Students Will Do or Demonstrate			
Students Will Use Academic Language or Vocabulary			

Unwrapping Template Using Key Words, Example 2

This template offers another way for teams to unwrap standards looking specifically at the key words; that is, nouns and verbs. This template also provides a space for teams to discuss what assessments (both formative and summative) teams might write.

Unwrapping Template				
Essential standard:				
What Will Students Do? (Skills or Verbs)	With What Knowledge or Concept? (Nouns or Direct Instruction)	In What Context?	What Is the Level of Thinking?	What Common Formative Assessment Will Students Have?
Summative assessment:				

Coaching Reflection for Action 4: Unwrap the Standards

Use the questions in this chart to reflect on the information you explored in Action 4.

Did teams work collaboratively to unwrap their standards? Did they do this work recently?	What role (facilitator, consultant, coach) should I play with each team?
How can I best communicate how valuable this step is to my teams?	What issues do I need to anticipate and plan for?
After examining their standards, what is the best process for each team I'm working with?	What is a reasonable time line for completing this step?

Coaching focus for PLC critical question 2:
How will we know if they have learned it?

ACTION 1: Build Understanding of a Balanced Assessment System
▸ Clarify the purpose of each assessment type.
▸ Ensure understanding of formative versus summative or end-of-unit measures.
▸ Support team clarity of standards versus learning targets in the assessment process.
▸ Clarify how common formative assessments fit into a unit of instruction.

ACTION 2: Design Assessments for Validity and Reliability
▸ Make your assessment valid by planning it first.
▸ Match the item type to the rigor of the learning target.
▸ Determine the number of items needed to ensure reliability.
▸ Set proficiency expectations.

ACTION 3: Write Quality Assessment Items
▸ Develop quality constructed-response items.
▸ Develop quality selected-response items.
▸ Choose the stimulus.
▸ Model samples and exemplars from high-stakes tests.
▸ Adapt the process for unique team structures.

ACTION 4: Collaborate Around Results
▸ Clarify scoring versus grading.
▸ Use strategies for quality feedback.
▸ Establish cut scores or proficiency expectations.
▸ Determine the frequency of common formative assessments.

A C T I O N S

How Will We Know if They Have Learned It?

Once teams commit to ensuring students learn essential standards, they need to decide how they will collectively monitor whether this learning is taking place. The second critical question in a PLC (How will we know if they have learned it?) leads to some of the most important work teams do. Together, teams must develop aligned and effective assessments to identify student proficiency on these standards.

To prepare for this work, coaches should consider the following.

- ▶ Teams that work within a balanced assessment system including various types of assessments are better able to ensure students get the support they need.

- ▶ Teams write common assessments based on the essential standards, which they unwrap to reveal specific learning targets.

- ▶ Common formative assessments, or any formative assessments, are written around learning targets rather than standards so they are more diagnostic.

- ▶ Collaborative teams are capable of writing valid and reliable assessments that provide quality information about how to respond.

- ▶ Teams use a backward-planning process to identify the evidence they will seek that demonstrates student learning of the essential standards.

- ▶ Teams must be clear on what that learning will look like, or the end in mind, for a unit of study to effectively design end-of-unit assessments.

- ▶ Once teams have designed their end-of-unit assessment, they can more effectively design meaningful formative assessments.

Explore Your Context

While this chapter focuses primarily on how collaborative teams write and use common end-of-unit and formative assessments, it's important to be aware of the entire balanced assessment system in which teams are working.

In some schools we've worked with, teachers feel the amount of testing they must do is overwhelming. In many of these situations, administrators tell them what assessments they need to give and then analyze these data and respond appropriately, sometimes with little professional development on the process or support on how to interpret the information. At some schools, teachers don't have any assessments other than end-of-year, high-stakes tests. Teachers feel overwhelmed with the responsibility of knowing what their students need and actually meeting those needs. In either case, it's important for coaches to understand the expectations around assessments before starting to guide the team's work. Coaches should become comfortable that they can address the following issues.

Expectations for Teachers Administering Assessments

Coaches may find it helpful to lay out the entire assessment system to examine redundancies or gaps in assessments. To do this, teachers should examine the pieces to include in a balanced assessment system to see which assessments they currently have access to and what they might need to add. They should understand which assessments are mandatory versus those they can use based on the school's discretion or specific need. It's important to understand the design, purpose, and frequency of each assessment piece. For example, how often do teachers administer benchmark or interim assessments? Does the district design them based on identified essential standards? Are the benchmarks developed along a pacing guide, assessing standards that have been taught, or are they miniature versions of the end-of-year, high-stakes assessment that evaluates all standards the teachers will address in a year?

Teacher Training for Data Use

What level of experience do teachers have disaggregating data from the various levels of assessment? How frequently do teachers engage in these conversations? Most often, the answer to both questions in the schools we work with is that someone goes through the reports available to teachers from district-required benchmarks or interim assessments and shares the results of end-of-year data, sometimes including trend analysis. Teams should actively engage in these analyses so they are able to use the information to identify critical areas of need and write quality SMART goals for their teams (Conzemius & O'Neill, 2014).

Reporting or Grading Systems

While we encourage teams to get a variety of different assessments in place before trying to change their reporting system, we also know that the current system may affect teachers' attitudes toward formative assessment. We've seen this play out from different perspectives. For example, some (mostly elementary) schools have moved to a standards-based reporting system, and these teachers may or may not have agreed about how to use them in a unified way. Other schools have a more traditional letter-grading system and embrace the idea that they should use formative assessments to respond to student learning but not as a part of students' grades. Some districts require teachers to put a certain number of grades into their system every week. All these factors affect how teachers react to the notion of designing and using common formative assessments.

So how does an instructional coach help this process? To support teams as they use benchmark and end-of-year data, coaches should dig into these reports themselves so they can ask teams the right questions as a guide to drawing accurate conclusions. They should find out which reports are most helpful for each step of the intervention process. They determine the connections between each major type of assessment and the reality of how teams are using the information. Coaches help teams prioritize their analysis based on what they discover.

Coaches should also be sure teachers understand that they will use data they get from these summative assessments differently than data from common formative assessments. Because they write formative assessments around smaller learning targets, the results are intended to be more diagnostic than the data from summative assessments. We'll dig into this process later in this chapter as well as discuss how to use the information in chapter 4 (page 131) and chapter 5 (page 175).

The Benefits of Common Formative Assessments

When Paul Black and Dylan Wiliam (1998) published their groundbreaking research concluding the impressive impact formative assessment can have on student achievement, teachers began to consider how they could include these assessments more frequently in their work. Black and Wiliam (1998) found that by using formative assessment during the learning process, teachers can raise student achievement and reporting effect sizes from 0.4 (the student would learn at the same rate as the top 35 percent of those not given formative assessment) to as high as 0.7. Effect sizes are statistical ways to measure the impact of a specific innovation on student learning and allow comparisons between different interventions or innovations. While effect sizes weren't as commonly used by practitioners in 1998, most educators are familiar with them through the work of John Hattie, as he has done extensive work in developing effect sizes for many of the educational practices we use and then comparing them to each other.

Since 1998, Hattie has also reported effect sizes for using formative assessment from 0.7 to 0.9 (Hattie, 2009, 2012; Hattie, Masters,

& Birch, 2016). In his book *Visible Learning for Teachers*, Hattie (2012) looks at more than eight hundred meta-analyses of research studies in the field of education that include fifty-thousand research studies. He acknowledges that almost everything he considers in his research has a positive impact on student achievement but suggests the real bar of student achievement should be set at a 0.4 effect size, which he calculates is the average improvement of all the strategies he studied. By listing all the innovations in rank order from those with greatest effect size through those which had a very small effect size—even a few that had a negative effect size—we can choose to focus our work on where the effect size is the highest.

Since this book was released, Hattie continues to move forward with additional meta-analyses as well as updated research (Goddard, Hoy, & Hoy, 2000; Hattie, 2017). You can follow his conclusions on the Visible Learning website (www.visiblelearningplus.com). In addition, many of the other significant influences Hattie includes in his research aggregation are strategies that formative assessments lead to: teacher clarity, feedback, response to intervention, and self-reported grades. Collaborative teams can easily see how using formative assessment in their classrooms can significantly impact student learning.

Most teachers embrace the need to use formative assessments in their classrooms. What they are often uncomfortable with, on the other hand, is the need to add additional common formative assessments into their already packed assessment repertoire. Be sure you are familiar and comfortable with the *why* behind these assessments, starting with the value of collaborative practices. More researchers are writing about the impact of collective teacher efficacy on student learning, an impact Hattie et al. (2016) report as a 1.57 effect size

1

(Donohoo, 2017). Megan Tschannen-Moran and Marilyn Barr (2004) define *collective teacher efficacy* as "the collective self-perception that teachers in a given school make an educational difference to their students over and above the educational impact of their homes and communities" (p. 190).

Common formative assessments uniquely allow teams to improve student learning through both ideas. The first is knowing *during* the learning process which students continue to need time and support on essential learning targets, as evidenced by the impact of formative assessments. The second is the belief that working collaboratively helps teams overcome any outside factors that negatively impact student learning, as evidenced by the impact of collective teacher efficacy.

Teams must see that this process has value to their work over and above the typical classroom formative and summative assessments teams use to measure student learning at a given point in time. Common formative assessments also uniquely provide feedback about the team's chosen essential learning targets, and they allow team members to compare the way instructional strategies impact student learning. Coaches should help team members see this. It's also important to emphasize that the team may be able to use items that individual teachers used previously on their classroom formative assessments. The key is that the team has agreement, and the assessments measure student learning for agreed-on targets.

The following actions support the work of PLC critical question 2: How will we know if they have learned it?

Action 1: Build Understanding of a Balanced Assessment System

Many teachers are confident in their understanding of the differences between formative and summative assessments and can usually list examples of those they are using. However, they often have questions about how to best use the results from these assessments and construct quality questions. When working with teams, we often discuss the importance of a balanced assessment system to access the right types of data. In order to build understanding of a balanced assessment system, coaches must work with teams to do the following.

▸ Clarify the purpose of each assessment type.

▸ Ensure understanding of formative versus summative or end-of-unit measures.

▸ Support team clarity of standards versus learning targets in the assessment process.

▸ Clarify how common formative assessments fit into a unit of instruction.

Clarify the Purpose of Each Assessment Type

When a school has a balanced assessment system, teachers have a variety of different assessments to guide their work. An assessment's purpose guides the way teachers write and use it. For example, within-unit assessments are designed to make sure students are learning the important content of each unit as it's being taught. Teachers use *classroom formative assessments* daily to obtain feedback on their students' learning and provide immediate feedback to students. In collaboration with their team, they use common formative assessments to assess essential learning targets shortly after they've been taught to make sure all students are learning the guaranteed curriculum. They make sure these assessments tightly align to the pacing guides they use. Common formative assessment items may resemble classroom formative assessments, such as an exit ticket, but require a tangible product that allows teams to gather and analyze evidence of each student's level of understanding or skill.

Teams also develop *end-of-unit summative assessments* to provide information about whether students master the standards in the unit. Teams administer *interim* or *benchmark assessments* (periodic) several times each year. Many districts use these three times a year for all students to monitor student growth during the school year. They may also use these assessments as progress-monitoring tools for students identified for Tier 2 or Tier 3 support to know whether they are getting the right level of assistance.

Response to intervention (RTI) includes three tiers of student support, as explained by Austin Buffum, Mike Mattos, and Janet Malone in *Taking Action: A Handbook for RTI at Work™* (2018). Tier 1 provides "*all* students access to essential grade-level curriculum and effective initial teaching" (p. 20), while Tier 2 offers additional time and support to learn the essential grade-level curriculum, often in small groups or teams. Finally, Tier 3 offers students who are struggling in several areas more intensive remediation in foundational skills. Buffum, Mattos, and Malone (2018) emphasize that teachers "must provide this level of assistance *without denying these students access*

to essential grade-level curriculum" (p. 22). For more detailed information about RTI, see chapter 4 (page 131).

Teams may move students to a more or less intensive tier as the team determines how students are progressing. Districts can develop benchmark or interim assessments and match the pacing and curriculum, or they can purchase them from an outside vendor and mirror the expectations from high-stakes tests. Finally, teams may rely on cumulative or annual assessments to guide their own work. In addition to providing information about how each student is doing relative to grade-level or course expectations, they can answer questions about the effectiveness of their curriculum, their instructional practices, and pacing. These assessments also provide a big-picture view to determine how specific student subgroups are performing. See table 3.1 (page 84).

As a coach, you can work with a collaborative team to identify the difference in purpose between assessments in a balanced assessment system. Without this basic understanding, teachers often see common formative assessments as one more thing they have to add to their already packed curriculum, one which provides little differentiated information. We use the following three-step matching activity with teams to help them see the difference.

1. Cut apart and mix up the cards in figure 3.1 (page 84). You should have one set of assessment-type cards and one set of assessment purpose cards.

2. Give each team a set of cards.

3. Ask teams to match the correct assessment type with its purpose. This helps them see that each assessment has a different purpose.

Table 3.1: Examples of Assessment Types

Current (Within-Unit) Assessments	Progressive or Periodic Assessments	Cumulative or Annual Assessments
These are: • Classroom formative assessments (designed by individual teachers) • Common formative assessments (designed by the team) • Common summative or end-of-unit assessments (designed by the team)	These are: • Quarterly or trimester benchmarks or interim measures • Periodic progress monitoring of Tier 2 and Tier 3 supports and interventions • End-of-course assessments	These are state or province high-stakes assessments (for example, SBAC and PARCC): • Language development assessments

Source: Adapted from Bailey & Jakicic, 2017, p. 8.

Types of Assessment	Purposes of Assessment
Common formative assessment	Teachers administer this assessment during instruction to check whether students have learned essential learning targets and understand what instructional strategies are most effective (used to guide Tier 1 support).
Summative assessment	Teachers administer this type of assessment at the end of a unit to check whether students can put all the skills and concepts taught during that unit together (used to guide Tier 2 support).
Benchmark assessments	Teachers administer these assessments periodically to check if students are making progress toward the end-of-year standards (can help identify the need for Tier 2 support).
State (or province) and national tests (like the ACT and SAT)	Teachers administer these assessments to measure overall student learning and effectiveness of pacing, curriculum, and instructional strategies.
Universal screeners	Teachers administer these assessments early in the year to identify students who are significantly below grade level so they can get intensive (Tier 3) support.
Preassessments	Teachers administer these assessments to gain information about what students already know and discover any gaps they have in their prerequisite learning before they start teaching a unit.
Classroom formative assessments	Teachers administer these assessments during instruction to check whether students have learned what they are teaching.

Figure 3.1: Card sort activity—Understanding the purposes of assessments in a balanced assessment system.

Visit go.SolutionTree.com/PLCbooks for a free reproducible version of this figure.

The following four coaching questions can help teams discuss their current assessments.

1. What information does this assessment provide us about student learning?

2. Can we act on that information to provide students the help they need?

3. Does this assessment provide us information specifically about student learning of our *essential* standards?

4. Can we learn more about how our instructional strategies are impacting student learning?

Here's the bottom line: we will only know whether students are learning if we specifically monitor them throughout the learning process. By keeping our fingers on the pulse of student learning through common formative assessments, we can gain useful information to make adjustments in instruction, provide additional time and support, and give students timely and specific feedback that empowers them to move forward in their learning.

Ensure Understanding of Formative Versus Summative or End-of-Unit Measures

As a coach, make sure team members understand the differences between formative and summative or end-of-unit assessments. Most teachers are pretty confident in this knowledge but don't always know how to write formative assessments differently than summative assessments. Usually, when teams receive explicit training on this, their ability to diagnose what students still need increases remarkably. In this chapter, we'll explore the difference between these two types of assessments as well as how to better design and write formative assessments.

You can use the checklist in figure 3.2 (page 86) to introduce writing and refining team assessments and gauge where teams are in their understanding and implementation of the common assessment process. This can be particularly helpful when comments about too much testing or insufficient results from tests are surfacing. Use the responses to gain insight about any misconceptions or lack of clarity around the information.

Teachers give formative assessments to students during a unit of instruction around essential learning. When students don't show proficiency, they get extra time and support before the class moves on. The purpose of formative assessment is more than just identifying students who need additional time and support; it also helps teachers understand where the learning stops or where student misunderstanding occurs. Educationist Dylan Wiliam's (2011) definition of formative assessment explains this difference:

> An assessment functions formatively to the extent that evidence about student achievement is elicited, interpreted, and used by teachers, learners, or their peers *to make decisions about the next steps in instruction that are likely to be better, or better founded*, than the decisions they would have made in the absence of that evidence. (p. 48, emphasis added)

This quote emphasizes the fact that formative assessments do more than just identify which students have or have not yet learned an important learning target. They help a team diagnose and learn from mistakes or misunderstandings a student might have so the response can be more effective.

1

Design	Yes	No
The targets come from identified power or essential standards.		
The assessment is written around learning targets, not standards.		
The assessment is written around a small number of learning targets.		
The purpose is to provide time and support rather than a grade.		
The type of assessment item the team uses matches the learning target's level of thinking.		
The team writes the selected-response items to find out what students know, not to trick them.		
Constructed-response items provide context and specific directions to make expectations clear to students.		
The team agrees on what proficiency looks like for each target.		
The team creates an answer guide for its assessment.		
Use		
The team collaboratively writes and administers the assessment in a common way.		
The team collaboratively scores items using a common rubric.		
The data meeting happens as quickly as possible after the assessment.		
All teachers bring their data, including student work, to the data meeting for discussion.		
The teachers use data for planning what to do next, not to judge their effectiveness.		
Students are involved; they know the learning targets and receive feedback on their work.		
Students get more time and support based on the results.		
Teachers reassess students after corrective instruction.		
Students who master learning targets receive more challenging work after teachers analyze the data.		

Figure 3.2: Common formative assessments checklist.

*Visit **go.SolutionTree.com/PLCbooks** for a free reproducible version of this figure.*

Teachers give formative and common formative assessments during the unit of instruction while students are still learning. This allows teachers to respond quickly and efficiently after instruction and before the class moves on to new material. Consider, for example, a common formative assessment consisting of a constructed-response question that asks students to explain how the text structure contributes to the meaning of the text. By using student responses, the team can figure out which students have difficulty identifying the text structure and which students can identify the structure but can't explain how that structure contributes to the meaning of the text. The responses for each group of students can be much more specific because they're based on a diagnostic look at student work.

We've addressed how powerful formative assessments can be in measuring specific learning targets. However, if teachers only use formative assessments to assess students, they cannot say with precision whether a student is learning what he or she should for that grade level. That is, if teachers are only assessing isolated learning targets, they might not gain a complete understanding of whether students have achieved the complete "end in mind" for the unit of study or end-of-year assessment.

Support Team Clarity of Standards Versus Learning Targets in the Assessment Process

In chapter 2 (page 35), we discussed the process of unwrapping standards into learning targets. This process is important because the team writes formative assessments around learning targets rather than standards to make them more diagnostic. Consider a team who is teaching the standard: "Conduct an investigation to provide evidence that living things are made of cells; either one cell or many different numbers and types of cells" (NGSS Lead States, 2013, p. 67). If the team assesses the standard in a summative assessment, it would look at the design and implementation of the investigation the student uses to demonstrate the concepts in the standard. For a common formative assessment, it would likely focus on one or more learning targets, such as what makes something living versus nonliving or the difference between multicellular and unicellular animals and plants.

Figure 3.3 shows the relationship between the two assessment types and how they evolve over the course of a unit of study. After identifying the essential standards being addressed in a unit of study, the team unwraps the standards to identify the learning targets, or the skills and concepts students must acquire to demonstrate the end-of-unit expectations. Teams use those learning targets to build one or more brief common formative assessments that specifically measure the learning targets after they're taught. The summative or end-of-unit assessment assesses standards or combinations of learning targets.

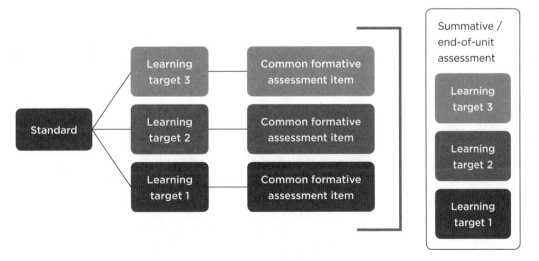

Figure 3.3: Relationship between assessment types and how they evolve over a unit of study.

One thing we've learned in our work is that some schools and districts face the goal of writing their own common formative assessments with a great deal of trepidation. They may worry about the amount of time it will take to do this work or that they don't know enough about assessment design to write valid and reliable items. We contend that writing and using common formative assessments is the heart of how teams learn together in a PLC. This chapter supports coaches who are working with teams through this process.

Clarify How Common Formative Assessments Fit Into a Unit of Instruction

Teams often want to understand how to find the time for giving and responding to common formative assessments. Many teams have been using their own classroom formative assessments as frequently as daily and their own end-of-unit assessments after instruction for that unit is complete. The graphic organizer for a generic unit (figure 3.4) may help their

understanding about what it would look like to add common formative assessments.

Notice that team members have five days to teach their content at the beginning of the unit. In a PLC, we don't expect all teachers to teach exactly the same way, so each teacher on the team makes instructional decisions about how to teach the content. On the sixth day, they use a short common formative assessment. Notice that there will still be time that day to do additional instruction. The team meets to share and analyze data so it can effectively plan its response. Time for that response with students is built into their pacing guide as a response day.

The graphic organizer in figure 3.4 is a generic one. It won't always take a full day to respond to an assessment, and teachers may not be able to meet and plan the response immediately following the assessment, as they have to score the student work and may not meet every day of the week. Also, many teams teach units that are much shorter or longer than this one. This means that they may only do one common formative assessment in a short unit

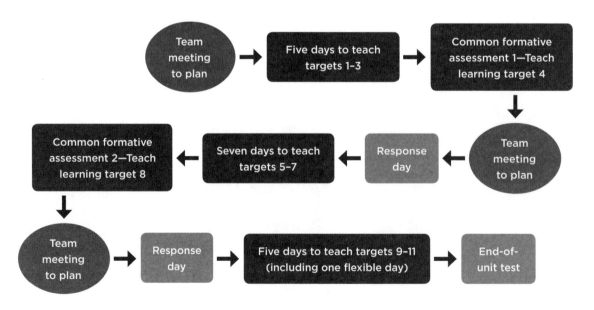

Figure 3.4: Process to develop a unit plan to include common formative assessments.

or more common formative assessments in a longer unit. One last consideration: As teams begin this work, they cannot possibly write all the common formative assessments they will eventually use during their first year engaged in this work. This is an ongoing process!

Some common questions teachers and teams have about using common formative assessments include the following.

▸ **How much time will it take to give a common formative assessment?** Teachers design common formative assessments to quickly determine whether students acquired a specific skill or piece of knowledge in a timely fashion after it was taught. Typically, they measure one or two learning targets at a time, so they are small in nature. Rather than major assessment events, they are brief measures teachers design to check in on each and every student and gather evidence of that learning. They should be quick enough to not interrupt the flow of instruction—in fact, that can feel like instruction. Teachers use them at the beginning, middle, or end of a lesson.

▸ **What should common formative assessments look like?** Common formative assessments don't always resemble traditional quizzes or tests. While teams can use selected-response items as a formative assessment, short-constructed items, such as bullet points, graphic organizers, sample problems, or brief explanations can provide great insight into whether students have learned a skill or concept. Furthermore, teams can get immediate insights by examining their students' work, including specific strengths, common errors, or misconceptions. The important thing is that the item provides tangible evidence of every student's learning of specific learning targets.

▸ **How frequently do teams give common formative assessments?** There is no prescribed frequency for giving common formative assessments. It's more important for teams to examine what they're teaching and decide when it would be important to check on their students' learning of critical learning targets. It may be appropriate for a team to check their students' learning with a common formative assessment after four days of instruction, because the team decides that it needs to ensure all students have a particular skill before moving on. Or, they might go a week or two between common formative assessments if appropriate for the targets being taught.

Use the Coaching Reflection on page 125 to reflect on the information you explored for Action 1.

Coaching the Issue

A middle school principal has worked diligently with his staff to effectively use a benchmarking assessment system the district purchased and requires its schools to use three times a year with students. Teachers can use this same benchmarking assessment to progress monitor students who are receiving additional time and

continued →

1

support to make sure they are getting the support they need. When the district purchased the system, the district trained teacher leaders to use the data and report with their teams. Since deciding to implement the PLC model, teachers are hoping to use the three assessments as their common formative assessments and believe that their teams are not as capable of writing good items as a testing company.

- **Coach's role:** The principal asks Mai Le, the school instructional coach, to facilitate data discussions with every team and help them identify students who need additional support in the areas of English language arts and mathematics. To make this happen, Mai Le realizes she needs to help teachers understand what a balanced assessment system should include and then support them as a coach in developing common formative assessments. Therefore, she chooses the role of a consultant and plans to prepare ideas and information as needed.

- **Team meetings:** Mai Le decides to set up meetings with each team to gather information and evidence of what's not working with the benchmarking assessments. When she first sits down with the mathematics team, team members share their concerns with her. For example, teachers might measure some students who are struggling as proficient on benchmark assessments and some as below basic but doing fine in the classroom. Some teachers claim that when students are taking the test, they have seen some of them attempting to answer questions about content that hasn't yet been taught. When asked about how they are using the data, they talk about their frustration with not having a designated time to work with students outside their regular class time. When Mai Le approaches the English language arts team members, they claim that assessment generally mirrors what they are seeing in the classroom—students who struggle to read and comprehend grade-level text do poorly on the assessment. In class, they've been providing simpler text for these students as they teach the standards. When asked about how students are responding, they share that they don't feel confident teaching students to read and wish they had a reading specialist who could work with these students.

- **Next steps:** Mai Le realizes that the next step for both teams is to engage them in discussion about the value of common formative assessments written around the learning targets they've identified as essential. She knows it is also important that the principal learns along with the teams about how the two types of assessment provide necessary information to respond to students. During her next meeting with these teams, she plans to share information about how a balanced assessment system that includes both benchmarking assessments and common formative assessments would help them better address student needs. She will ensure teachers have the information they need to write the assessments and feel comfortable analyzing these data. Additionally, Mai Le realizes it is important to share this work with the principal so he is part of the process.

Action 2: Design Assessments for Validity and Reliability

While we've worked with teams in all grade levels and subject areas, the one thing they all seem to have in common is a concern about their ability to write valid and reliable assessments. When Chris was principal at Woodlawn Middle School, the mathematics team pointed this out to staff after spending a great deal of post-assessment time looking at items that provided useless information either because the answer was too obvious (lack of rigor) or the question was confusing to students. We wanted a way to write questions that would provide good information about whether students had learned the targets. At the same time, most of the teachers didn't want to have to use a statistical analysis of their results to interpret whether the data were accurate. And, of course, they didn't have access to thousands of students with which to pilot items. They wanted to create assessments that, from the beginning, were valid and reliable as well as meaningful and doable.

Doug Reeves's (2007) insights about the role of validity and reliability in teacher-created assessments encouraged us on this journey.

> When our purpose is a quick determination of the extent to which students understand skills and concepts, and the equally important purpose of adjusting teaching strategies to help students who have not yet mastered those skills and concepts, then practical utility takes precedence over psychometric perfection. (p. 235)

Christopher Gareis and Leslie Grant (2008) provide guidelines that explain what the term *validity* means and how to make teacher-created assessments valid. We learned that valid assessments mirror the content taught as well as the expected rigor for learning. If our learning target says students need to be able to analyze how rhetoric impacted the meaning in a speech, we can't settle for having students just list different ways authors use rhetoric in their writing or a piece of text. We recognized that when our items weren't valid (or didn't accurately assess what we wanted them to), they were most likely designed to match the content we wanted to assess but lacked the rigor we intended for assessment.

So, our task became to develop questions and items at the appropriate rigor level. This caused us to focus again on the unwrapping process through which we had identified learning targets. During this process, we had discussed DOK levels of each learning target. This discussion originated as a way for team members to make sure they were interpreting the learning targets in the same way. However, we also realized that this was vital information for ensuring validity of the assessment items we would write. While we were getting closer to valid items, we also needed to understand better how to choose the right type of item to assess at the rigor our learning target demanded. Following are two steps for helping teams make their common formative assessments more valid.

1. Unwrap the standard into a learning target and agree on the DOK level required for mastery of that target.

2. Develop an assessment plan prior to writing the assessment that ensures the types of items teams use match the rigor of the learning target.

That led us to put a new process in place to ensure validity and reliability. This four-step process includes:

1. Make your assessment valid by planning it first.

2. Match the item type to the rigor of the learning target.

3. Determine the number of items needed to ensure reliability.

4. Set proficiency expectations.

Make Your Assessment Valid by Planning It First

Teams can use the assessment-planning template in figure 3.5 to create an assessment map to help with choosing which learning targets to assess and which types of items to use for assessing targets before writing the assessment items. When teams use this assessment-planning template, their assessments will likely be more valid.

Figure 3.6 shows an example of how a fourth-grade team might plan a common formative assessment in ELA.

Content or Targets	Level of Cognitive Demand				
	Knowledge Retrieval DOK 1	Comprehension Application DOK 2	Analysis DOK 3	Synthesis Evaluation DOK 4	Expectations for Proficiency

Figure 3.5: Blank assessment-planning template.

*Visit **go.SolutionTree.com/PLCbooks** for a free reproducible version of this figure.*

Learning Targets	Level of Cognitive Demand				
	Knowledge Retrieval DOK 1	Comprehension Application DOK 2	Analysis DOK 3	Synthesis Evaluation DOK 4	Expectations for Proficiency
Compare and contrast a firsthand and secondhand account of the same event or topic. (Step 1)		Four multiple choice (Step 2)			Three of four questions correct
Describe the difference in focus.			One constructed response (Step 3)		Proficiency level on the rubric (Step 4)

Note: DOK 3 and 4 are shaded to remind teams that if the learning target is DOK 3 or 4, it probably won't be effectively assessed using a selected-response question.

Figure 3.6: Example common formative assessment plan for ELA.

When a team is designing a common formative assessment, it should assess a maximum of three learning targets at a time. In fact, we've often worked with teams who assess only one target on a common formative assessment because they believe that one target is absolutely essential to student learning, and they don't want to move on in the unit until they are confident students have learned that target. As you would imagine, the assessments themselves are short and focused—maybe twenty minutes or less, depending on whether students need to read and comprehend a piece of text or analyze graphs or charts.

Coaching Insight

It isn't necessary to assess every learning target identified when unwrapping a standard. Consider the following five targets that come from a ninth- and tenth-grade informational text standard: (1) delineate the argument and specific claims in a text, (2) evaluate the argument and specific claims in a text, (3) assess whether the reasoning is valid, (4) assess whether the evidence is relevant and sufficient, and (5) identify false statements and fallacious reasoning (RI.9–10.8, NGA & CCSSO, 2010a). Keeping in mind that assessments should be short and focused, team members discuss which of these five targets are most important. For example, they may determine that high school students should be proficient in delineating an argument and claims, so they may decide to assess the second target requiring students to evaluate the argument and claims. They may look at targets three through five and choose to assess targets three and four. Give teams three ideas to consider when deciding which targets to assess: (1) targets that are difficult and often lead to misconceptions; (2) targets that are prerequisite to future learning; and (3) targets that are absolutely necessary for students to know.

Match the Item Type to the Rigor of the Learning Target

In this step, teams plan to ensure that the items they write for their assessment match the type and rigor of the learning targets they will assess. Therefore, part of the process involves teams reaching consensus about the DOK level for each learning target they have on the assessment and implications for the type of item they plan to write.

When teams begin learning about assessment design, it's important that they understand the pros and cons of using different types of items. Generally, they can categorize these types of items into performance, performance tasks, selected response, or constructed response.

Performance items are those that assess specific skills, such as using the bow correctly on a violin, doing a roundoff in physical education, using specific techniques to show perspective in an art project, measuring accurately in science, or writing an essay. Note that any of these require a student to demonstrate the skill either directly to the assessor or create a product for the assessor to examine.

Performance tasks, on the other hand, are generally used for summative assessments because they require students to use a combination of multiple learning targets to complete. Teams generally establish the task as a realistic problem one might encounter in real life. In order to complete the task, students must carry out multiple activities using a variety of stimulus information. There are generally a number of different ways to solve the problem and likely multiple correct answers.

Selected-response questions have the answer on the page, and the student must select the correct answer. Multiple-choice questions, matching questions, and true-or-false questions fit into this category. Teachers often favor these items because they are efficient to administer, easy to score, and require no collaborative scoring practices. However, teachers typically can't use them to assess learning targets beyond level DOK 2.

Constructed-response questions require students to supply the answer without the benefit of choices. They may include short answer, extended response, graphic organizers, or diagrams. Often, teachers give students some kind of stimulus to read or analyze (for example, piece of text, graphs) requiring complex thinking. The student then responds to a question based on this stimulus. These questions are often more difficult and time-consuming for teachers to score. However, because students must use more complex reasoning, constructed-response questions are often the choice for any learning target that is a DOK 3 or 4. These questions often provide information to teams about misconceptions or misunderstandings when students show their thinking.

Rick Stiggins, Judith Arter, Jan Chappuis, and Steve Chappuis (2004) suggest that teams match the rigor of the learning target to the type of item they choose to use. That is, teachers can assess learning targets that require only knowledge or simple reasoning with selected-response items, but those that require more complex reasoning are better assessed using constructed-response questions. Skills will likely need to be assessed with performance items. We believe that this matching process is an important step in making assessments valid. Notice that we believe defining proficiency in the unwrapping process leads to better quality assessments.

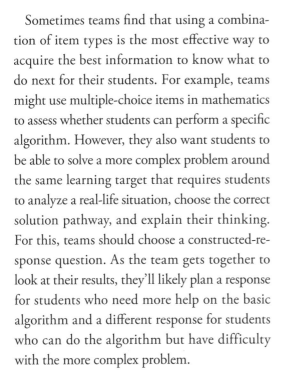

Coaching Tip

Generally, questions that have only one correct answer are used in assessing DOK 1 or 2 learning targets. If the question has more than one right answer, it is likely assessing a DOK 3 or 4 learning target. DOK 3 and 4 are shaded in the assessment-planning template (see figure 3.5, page 92) to remind teams that if the learning target is a DOK 3 or 4, it probably won't be effectively assessed using a selected-response question.

Sometimes teams find that using a combination of item types is the most effective way to acquire the best information to know what to do next for their students. For example, teams might use multiple-choice items in mathematics to assess whether students can perform a specific algorithm. However, they also want students to be able to solve a more complex problem around the same learning target that requires students to analyze a real-life situation, choose the correct solution pathway, and explain their thinking. For this, teams should choose a constructed-response question. As the team gets together to look at their results, they'll likely plan a response for students who need more help on the basic algorithm and a different response for students who can do the algorithm but have difficulty with the more complex problem.

As teams build consensus around DOK levels and the appropriate item type for each learning target, they complete those sections of the assessment-planning template (figure 3.5, page 92). Note that teams may also create this chart as a shared electronic document they can reproduce for each unit of study.

Determine the Number of Items Needed to Ensure Reliability

Teams must decide how many questions they need to reliably measure each learning target. A greater number of items usually results in a more reliable assessment. Assessments with greater reliability mean that you will have greater

confidence in the results teams get back. For example, consider what happens when a team has only one multiple-choice question. The student might guess the correct answer and appear to have mastered the learning target. So, we must use more than one item to assess the learning target if we use multiple-choice questions.

However, common formative assessments should take a minimum amount of time to administer so teams need to find the sweet spot for the number of items to use. While we've found lots of research saying that the more items used the more reliable the result, we haven't found a definitive answer to the question of how many we need. For example, Stiggins et al. (2004) remind us we need enough items for each learning target to ensure students learn. Gareis and Grant (2008) add that, in general, the more items we have the more reliable the assessment. They suggest that teachers rely on common sense in choosing the number of items but that a minimum of three is necessary. Working collaboratively with teams developing common formative assessments, we've generally suggested that they use three to four multiple-choice questions or one well-designed constructed-response question per learning target.

Set Proficiency Expectations

The far-right column in the assessment-planning template (figure 3.5, page 92) addresses the final decision a team must make: the level of expected proficiency for each learning target. So, for example, if the team uses four multiple-choice questions, teachers might expect a student to get three of those questions correct. Only a very lucky student would be able to guess three questions correctly, and this allows a student to misread a question and still show proficiency. For constructed-response questions, the team may want to develop a rubric with a description of proficiency as one level. When teams come back together after administering the assessment, they start with the information from this planning chart. They'll remind themselves which learning targets they're assessing and the expectations of proficiency for each.

Table 3.2 summarizes the protocol and provides additional information about the type of coaching support teams might need for creating a protocol for developing an assessment plan.

Let's look at the example in figure 3.7 of how a sixth-grade science team develops a common formative assessment and a common summative assessment for its upcoming cell unit. Team members begin by unwrapping the two standards they will include in the unit. As they unwrap the standards, they note any ideas for assessment items so they can build on these ideas later.

Table 3.2: Protocol for Developing an Assessment Plan

Step	Description of Process	Coaching Support
1. Make your assessment valid by planning it first.	Teams agree on which learning targets to assess, choosing essential learning targets that have been taught.	Coach may need to help teams identify which targets they should assess. Teams can't assess *every* learning target that comes from an essential standard, so they must choose the most important.
2. Match the item type to the rigor of the learning target.	Teams agree on the rigor level of the learning target. This information may come straight from their unwrapping template.	Coach points out that teams must go back to this step in the unwrapping process so they don't miss the rigor the target implies.
3. Determine the number of items needed to ensure reliability.	Teams determine what type of items to write and how many they will use based on the rigor level of the target.	Note that the DOK 3 and 4 levels on the assessment-planning template are highlighted to remind teams that teams will probably not be able to assess targets using multiple-choice questions. Coaches should point this out as teams begin their work together. When using multiple choice, teams need a minimum of three to four questions for each learning target. Targets with constructed response only need one question but it needs to be well written. (See advice in Action 3).
4. Set proficiency expectations.	Teams complete the "Expectations for Proficiency" column in figure 3.5 (page 92) by agreeing how many multiple-choice items students must get correct or what the rubric level expectation is for constructed response.	At this step, it's critical for teams to examine the data *learning target by learning target*. That is, they want to know which students were not proficient on each of the learning targets being assessed. On formative assessments, there isn't any value to an overall assessment score. We can't find any research that determines how many multiple-choice items a student must get correct, but most teams are comfortable with two out of three or three out of four.

*Visit **go.SolutionTree.com/PLCbooks** for a free reproducible version of this table.*

Standard or standards to address:

Conduct an investigation to provide evidence that living things are made of cells; either one cell or many different numbers and types of cells (MS-LS1-1).

Develop and use a model to describe the function of a cell as a whole and ways the parts of cells contribute to the function (MS-LS1-2).

Context and Conditions (Explain what text, problem type, or situation students will encounter.)	Students have learned to use a microscope and the steps of the scientific method. In this unit, they will use both of those skills. They use models to explain phenomena but never develop their own model.		
Learning Target		**DOK**	**Assessment**
Students Need to Know Concepts or Information	• The definition of a cell	1	Have students define important vocabulary.
	• What makes something living	1	Have students list the factors that make something living.
	• Unicellular organisms versus multicellular organisms	2	Have students explain the difference between unicellular and multicellular organisms.
	• Cell organelles	1	
	• Definition and description of osmosis and diffusion	2	Have students explain the difference between osmosis and diffusion.
	• Plant cells versus animal cells	2	Provide slides of plant and animal cells, and have students identify them.
	Big idea: All living things are made up of cells. More complex animals and plants have many different kinds of cells. Cells have parts called organelles that carry out a variety of functions.		
Students Will Do or Demonstrate	• Distinguish between living and nonliving things.	2	Provide a table with evidence, and have students determine if the item is living or nonliving.
	• Develop and use a model to describe the function of a cell as a whole.	2	
	• Develop and use a model to describe how parts of a cell contribute to the function.	3	
	• Explain how osmosis and diffusion affect cell transport.	3	Have students draw a model to explain cell transport with osmosis and diffusion.
Students Will Use Academic Language and Vocabulary	Cell, nucleus, chloroplasts, mitochondria, cell wall, cell membrane		

Source for standards: NGSS Lead States, 2013.

Figure 3.7: Example of unwrapping standards for cell unit.

Visit go.SolutionTree.com/PLCbooks for a free reproducible version of this figure.

Knowing that they won't be able to get everything done that they want to for this unit during the first year, the team members agree to write one common formative assessment shortly after the first lab during which students examine slides of cheek cells, onion skin cells, elodea leaves, cork, and sugar. For the assessment, the teacher will give them a table with data from a similar investigation with different items and ask them to determine if these items are living or nonliving. He or she will also ask them to explain the difference between unicellular animals and plants and multicellular animals and plants. Figure 3.8 shows the assessment plan the team develops.

Content and Targets	Level of Cognitive Demand				
	Knowledge Retrieval DOK 1	Comprehension Application DOK 2	Analysis DOK 3	Synthesis Evaluation DOK 4	Expectations for Proficiency
Explain the difference between living and nonliving things based on evidence from an investigation.		One constructed response			Proficiency on the rubric
Explain why some animals and plants are unicellular and some are multicellular.		One constructed response			Proficiency on the rubric

Figure 3.8: Common formative assessment planning chart for cell unit.

*Visit **go.SolutionTree.com/PLCbooks** for a free reproducible version of this figure.*

As soon as team members complete the pacing guide for the unit, they develop the plan for their end-of-unit summative assessment. They intend this assessment to ensure students master the most important concepts taught. They will build on some of these learning targets in the next unit: tissues, organs, and systems. Others are important concepts for future life science units. Figure 3.9 shows the team's summative assessment plan.

Coaching Tips

1. Encourage teams to create an answer guide at the same time as they create the assessment. Surprisingly, teams score items differently, even multiple-choice questions. As they create the answer guide they discuss what are correct and incorrect answers. The same goes for rubrics for constructed-response and performance items. It's important that students as well as teachers understand what proficiency looks like.

2. While using multiple-choice questions might be appealing for teams, as they make scoring easier and they avoid having to use collaborative scoring methods, they may reveal little about student thinking and misunderstanding.

3. Teams may find scoring constructed-response questions easier by including a graphic organizer in which students can write their answers. This helps students frame their responses, and they are likely to provide every part of the answer the team is looking for. Consider a question that asks teams to list three examples of data the author uses to support an argument and evidence of where that information appears in the text. With a graphic organizer, the team knows students will likely pay more attention to the expectation of three data points as well as the need to supply the source from the text. Teachers also find this information easier to score because of the way it's organized.

Content and Targets	Level of Cognitive Demand				
	Knowledge Retrieval DOK 1	Comprehension Application DOK 2	Analysis DOK 3	Synthesis Evaluation DOK 4	Expectations for Proficiency
Distinguish living things from nonliving things based on evidence from an investigation.		Table with information—student draws conclusions			Four out of five correct
Explain the function of cell membrane and cell wall.		One constructed response			Proficiency on the rubric
Distinguish plant cells from animal cells.		Identify four slides.			Three correct
Draw a model to explain osmosis and its effect on cell transport.			One constructed response		Proficiency on the rubric
Critique an investigation designed to provide evidence that living things are made up of cells.			One constructed response		Proficiency on the rubric
Definitions: *cell, organelle, cell wall, cell membrane, chloroplasts, mitochondria*	Four multiple choice				Three out of four correct

Figure 3.9: End-of-unit or summative assessment planning chart for cell unit.

Visit go.SolutionTree.com/PLCbooks for a free reproducible version of this figure.

2

The process of writing and using common formative assessments must be something teachers can realistically accomplish during their regular common planning time. When we are coaching teams through the process of designing common formative assessments, the first couple of assessments may take much longer to write. But as teams become proficient, they can easily write a common assessment and its scoring guide in a fifty-minute planning time.

The following are four ways coaches can prepare for and work with teams to write common assessments.

1. If the team doesn't already have a way to save their documents, set up a folder or share site with easy access so team members can work together on each document and have an archived product of their work.

2. Make sure each team member has access to the templates he or she will use during this process—most likely in an electronic format.

3. Provide a copy of figure 3.5 (page 92) for team use.

4. Bookmark the sites you and team members have identified to make their work easier, including sites with appropriate text, sites for sample mathematics items, primary source documents, and so on.

In chapter 2 (page 35), we discussed how a team moves from essential standards to assessment design. In this chapter, we explored how teams plan for formative and summative assessments. High-performing teams integrate these steps in their work. The critical questions in figure 3.10 serve as the framework for this unit

development, and the facilitator questions provide guidance as teams address each step of the process. Teams can use the five-step process for unit planning outlined in figure 3.11. It provides a protocol for teams as they walk through the backward-planning process.

As teams develop their units of study, they should see evidence of:

▸ Clear identification of the essential standards and their subset learning targets (knowledge, skills, conceptual understandings) to be achieved by the end of the unit

▸ Clear expectations for the end-of-unit / summative performance and proficiency (By the end of the unit, students should be able to . . .)

▸ An instructional plan that aligns and intentionally facilitates learning of the essential learning targets (knowledge, skills, conceptual understanding) to be attained by the end of the unit

▸ Specific text or stimuli to be used within the unit instruction

▸ Integration of shared quality instructional practices used to support high levels of learning

▸ Embedded common formative assessments designed to monitor essential learning targets at key points within the unit

▸ Intentionally planned activities that engage students in using feedback coming from their formative assessments, including peer reviews and editing, in order to improve learning

Question 1: What do we want students to know and be able to do? Identify priority standards and learning targets.

Question 2: How will we know if they have learned it? Determine what evidence team members should see by the end of the unit (summative), and identify the skills or concepts they must monitor along the way to make sure students get to that end in mind (formative).

Question 2.5: What strategies will we use to help students learn? Draft a time line for instruction and assessment.

Figure 3.10: Critical questions as framework for unit development.

*Visit **go.SolutionTree.com/PLCbooks** for a free reproducible version of this figure.*

Question 1: What do we want students to know and be able to do?

Step 1: Identify the essential or power standards for the unit.

> **Essential standards taught in this unit:**
>
>
> **Supporting standards taught in this unit:**

Question 2 (summative or end of unit): How will we know if they have learned it? What evidence will tell us they meet the standards by the end of the unit?

Step 2: Discuss evidence of the end in mind (summative measure)—How you will know if students achieved these standards? What type of task could they perform or complete by the end of the unit? With what level of proficiency? With what type of problem or text (stimulus)? (Note: Use released items, and look at prior and subsequent grade levels or other information to gain insight about the types of tasks you expect students to perform and the stimuli [problems, text, and so on] they will use.)

Figure 3.11: Five-step team unit planning process.

Step 3: Share the specific learning targets (bite-sized pieces of learning) that lead to students accomplishing the unit goals. Be sure to identify the main ideas emphasized in the unit. (Note: Not everything is written in the standard—teams should use their professional judgment to identify the learning targets. Read "between the lines" of the standard language.)

Learning Targets		Assessment Items
What should students know? (Information, definitions, processes, concepts, main ideas that students must know or understand)	Big idea:	
What should students be able to do? (Performance, skills, or actions students must do or demonstrate)		
What academic language / vocabulary should students acquire and use?		

Alternatively, teams can use the Unwrapping Learning Targets Through DOK Analysis (figure 2.13, page 70) to identify the learning targets.

Question 2.5 (formative): Where in the unit does it make sense to see if our students are learning what we are teaching? What evidence will we collect along the way?

Step 4: Do the following—

• Identify specific targets the team will commonly assess (formatively). Your team should collectively monitor learning targets that are typically challenging for students.

• Identify or develop brief but aligned assessment items that will provide useable evidence to the team about their students' understanding and skill. Discuss the level of proficiency you would expect for the assessment item or items.

Step 5: Plan the sequence of instruction and the timing for common formative assessments—As the team designs the plan, they should include the quality instructional practices that support high levels of student learning (Question 2.5: What are best instructional practices or strategies we will embed in this unit?).

Sequential Plan for Unit Instruction and Monitoring Learning		
Days	**Lessons or Activities** (What learning targets will you teach? How will you teach them?)	**Embedded Assessment Checkpoints** (What are the formative and summative checkpoints?)

Notes:

*Visit **go.SolutionTree.com/PLCbooks** for a free reproducible version of this figure.*

Figure 3.12 (pages 104–106) shows an example of a completed five-step team unit-planning process chart. Note how the team answered critical questions 1, 2, and 2.5 in this planning process.

Teams engaging in collaboratively designing instructional units are continually addressing the critical questions of learning. Throughout the unit, members come together to share and analyze evidence of their students' learning to determine who is acquiring the learning targets, what instructional strategies are effective, and how they might support students moving forward. The process is never quite finished. It may begin as a rough outline with specific pausing points designated for common formative assessments, but each year they teach this instructional unit, teams can refine it and make it more effective.

Use the Coaching Reflection on page 126 to reflect on the information you explored for Action 2.

Sample Unit for Grade 5 History / Social Studies: Unit of Study Team Planning (With Facilitator Points)

Question 1: What do we want students to know and be able to do?

Step 1: Identify the priority standards (essential or power) for the unit.

Essential or Power Standards	Supporting Standards
Literacy standards: • Explain the relationships or interactions between two or more individuals, events, ideas, or concepts in a historical, scientific, or technical text based on specific information in the text (RI.5.3). • Integrate information from several texts on the same topic in order to write or speak about the subject knowledgeably (RI.5.9). • Write informative/explanatory texts to examine a topic and convey ideas and information clearly (W.5.2). History / social studies standards (California): • Describe the entrepreneurial characteristics of early explorers (for example, Christopher Columbus, Francisco Vázquez de Coronado) and the technological developments that made sea exploration by latitude and longitude possible (for example, compass, sextant, astrolabe, seaworthy ships, chronometers, gunpowder) (CAHSS 5.2.1). • Explain the aims, obstacles, and accomplishments of the explorers, sponsors, and leaders of key European expeditions and the reasons Europeans chose to explore and colonize the world (for example, the Spanish Reconquista, the Protestant Reformation, the Counter-Reformation) (CAHSS 5.2.2).	Supporting standards: • Draw on information from multiple print or digital sources, demonstrating the ability to locate an answer to a question quickly or solve a problem efficiently (RI.5.7). • Analyze multiple accounts of the same event or topic, noting important similarities and differences in the point of view they represent (RI.5.6).

Question 2 (summative)—How will we know if they have learned it?

Step 2: Discuss evidence of the end in mind (summative measure)—How will you know if students achieved these standards? What type of task could they perform or complete by the end of the unit? With what level of proficiency? With what type of problem or text (stimulus)?

This means a student would be able to do the following.

Present a piece of writing or multimedia project to demonstrate his or her understanding of the entrepreneurial characteristics of early explorers, including the technological development, economic influences, and obstacles that impacted their exploration and discoveries.

Question 3: What are the specific learning targets (bite-sized pieces of learning) that lead to students being able to accomplish the unit goals?

Step 3: Unwrap the essential or power standards.

Learning Targets		Assessment Items
What should students know? (Information, definitions, processes, concepts, main ideas that students must know or understand)	Students will know: • The entrepreneurial characteristics and motives of early explorers • The connection between sponsoring countries and the explorers • Technological innovations taking place that enabled explorers to advance in their work • Motivation and obstacles related to the exploration Big idea: There were economic, political, and religious motivations for European countries to explore new lands. Exploration influenced how the New World was settled.	Items include: • Exit ticket with prompt regarding motives • Tree map of explorers in which students are to: Identify their sponsoring country for each (have blanks there) • Cause-and-effect graphic organizer showing tech development and what it allowed (students complete) Add to tree map.
What should students be able to do? (Performance, skills, or actions students must do or demonstrate)	Students will: • Read and extract information from credible sources. • Group, organize, and summarize the information gathered from a variety of resources. • Identify the cause-and-effect relationship related to the explorers and their success, obstacles, or both. • Present the information in written form and in an oral or multimedia project.	Items include: • Google Classroom notes • Google Classroom outline and citations Add to tree map or outline. • Exit tickets • Info writing or presentation rubric
What academic language / vocabulary should students acquire and use?	*generalization, summarize, compare and contrast, perspective, expedition, navigation, exploration, monarch, magnetic compass, astrolabe, chronometer, latitude, biography, longitude, circumnavigation, cartographer, caravel, tributary, trading post, charter, settlement*	

Figure 3.12: Sample grade 5 history unit.

continued →

Question 2 (formative): What evidence will we collect along the way for these learning targets? Where in the unit does it make sense to see if our students are learning what we are teaching? What evidence will we collect along the way?

Step 4: Do the following—

- Identify specific targets the team will commonly assess (formatively). The team should collectively monitor learning targets that are typically challenging for students.

- Identify or develop brief but aligned assessment items that provide useable evidence to the team about their students' understanding and skill. Discuss the level of proficiency you would expect for the assessment items.

Step 5: Plan the sequence of instruction and the timing for common formative assessments—As the team designs the plan, it should include the quality instructional practices that support high levels of student learning. (Question 2.5: What are best instructional practices or strategies we will embed in this unit? Where will we check in on specific learning targets using our formative assessments?)

Sequential Plan for Unit Instruction and Monitoring Learning		
Days	**Lessons or Activities** (What learning targets will you teach? How will you teach them?)	**Embedded Assessment Checkpoints** (What are the formative and summative checkpoints?)
Day 1	Launch activities (individual teacher determination)	
Days 2–8	Read the *The Age of Exploration* with students, available on ReadWorks (2016; https://bit.ly/2zDSe8Y). Have students work in teams to answer text-dependent questions and identify the relationship between specific explorers and countries of sponsorship.	Note-taking on Google Classroom Exit ticket Tree map for explorer information
Days 8–13	Continue engaging students in close reads of articles on explorers and referencing information in the textbook. Add information to a time line and reference a world map. Discuss information sources and strategies for organizing information coming from multiple sources; identify key sources to use for gathering information on explorers. Students will work online to identify information sources. They will identify information on the cause-and-effect relationship between entrepreneurial motivation and obstacles getting in the way of explorers' successes.	Updated notes on tree map Obstacle cause-and-effect map
Days 14–19	Discuss organization of informational text and multimedia presentations. Have students submit outlines for their informational presentations and sources on Google Classroom.	Google Classroom: Students submit outline and citations.
Days 20–25	Review the rubric with students. Have students continue working on informational reports and presentations or multimedia projects. Students will revise information based on peer and teacher feedback.	Peer review of information and feedback using the rubric
Days 25–30	Student presentations and peer rating	Grade-level informational report scoring rubric

Source for standards: California Department of Education, 2000; NGA & CCSSO, 2010a.

*Visit **go.SolutionTree.com/PLCbooks** for a free reproducible version of this figure.*

2

Coaching the Issue

Tim is an elementary school instructional coach. He is working with a fourth-grade team to develop a common formative assessment for its unit on common denominators—based on an essential standard. (Compare two fractions with different numerators and different denominators, for example, by creating common denominators or numerators, or by comparing to a benchmark fraction such as ½. Recognize that comparisons are valid only when the two fractions refer to the same whole. Record the results of comparisons with symbols >, =, or <, and justify the conclusions, such as, by using a visual fraction model; 4.NF.2, NGA & CCSSO, 2010b). He knows that this is the first true assessment the team has planned using a protocol he suggests, and he offers to co-plan the assessment with the team.

- **Coach's role:** Tim wants to co-plan this assessment with the team because he's confident these teachers understand both the purpose of the work and the process they need to follow. Tim can facilitate the discussions and keep the team on track as they follow the protocol.

- **Team meeting:** The team is made up of three teachers—Martina, Tammy, and Terrance. When they unwrapped this standard, they found five learning targets explicitly written in the standard.

  a. Compare two fractions with different numerators and different denominators by creating common denominators or numerators.

  b. Compare two fractions with different numerators and different denominators by comparing to a benchmark fraction.

  c. Recognize that comparisons are valid only when the two fractions refer to the same whole.

  d. Record the results of comparisons with symbols >, =, <.

  e. Justify the conclusions.

Teachers come to the meeting prepared with examples of questions they use in their classrooms. Tim starts by asking team members to determine which learning targets they want to assess and reminds them that they don't have to assess every learning target from an essential standard. Martina starts by suggesting that the first learning target is really the most important because if students haven't mastered this one, they won't be able to add and subtract fractions with unlike denominators. Her teammates agree, and then Terrance suggests they also assess target five. He says that this is an important target because it demonstrates whether students understand the process. This gives the team insight into any misunderstandings students might have.

Tim displays the template from figure 3.5 (page 92) on the screen at the front of the room so everyone can see and enters the learning targets in the template. He asks members to identify the DOK levels they've agreed on as a team. Team members suggest that the first target is DOK 2 because students must complete multiple steps to determine the answer, and the second target is DOK 3 because students must go beyond the process to explain their thinking about the outcome.

continued →

Tim starts with the first learning target and reminds teachers that they can use multiple choice on this question because it's DOK 2. Team members agree to write four questions in total because a student might misread one but still understand the concept. They agree students must get three of the four correct for students to master the target. As members discuss the second learning target, they realize they will have to write a constructed-response item for it. They agree that they need a rubric to score this question.

- **Next steps:** Tim feels good about this work and asks team members if they feel comfortable with the plan. They agree and are eager to start developing the assessment items.

Action 3: Write Quality Assessment Items

We've already addressed one way a team can increase reliability, that is, have a sufficient number of items to prevent students from guessing and looking proficient. The second way a team can increase reliability is to write questions that are clear and easy for students to interpret so they can show what they've learned.

The first piece of advice we offer teams on developing assessment items comes from Stiggins et al. (2004): "Keep wording simple and focused. Aim for the lowest possible reading level" (p. 139). This recommendation allows students to clearly understand what they are being asked to do. In addition, we recommend that teachers write items with appropriate academic and domain-specific vocabulary. It's important to clarify here, however, if the item includes as a stimulus any written text, that text should be at the appropriate rigor for students. In other words, if the item is an eighth-grade English language arts learning target that requires students to read a piece of text, the text itself should be at the eighth-grade level. The question about the text, however, should read as simply as possible.

In order to write quality assessment items, coaches must work with teams to:

▸ Develop quality constructed-response items.

▸ Develop quality selected-response items.

▸ Choose the stimulus.

▸ Model samples and exemplars from high-stakes tests.

▸ Adapt the process for unique team structures.

Develop Quality Constructed-Response Items

When they are well-designed, constructed-response items can tell teachers not only if a student has mastered a learning target, but also whether that student has misconceptions or misunderstandings related to that target. Stiggins et al. (2004) provide two suggestions about writing these items. The first is teams should be clear about their expectations for student responses. For example, if students must supply examples from a text, the item must be clear about how many examples they must provide and what they need to supply for each example (for instance, quote from text, evidence from text, page number).

The second way teams can make their constructed-response items more reliable is to consider whether providing some kind of context for the item will help clarify exactly what students must do to demonstrate mastery (Stiggins et al., 2004). Teams do this by including some information that helps students narrow down the expectation for the item. Consider the following examples.

- A science team writes, "Use the graph on page 68 to explain what happens to temperature during a chemical change." This context tells students that they can find the information they need for their answer in the graph on page 68 rather than elsewhere in the text, but it doesn't tell them how to interpret the graph.

- Another team writes, "In class, we studied how authors use facts and details to get the reader to agree with them. How does this author use facts and details?" This question narrows down the information students should use to answer the question to the information learned in class.

- Another team writes, "After analyzing the primary-source documents, discuss

how this information affected U.S. President Harry S. Truman's decision to use the atomic bomb on Japan. Provide three examples of information he had and how that information affected his decision." With this question, students must use information from the primary source documents rather than information they learn in class or from other sources.

When appropriate, teams must include a rubric to help students understand what proficiency looks like. Note that not all constructed-response questions need a rubric. Sometimes the answer is either right or wrong. For example: Describe the setting of the story, or list three problems Sarah faced on her first day of school. However, when there are gradients of proficiency, a rubric helps teams decide what students need next. Teachers base gradients on the quality of the answer rather than the quantity the students provide. For example, let's consider the above question about primary source document information. A team might be tempted to develop a rubric that differentiates based on quantity rather than quality. Figure 3.13 shows an example of a poor rubric.

Proficiency	Partial Proficiency	No Proficiency
The student provides three examples.	The student provides one or two examples.	The student provides no examples.

Figure 3.13: Example of a poor rubric.

However, the student may be proficient on the learning target (using text evidence) but not persistent enough to supply all three examples. Since the purpose of the assessment is to provide needed time and support if a student can't read and interpret the primary-source documents, teams should decide how to respond to students who didn't follow the directions,

perhaps returning the paper and asking students to complete the question.

A better way to develop the rubric is to start with the proficiency level and describe what that looks like without giving away the answer. This may lead more easily to describing the other levels, as shown in figure 3.14 (page 110).

Proficiency	Partial Proficiency	No Proficiency
The student is able to give specific examples of information from the primary-source documents and provides precise reasons why this information impacted President Truman's decision.	The student is able to give specific examples of information from primary-source documents but is unable to provide precise reasons why this information impacted President Truman's decision.	The student is unable to give specific examples of information from the primary-source documents.

Figure 3.14: Example of a quality rubric.

Develop Quality Selected-Response Items

Because a selected-response question is designed for students to pick the correct answer from different choices, it's important that it is written so students can't guess the correct answer and appear to be proficient on that learning target. In fact, there are many resources students can find that provide advice on what to do when they don't know the answer to a question and must make a guess.

There are generally three major types of selected-response questions: (1) multiple choice, (2) true or false, and (3) matching. Because so many high-stakes tests primarily use multiple-choice questions, many teams like to use these for their classroom assessments. Multiple-choice questions have two parts: the item stem, which is the statement or question that precedes the answer choices, and several answer choices. A traditional multiple-choice question has one correct answer, and the other choices are called distractors. In some multiple-choice questions, students can choose more than one correct answer.

One way teams can make multiple-choice items more reliable is to write the item stem as a full question or sentence. This helps students think about the topic before they get to the answer choices. To obtain the best information about student learning, it is best not to use negatives in the stem, as this may confuse some students who actually know the answer. For example, *Which of these is not an example of figurative language?* might confuse a student who really does know what figurative language is. In order not to give away the answer, make sure you haven't included grammatical clues in the stem, such as plural verbs, which indicate the answer must be plural. Finally, if you are asking for the *most likely* or *best* answer, emphasize these words by using boldface or italics. Research supports several ways to write answer choices effectively (Gareis & Grant, 2008; Popham, 2003; Stiggins et al., 2004).

▸ **Answer choices should be reasonable:** Each of the answer choices should be reasonable so students can't easily eliminate an obviously wrong choice. If one choice is clearly wrong, it makes guessing the correct answer more likely. A teacher might think that having a funny answer choice helps lighten the mood during the test, but it's more likely to get students looking for more funny choices.

▸ **All the answer choices should be similar length and have parallel grammar:** Having worked extensively with teams as they write questions, we have observed that teachers tend to write the correct answer more carefully than the distractors. This sometimes results in longer correct answer choices.

You might want to go back over some of your own questions to see if this happens.

▶ **Be careful not to overuse *all of the above* and *none of the above* as answer choices:** While appropriate in some instances, they can lose their effectiveness when used as fillers. In addition, there is no evidence that all multiple-choice questions must have the same number of answer choices to make them reliable.

▶ **Put the answer choices in logical order:** Teachers can order them alphabetically, numerically, historically, and so on. They rarely put the correct answer early on their list of choices. In fact, we've heard and experienced that we tend to put the correct choice as answer "c." While we haven't found any research to support this, we have observed this in our own work. If you use a logical order for choices, students won't waste time trying to guess based on the order.

▶ **Make sure the correct answer is the *only* correct answer (unless you're asking students to choose the *best* answer):** When developing distractors, it's easy to come too close to the correct choice when trying to develop reasonable incorrect choices.

Finally, we've found that including distractors that represent common misunderstandings or errors a student might make allows teachers to more easily figure out how to respond when students choose the wrong answer.

Choose the Stimulus

When developing assessment items, one way to increase the rigor of the question is to choose a stimulus that students must analyze before they can answer the questions. In English language arts, this might be a passage or a video that students need to read or watch. In mathematics, it might be tables or graphs to investigate or a picture to help understand the problem. In science, it might be a text, tables, or graphs or an experimental design. In social studies, it might be maps, tables, charts, texts, or primary-source documents. The stimulus must align to the learning target being assessed (think, "Analyze two versions of the same story"), and it must be at the appropriate reading level and length for students' grade level.

3

Coaching Tip

Remind teachers that the stimulus they use for common formative assessments must be new to students if they're assessing a reading learning target. They can't simply ask students, "What is the theme of *Romeo and Juliet*?" if they've had that discussion already during class. If so, they are assessing listening or memory skills, not whether students can use text evidence to determine the theme of a story.

While we know that text complexity is more than just a quantitative number, we suggest that teams keep their assessment texts somewhere around suggested Lexile levels so students are exposed to texts that might appear on high-stakes tests. Table 3.3 (page 112) provides more information on the Lexile range targeted for each grade-level band.

Table 3.3: Lexile—Typical Reader Measures to Guide Reading for College and Career Readiness

Grade Band	Lexile Range
Grade 1	Beginning reader (BR) 120L–295L
Grade 2	170L–545L
Grade 3	415L–760L
Grade 4	635L–950L
Grade 5	770L–1080L
Grade 6	855L–1165L
Grade 7	925L–1235L
Grade 8	985L–1295L
Grade 9	1040L–1350L
Grade 10	1085L–1400L
Grades 11–12	1130L–1440L

Source: Lexile Framework for Reading, n.d.

Teams also must consider the length of the text they'll use for the assessment. In writing assessments, we've found that if the text is too short, it's hard to build enough rigor into the question. Two of the more common high-stakes tests publish their expectations about the anticipated length to use. Table 3.4 and table 3.5 provide information related to PARCC and SBAC text lengths.

Table 3.4: Length of Text Per PARCC

Grade Band	Minimum and Maximum Length of Text
Grades 3–5	200–800 words
Grades 6–8	400–1,000 words
Grades 9–11	500–1,500 words

Source: PARCC, n.d.

Table 3.5: Length of Text Per SBAC

Grade	Word Count (Short Text)	Word Count (Long Text)
Grade 3	200–487	488–650
Grades 4–5	450–562	563–750
Grades 6–8	650–712	713–950
Grade 11	800–825	826–1,100

Source: SBAC, 2015b.

Teams find it helpful when someone provides this kind of information in a short handout or makes it readily available in a shared folder. Many states publish this information, along with test specifications on their assessment websites. Table 3.6 shows guidelines for effective question writing.

One thing that has changed in the last few years is the plethora of resources that align to the Common Core standards. Practitioners can easily share resources since they are working on the same standards. The opportunity to find resources aligns with one role of an effective coach; that is, to help locate quality resources.

Table 3.6: Guidelines for Question Writing

General guidelines for all formats include:
1. Unwrap (or unpack) standards into learning targets and write questions around the most important targets.
2. Create an assessment-planning chart to ensure adequate cognitive demand and number of questions asked per target.
3. Remember the goal is to determine whether students know the material, not whether they can use good test-taking strategies to guess the right answer.
4. Provide a sufficient number of items to know whether a student learned, but not so many that the assessment takes too long.

Multiple-choice guidelines include:
1. Make sure that each item assesses only one target.
2. State the whole question in the item stem.
3. Put the answer choices in an order that makes sense, such as largest to smallest or alphabetical.
4. Be sure there is only one correct or best answer.
5. Keep response options brief and parallel in: • Length   • Grammatical construction
6. Limit use of *all of the above* or *none of the above*.
7. Use *always* and *never* with caution.
8. Questions can have different numbers of responses; don't add answers just to make them even.

True-or-false guidelines include:
1. Make them entirely true or entirely false as stated.
2. Avoid negatives which make questions ambiguous.
3. Make sure there is only one target per question.

Matching guidelines include:
1. Provide clear directions for the match to be made. Indicate if a response can be used more than once or if an item has more than one match.
2. Include no more than ten items.
3. Put the responses on the left and the trigger on the right.
4. Include only homogeneous items. Do not mix dates, events, and names in a single exercise.
5. Provide more responses than trigger items.

3

continued →

Completion or fill-in-the-blank guidelines include:

1. Ask a question.
2. Provide one blank per item.
3. Do not make length a clue.
4. Put blank toward the end.

Constructed-response guidelines include:

1. Creating questions:
   a. Make the context and the expectations clear to the student.
   b. Don't provide options that allow students to choose areas in which they feel most competent. (You want to know what they really know!)
2. Scoring:
   a. Establish scoring criteria in advance.
   b. Set a policy about non-achievement factors, for instance, writing skills.
   c. Score collaboratively, if possible.
   d. Score all responses to one exercise at a time. (It's faster!)

Formatting and arranging assessment items include:

1. Be consistent in the presentation of an item type.
2. List the learning target the team is assessing.
3. Avoid crowding too many questions onto one page.

Writing directions include:

1. Write clear, explicit directions for each item type.
2. Indicate how students should express the answer (for instance, should students write *true* or *false*, or *T* or *F*? Should students round numbers to the nearest tenth? Should students include units such as months, meters, or grams in the answer?)

Producing the test:

1. Proof carefully and double check the answer key.
2. Ask a colleague to review or take important tests.

Sources: Ainsworth & Viegut, 2006; Gareis & Grant, 2008; Popham, 2003; Stiggins et al., 2004.

Model Samples and Exemplars From High-Stakes Tests

One of the best ways to make sure your team is accurately interpreting the proficiency expectations for the standards is to investigate sample released items from high-stakes, end-of-year tests. While we occasionally hear teachers worry that they are "teaching to the test" by looking at these items, unless we know what the end product looks like, it's nearly impossible to hit that end product with accuracy.

Teachers should work through sample items together, discussing the types of stimulus they use, the wording of questions, and the anticipated reasoning students have to do to answer correctly. Teams tell us that sometimes they teach a concept using a particular vocabulary term (either academic or domain specific) but that the test uses a different term. They can avoid this problem if they know prior to instruction the questions' wording. Then, even if their instructional materials use different terminology, they can use terms students will see on the assessments.

Teams also ask whether they should use sample items for the assessments themselves as common formative assessment items. See the following websites for sample items: Smarter Balanced Assessment Consortium (http://sample items.smarterbalanced.org), PARCC (https://parcc-assessment.org/practice-tests), and ACT Aspire (http://actaspire.pearson.com/exemplars .html). It's best to be cautious about this practice because students might have to use several different learning targets to respond to the question. This, of course, works better for summative assessments but might affect a team's ability to diagnose what students need next if used for formative assessments. Teams should make sure the item they want to use is actually assessing the learning target they want to assess.

This same caution goes for using any items from other sources such as test banks or textbook questions. We sometimes encourage teams to look for quality items online because there are many ways they work better than items a team writes itself. Some websites we've found helpful include Inside Mathematics (www.insidemathematics.org), ReadWorks (www.readworks.org), and EDSITEment (www.edsitement.neh.gov). For example, when you want to use a real-life mathematics example, it may be much easier to use one from a source rather than starting from scratch. Be sure the item assesses what you want it to assess *and* at the appropriate rigor level.

Consider this example from a sixth-grade English language arts team. The team wants to assess the learning target "Interpret figures of speech in context." It finds a test-bank question that asks students to find four figures of speech in a text excerpt. Identifying and interpreting are two different levels of cognitive demand.

So while the content is the same (figures of speech), the rigor doesn't match the learning target.

Adapt the Process for Unique Team Structures

As we discussed in chapter 2 (page 35), a singleton is the only teacher in the school who teaches a particular course or content. Involving singletons in developing and using common formative assessments is a complex but worthwhile endeavor. When teachers work collaboratively on this process, they learn together—about their standards, quality assessment, effective response to students, and their instructional practices. But as William Ferriter (2011) puts it, "One of the greatest challenges in any professional learning community is finding meaningful learning partnerships for the singletons." A team of singletons should first consider what members have in common rather than what their differences are.

Vertical Teams

Let's first look at vertical teams. These teachers teach common content, but each has a different grade level or course level. Examples include a grades 3–5 elementary team of one teacher at a grade level, a middle school science team of one teacher at a grade level, or a high school mathematics team of one teacher per course. At first glance, these teachers might think they have little in common because each grade level or course has different standards. However, when looked at more closely, these teachers have numerous skills in common so they can discuss how to teach, how to assess, and how to respond. Consider, for example, a grades 6–8 science team. In the NGSS standards, there are common science process skills such as *develop a model*, *analyze and interpret data*, *plan an investigation*, and so on (NGSS Lead States, 2013). The team members might work together to discuss both how to teach and then how to assess these processes. Each

3

teacher then applies the processes to his or her own standard but will have established common expectations through assessment.

We can apply this same idea to mathematics teachers who teach different courses. The math practices are the same for all mathematics courses and can be considered the same skills. The vertical team works together to figure out how to assess each practice, asking itself, for example, "What does it look like for students to critique the reasoning of others?" The team develops a rubric that defines the expectations for proficiency for this practice. Then, each teacher applies it to the course content but has the same expectations as all the mathematics teachers for this practice.

High school social studies teachers might apply a similar idea when they consider how they teach and assess students to read primary-source documents. Each teacher could choose primary-source documents appropriate to the content in his or her course, but all social studies teachers can teach students how to read and understand primary source documents in a similar way.

Considering the progressions within their standards is another way vertical teams can develop common formative assessments. For example, a grades K–2 team of teachers can look at anchor standard one for informational text to see what's alike and what's different. See figure 3.15.

Kindergarten	First Grade	Second Grade
With prompting and support, ask and answer questions about key details in a text (RL.K.1).	Ask and answer questions about key details in a text (RL.1.1).	Ask and answer such questions as *who*, *what*, *where*, *when*, *why*, and *how* to demonstrate key details in a text (RL.2.1).

Source for standards: NGA & CCSSO, 2010a.

Figure 3.15: Progressions within a grades K–2 team standard for informational text.

The team might want to discuss the phrase *with prompting and support* so each member understands what that support might look like for kindergarten students. Most teachers are pretty comfortable having students *answer* questions about a text but sometimes are unsure how to teach and assess having students *ask* questions about a text. You can support teachers with this standard by investigating how to write good text-dependent questions, such as answering questions about details in a text. Teams use a text passage appropriate for their grade but will assess the standard in a similar way.

Horizontal or Interdisciplinary Teams

Horizontal teams can also use the ELA progressions documents by working together to see

how the ELA standards in history / social studies and science and technical subjects overlap with those for ELA at a particular grade level. In this situation, each content-area teacher teaches the standard at the same time in the pacing guide but specific to his or her content. For example, consider how a sixth-grade interdisciplinary team might use the idea of learning progressions to teach and assess students on a particular standard.

In this case, the team is composed of a sixth-grade ELA teacher, a sixth-grade social studies teacher, a sixth-grade science teacher, and a sixth-grade mathematics teacher. The team decides to look specifically at the standard for point of view—standard six in the Reading Standards for Informational Text at the sixth-grade level

(RI.6, NGA & CCSSO, 2010a). Members consider what students should already know about point of view and what they should learn this year in each of their classes. By reading down the column for sixth grade (including the ELA standard, the history / social studies standard, and science and technical subjects standard) in figure 3.16 (page 118), each teacher is able to identify the outcome for the students in his or her subject area. The ELA teacher is looking at how the author of the text conveys his or her point of view; the social studies teacher looks at things like loaded language and information excluded in a particular piece of text; and the science teacher examines why the author includes specific data or conclusions in a text.

Team members can then either each develop an assessment around a piece of text appropriate for their content area, or choose to write one assessment together that uses a few short pieces of text requiring students to examine point of view and its impact on the text.

Coaching Tip

Laying out the ELA standards for middle school and high school teachers, as in figure 3.16 (page 118), helps teams see how their content connects both to the grade or course before the one they teach as well as to the grade or course that follows. This organizer also helps teams see who owns which standards. For example, standard 6 in Common Core ELA for history / social studies is the same for grades 6, 7, and 8.

Of course, each grade level or course will use a different but appropriate text passage to assess its standard, but the proficiency expectations will be the same.

Horizontal teams or interdisciplinary teams can use both of the preceding strategies as well in their work. Consider a middle school seventh-grade team that wants to focus on writing arguments. The team organizes the writing standards for seventh grade in each subject area (see figure 3.17, page 119). Because team members have been working as an interdisciplinary team for several years, they are aware that writing standards for science and social studies are the same for both departments. They are also the same for grades 6–8.

Team members agree that they will work on argument writing during the same month and create a common formative assessment for the learning targets: introduce claim or claims about a topic or issue, acknowledge and distinguish the claim or claims from alternate or opposing claims, and organize the reasons and evidence logically. Allow students to choose a topic from any content area but assess it using a team-developed rubric.

Cross-school and district teams, as well as electronic teams, generally have a composition similar to typical collaborative teams in a PLC, for example, band directors across the district or physics teachers in several different settings. These teams may meet in person or electronically, however, the way they work is similar to a school-based team. They typically have all the same considerations for writing and using common formative assessments. The issue they face is finding a time that they are all available since multiple master schedules are in play. If the team works electronically, it will likely meet online and use software to exchange documents. The issues it faces are how to share documents, particularly student work samples.

Grade 5	Grade 6	Grade 7	Grade 8	Grades 9–10	Grades 11–12
Analyze multiple accounts of the same event or topic, noting important similarities and differences in the point of view they represent (RI.5.6).	Determine an author's point of view or purpose in a text and explain how it is conveyed in the text (RI.6.6).	Determine an author's point of view or purpose in a text and analyze how the author distinguishes his or her position from that of others (RI.7.6).	Determine an author's point of view or purpose in a text and analyze how the author acknowledges and responds to conflicting evidence or viewpoints (RI.8.6).	Determine an author's point of view or purpose in a text and analyze how an author uses rhetoric to advance that point of view or purpose (RI.9–10.6).	Determine an author's point of view or purpose in a text in which the rhetoric is particularly effective, analyzing how style and content contribute to the power, persuasiveness, or beauty of the text (RI.11–12.6).
History / social studies	Identify aspects of a text that reveal an author's point of view or purpose (for example, loaded language, inclusion, or avoidance of particular facts) (RH.6–8.6).			Compare the point of view of two or more authors for how they treat the same or similar topics, including which details they include and emphasize in their respective accounts (RH.9–10.6).	Evaluate authors' differing points of view on the same historical event or issue by assessing the authors' claims, reasoning, and evidence (RH.11–12.6).
Science and technical subjects	Analyze the author's purpose in providing an explanation, describing a procedure, or discussing an experiment in a text (RST.9–10.6; RST.6–8.6).			Analyze the author's purpose in providing an explanation, describing a procedure, or discussing an experiment in a text, defining the question the author seeks to address (RST.9–10.6).	Analyze the author's purpose in providing an explanation, describing a procedure, or discussing an experiment in a text, identifying important issues that remain unresolved (RST.11–12.6).

Source for standards: Adapted from NGA & CCSSO, 2010a.

Figure 3.16: Informational text standard 6 for grades 5–12 in ELA, history / social studies, and science and technical subjects.

English language arts	Write arguments to support claims with clear reasons and relevant evidence. a. Introduce claim or claims, acknowledge alternate or opposing claims, and organize the reasons and evidence logically (W.8.1.a). b. Support claim or claims with logical reasoning and relevant evidence, using accurate, credible sources and demonstrating an understanding of the topic or text (W.8.1.b). c. Use words, phrases, and clauses to create cohesion and clarify the relationships among claim or claims, reasons, and evidence (W.8.1.c). d. Establish and maintain a formal style (W.8.1.d). e. Provide a concluding statement or section that follows from and supports the argument presented (W.8.1.e).
Science and technical subjects and history / social studies	Write arguments focused on discipline-specific content. a. Introduce claim or claims about a topic or issue, acknowledge and distinguish the claim or claims from alternate or opposing claims, and organize the reasons and evidence logically (WHST.6–8.1.a). b. Support claim or claims with logical reasoning and relevant, accurate data and evidence that demonstrate an understanding of the topic or text, using credible sources (WHST.6–8.1.b). c. Use words, phrases, and clauses to create cohesion and clarify the relationships among claim or claims, counterclaims, reasons, and evidence (WHST.6–8.1.c). d. Establish and maintain a formal style (WHST.6–8.1.d). e. Provide a concluding statement or section that follows from and supports the argument presented (WHST.6–8.1.e).

Source for standards: Adapted from NGA & CCSSO, 2010a.

Figure 3.17: Seventh-grade writing standards for grades 6–8 in ELA, history / social studies, and science and technical subjects.

We haven't yet addressed how singletons who work on electronic teams create their common formative assessments. In these situations, team members are the only ones in their school who teach a certain grade level or course, but the team itself is usually composed of members who *do* teach the same content (for example, they all teach AP physics). For these teams, the process of writing common formative assessments is similar to that of a typical collaborative team because they are working with the same standards as the other members. Working with these teams, we found that there are so many ways to share information electronically, team members rarely have trouble writing

assessments (for example, everyone works within a Google Doc). However, sharing their results can be more cumbersome when using actual student products in the discussion. When the team members are sitting at a table together, they can look at specific student work samples. For electronic teams, the work has to be uploaded for all to see. Most teachers who work in these team configurations overcome these minor problems once they see the benefits of having collaborative partners.

Use the Coaching Reflection on page 127 to reflect on the information you explored for Action 3.

3

Coaching the Issue

A fifth-grade team is developing a common formative assessment in reading for the learning target "Integrate information on the same topic for two texts." As the team develops the item, it realizes that team members have different interpretations of what students need to do to be proficient.

- **Coach's role:** Josh is the instructional coach for this team and, while he's taught third grade for a number of years, he isn't as familiar with expectations for fifth grade. He offers to meet with the team and facilitate the discussion. Before the meeting, Josh goes to the ACT Aspire webpage (www.actaspire.org) and looks for sample reading questions for fifth graders and finds one for this learning target to bring to the team.

- **Team meeting:** Josh starts the conversation by asking the team members to read the stimulus information and answer the question individually. He then shares with them the way that this assessment company would score different student responses demonstrating different levels of proficiency. As they work through this process, team members consider the sample stimulus items (much shorter than they originally expected) and how the questions themselves are worded. They build their own rubric based on the rationale supplied with this question. They look for sample text excerpts for their own assessment, use the same question structure they found on the sample item, and develop an answer guide with possible correct and incorrect answers.

- **Next steps:** After giving the assessment, the team discusses how its students responded and considers the clarity of the question and the rubric supplied. Team members concur that they wish they had done this work before they started to teach the item, because they realize how knowing the expectations for proficiency would make the instructional process much more effective.

Action 4: Collaborate Around Results

When high-performing teams effectively use data from their common formative assessments they are able to increase student learning because they know which students still need help as well as what kind of help they need. But more than that, team members learn together about effective instructional strategies. They are also able to engage in action research around problems they encounter and continuous improvement in their teaching. When we've had the opportunity to work with teams over an extended period of time, we get to see how they use their assessment results to plan effective responses as well as consider better instructional strategies.

For example, Angie Walker, a mathematics teacher and team leader at Sherman Junior High in Boone County, West Virginia, reflected on the changes she saw with her teammates after several years working together:

> Common formative assessments have simplistically focused my teaching to the most important concepts we want to guarantee our students

learn. Within a year of using common formative assessments, I noticed our mathematics team growing professionally and addressing specific student misconceptions. Students are more focused in class, student content knowledge has increased, and team members have noticed many other successes with our students and our collaborative mathematics team like I have never seen before! (A. Walker, personal communication, May 9, 2018)

In order to collaborate around results, coaches must work with teams to do the following.

▸ Clarify scoring versus grading.

▸ Use strategies for quality feedback.

▸ Establish cut scores or proficiency expectations.

▸ Determine the frequency of common formative assessments.

Clarify Scoring Versus Grading

In chapter 4 (page 131), we discuss how teams plan and carry out the response to common formative assessments to support students in learning the essential standards. However, before we tackle that topic we want to recommend coaches become clear about what we refer to as the difference between scoring and grading. Because formative assessments are intended to guide instruction while students are still learning, we believe that teachers shouldn't grade them. By this, we mean that teachers shouldn't record the results in the gradebook as a final score.

In a PLC, teachers believe all students can learn at high levels but say nothing about how quickly they must get to proficiency. Instead, we believe teachers need to *score* the assessments. That means they read student responses and provide feedback to students about next

steps. They also work with the rest of the team to plan how they will respond so students who are not yet proficient have an opportunity to get there. Teachers provide an opportunity to go beyond that expectation for students who demonstrate proficiency.

We often hear from teachers that if they don't put a grade on an assessment, students won't do their best work. They also worry that if students know they can retake an assessment they won't study for the first one. They see these things as burdensome in the amount of additional grading they will need to do. However, it's important to know the research behind these ideas to convince teachers that grades are not intrinsic motivators.

In their studies of whether grades affect student motivation and how students respond to grades versus teacher comments, Ruth Butler and Mordecai Nisan (1986) find that while students who got grades showed no motivation to do better on a similar task, those who received comments improved their work on the second task by 30 percent. Since this time, researchers have continued to study how effective feedback can promote student learning (Hattie, 2009; Wiliam, 2011).

We like to remind teachers about what students often do when getting back an assignment with lots of comments but also a grade at the top. Teachers laugh with us when we remind them that students immediately look at the grade and then put the assignment away without reading all the comments. Grades send the message that learning is done.

Use Strategies for Quality Feedback

On Hattie's (2012) list of strategies that improve student learning, *feedback* is number ten, with an effect size of 0.75. When coupled

4

with the work of D. Royce Sadler (1989), we have a powerful learning opportunity. Sadler (1989) suggests that students should be able to answer three questions: Where am I going?, Where am I now?, and How can I close the gap? Quality feedback supports students in answering with precision the second and third questions by making them a partner in the process. This is where we see assessment as something we do *with* students rather than something we do *to* students.

Knowing what makes feedback effective is something teams can learn together as they work with common formative assessments. Educational consultant and author Susan Brookhart (2008) shares a number of strategies teachers should consider in providing quality feedback. She suggests that teams consider the timing of the feedback. Students need immediate feedback for correct and incorrect answers and short-term feedback on more complex tasks. Teachers should provide feedback on the learning targets they're assessing students on as often as possible. Finally, the feedback must be specific enough for students to know what to do next, but not so specific that the teacher does the work for them.

Establish Cut Scores or Proficiency Expectations

When we work with teams as they start to look at their results, teachers often ask, "What should our cut score be?" Teams who ask this question often have had experience with summative assessments, either one they've written themselves or a standardized test. These tests set a cut score as the number correct or percent a student has to earn to achieve grade-level proficiency. Traditional tests often set 60 percent or 70 percent as a passing score. When we are working with common formative assessments, we don't look at the entire assessment and set a cut score for proficiency. Instead, the team looks at each learning target separately to determine if a student is proficient on that target. Going back to the planning chart in figure 3.5 (page 92), the team uses the far-right column and identifies—for each target on the assessment—which students *are* or *are not yet* proficient.

As we've mentioned previously, it's important for the team to create an answer guide as it is writing the questions. This way everyone agrees what the answers should be. For constructed-response questions, team members might predict what answers students might come up with—both correct and incorrect.

Coaching Insight

Be cautious of teachers who want to give half credit or a certain number of points for student answers. This usually occurs when teachers are still thinking about grading or cut scores. It's important that common formative assessments provide information about levels of proficiency.

4

Finally, teams should engage in collaborative scoring in which team members calibrate their scoring practices to make sure different teachers aren't scoring student work differently. There are a number of protocols available to do this work, but one we often recommend is to

have each teacher bring three student samples randomly pulled from an assessment. Team members then individually score all the student samples and put their score on a sticky note on the back of the work sample. Once team members score all the samples, they review any samples that have discrepant scores to build consensus on what the correct score should be.

Determine the Frequency of Common Formative Assessments

"Where do we start?" This may be the most frequently asked question we encounter in our own work. Underlying this question is also a question about frequency. Teams want to know upfront how often teachers should give these assessments, which also helps them understand how large the assessments should be. What we've discovered about frequency is that it is idiosyncratic to the content area, grade level, team composition, and many other factors.

In other words, there's no one right answer to this question.

Basically, teams should start wherever they are and complete one cycle of choosing which learning targets to assess, developing an assessment plan, writing questions, giving the assessment, planning next steps, and reflecting on the work. However long it takes your team to work through this cycle, know that the work gets easier and your team gets more efficient with more experience. Each year, you will build on the assessments you have and assess more frequently. Some teams administer common formative assessments almost weekly, but others might administer them approximately every three weeks. Teams should still keep these assessments short and focused on the most important learning targets from their essential standards.

Coaching Insight

While we have provided a step-by-step sequence for developing aligned and accurate common assessments with teams, there may be times when coaches must enter into a conversation differently. For example, the high school history team has spent a great deal of time developing its curriculum and writing extensive units of study, which include common assessments. As you review them, you discover that the assessments don't reflect the level of rigor and consist primarily of DOK 1 items. How might you proceed to ensure that the team's assessments indeed align and are effective measures of its students' learning without frustrating a team who has put a lot of work into the process?

Rather than asking a team to throw away its previous work, effective coaches meet their teams where they are. For example, in the previous scenario, one could familiarize the team with the concept of DOK and then use an existing assessment to see what levels each item focuses on. You can analyze items for their level of rigor or specific alignment to learning targets the team identifies once it unwraps the standards. Team members can then discuss their findings, discuss ways to adjust the items to more accurately align with the intended rigor, and set the stage for future assessment development.

4

Teams should always take some time after they plan the response to the assessment to discuss what worked particularly well and what didn't work so well with the questions

themselves. Were any questions unclear or not rigorous enough? If they need to make changes, they should take notes during this meeting rather than rely on memory when they use the assessments the following year. In addition, as teams gain experience with assessments, they will want to consider building opportunities for action research into their work. For example, consider how a team might ask the question, "How can we help students who are not able to read text at grade level?" The team decides to teach specific strategies (for example, chunk the text, annotate vocabulary, and reread unclear paragraphs). They then use the results of their common formative assessments to see if students are growing in this skill. The data have now morphed from being solely about student success to also being about team success.

Use the Coaching Reflection on page 128 to reflect on the information you explored for Action 4.

Conclusion

This chapter focused on how coaches support teams as they answer critical question 2 (How will we know if they have learned it?), which is the incentive for teams to develop aligned and effective assessments to identify student proficiency on the standards. By implementing the four actions in this chapter, teams accomplish the following.

▸ Build an understanding of a balanced assessment system, including the difference between formative and summative / end-of-unit assessments.

▸ Learn how to design assessments for validity and reliability, matching item type to learning target rigor and setting proficiency expectations.

▸ Write a variety of appropriate and quality items for assessments, adapting the process for unique team structures.

▸ Collaborate around assessment results, using strategies for quality feedback.

With these actions in place, teams can analyze student assessment results and data, turning their attention to PLC critical question 3 (How will we respond when some students do not learn?), the focus of the next chapter.

4

Coaching Reflection for Action 1:
Build Understanding of a Balanced Assessment System

Use the questions in this chart to reflect on the information you explored in Action 1.

Does our school have all the components of a balanced assessment system? Do teachers understand the purpose of each assessment type?	What role (facilitator, consultant, coach) should I play with each team?
What kind of support will my teams need to be confident in their assessment work?	What issues do I need to anticipate and plan for?
Are we using our current assessments effectively?	What is a reasonable time line for completing this step?

Coaching Reflection for Action 2: Design Assessments for Validity and Reliability

Use the questions in this chart to reflect on the information you explored in Action 2.

What do teachers in this school already know about assessment design?	What role (facilitator, consultant, coach) should I play with each team?
Does each team I'm working with understand *why* it's so important to plan for validity and reliability? If not, how can I support its understanding?	What issues do I need to anticipate and plan for?
What can I do to make templates more accessible and understandable?	What is a reasonable time line for completing this step?

Coaching Reflection for Action 3: Write Quality Assessment Items

Use the questions in this chart to reflect on the information you explored in Action 3.

How confident do teams feel about writing their own questions? How can I support this?	What role (facilitator, consultant, coach) should I play with each team?
Are teams using a variety of item types or relying primarily on one type?	What issues do I need to anticipate and plan for?
What materials and resources are available for the teams I'm supporting?	What is a reasonable time line for completing this step?

Coaching Reflection for Action 4:
Collaborate Around Results

Use the questions in this chart to reflect on the information you explored in Action 4.

Are teachers in this school comfortable sharing data with each other?	What role (facilitator, consultant, coach) should I play with each team?
Do teachers see the difference between scoring and grading, or do we need to have a discussion?	What issues do I need to anticipate and plan for?
Are teachers using feedback effectively? If not, how can I support them?	What is a reasonable time line for completing this step?

Coaching focus for PLC critical question 3:
How will we respond when some students do not learn?

1

ACTION 1: Build Shared Knowledge About a System of Supports
▸ Understand the importance of culture and collective vision for supporting learners.
▸ Clarify schoolwide versus team-level responsibilities.
▸ Explain features of an effective system of supports.

2

ACTION 2: Use Common Assessments to Identify Students Who Struggle
▸ Understand the role of assessment data in the RTI process.
▸ Find the time.
▸ Use a protocol to analyze common formative assessment data.
▸ Use a protocol to analyze summative data.

3

ACTION 3: Develop the Response
▸ Select from various strategies to plan the response.
▸ Identify which teacher will work with which group.
▸ Use data to reflect on instruction.
▸ Include singletons in the process.

4

ACTION 4: Take Into Account Other Considerations for Effective Responses
▸ Evaluate the current response system.
▸ Make the system mandatory rather than invitational.
▸ Respond to academic and social behavior issues.
▸ Take a proactive stance.

A C T I O N S

How Will We Respond When Some Students Do Not Learn?

Teams who have access to a balanced assessment system that provides quality information about their students still have work to do to make all students successful. The next two PLC questions, which we discuss in this chapter and the next, will drive this work: *How will we respond when some students do not learn?* and *How will we extend the learning for students who are already proficient?* These two questions allude to the notion of differentiated instruction.

In their book *Leading for Differentiation* (2015), Carol Ann Tomlinson and Michael Murphy describe the various features of differentiated instruction.

1. Offer each student a positive, secure, challenging, and supportive learning environment.

2. Provide a meaning-rich curriculum that is designed to engage learners and built around clearly articulated learning goals known to both teacher and students.

3. Use persistent formative assessment to ensure that teacher and students alike are aware of student status relative to the specified learning goals, and that teacher and students alike know what next steps are most likely to propel a given learner forward.

4. Plan instruction based on formative assessment information to attend to whole-class, small-group, and individual differences in readiness, interest, and approach to learning.

5. Work with students to create and implement classroom management routines that allow both predictability and flexibility. (pp. 1–2)

Each of these non-negotiables describes the work of PLCs. In this chapter, we examine how a PLC school develops and uses a systematic and responsive system to help students who require additional time and support to be successful learners at high levels. It's important to note that the focus now shifts from the work of the collaborative team to the whole school in making this systematic response happen.

Following are the foundational concepts behind the development of a system of supports for student learning.

▸ The goal of a PLC is to ensure student learning of essential standards; therefore, when students aren't learning, the school's focus must be to ensure that they receive additional time and support.

▸ There will always be students who struggle in some aspect of learning, so we need to build in structures and expectations for providing additional time and support.

▶ There isn't one right way to provide interventions, and the model may look different from school to school depending on the resources, size of school, and so on. However, there are some guiding principles teachers should follow.

    ▶ Students should never miss core instruction.

    ▶ Teachers must monitor student progress regularly so students continue to get the amount and type of support they need.

    ▶ Students should have access to all three levels of support if that is what they need.

▶ Schools will prioritize their available resources to meet their students' needs.

▶ The RTI or multitiered system of supports (MTSS) model represents a systems approach to organizing and providing supports and services students receive at a school. As explained in chapter 3, these models provide a pyramid of intervention at multiple levels in both academic and social-emotional areas. The foundational piece of this pyramid is core instruction and should be the first line of attack when supporting student learning. (For more detailed information on RTI, see page 136.)

▶ The school is responsible for the successful learning for all students. However, the team takes primary responsibility for academic learning in RTI Tiers 1 and 2. This means it isn't up to individual teachers to figure out how to support students who are struggling.

When collaborative teams answer PLC critical question 3, they are deciding how to respond when students need extra time and support to learn essential standards, including both corrective instruction and interventions.

Explore Your Context

We call the response created for students who have not yet mastered essential learning targets for the current school year *corrective instruction* to distinguish it from the other levels of intervention. Corrective instruction occurs closely following the assessment (as soon as the team has time to meet and plan next steps) and is intended to be part of a good instructional process rather than a separate event. Team members take collective responsibility for the learning of all students on their team whether or not the school assigns those students on their class list when they plan and carry out their response to data together.

Coaching Insight

One of the hallmarks of a PLC is that collaborative teams take collective responsibility for student learning. This means that all team members are responsible for all students on the team rather than only those students on their class lists. They can do this by sharing students for additional time and support, rotating who takes each student group, sharing ideas and strategies, and, as discussed in chapter 1 (page 11), writing SMART goals.

Coaches will be able to gather information about the context within a school by asking the following questions.

- Is there a schoolwide model of providing intervention?

- What are the basis and process for identifying students who are struggling? What assessments do teachers use?

- What are the frequency and intensity of this intervention?

- How do teachers monitor their students' progress?

In a PLC at Work, the conditions for teachers to take collective responsibility are not left solely to the collaborative teams but, rather, the entire school must have a unified process designed to make this happen. The school must allocate resources and time fairly for access by all students. In order to do this, the school leadership team works together to build a master schedule, allowing each team access to the resources or staff it needs as well as determining how to ensure all students have the time they need for intervention.

Coaches should be familiar with how teachers planned the master schedule to support this response. In addition, an important step a coach will want to take is to assess the culture of the school as well as the culture of each collaborative team he or she will work with. Most schools who claim to operate as a PLC at Work take time early in their conception to build the culture to support this belief. They do this by creating a vision as well as by making collective commitments about the actions they would take to ensure this happens. Without regular check-ins on their culture, schools may see strong beliefs wane and staff motivation decrease as the work gets hard. Occasionally, we encounter staff members whose actions don't support their school's vision. For example, a teacher might explain that stakeholders shouldn't expect special education students to learn at the same high levels as other students. Or teachers might bemoan the lack of parent support they get when students struggle. When coaches encounter these situations, it's important to note this discrepancy and respond in a way that moves the staff member or team forward.

In chapter 3 (page 79), we described John Hattie's research about the impact of various strategies on student achievement (Hattie, 2009, 2012; Hattie et al., 2016). This research also supports the significant positive impact of providing additional time and support for students. In his book *Visible Learning for Teachers*, Hattie (2012) identifies RTI as the third strategy out of 150 strategies that influence student learning, with an effect size of 1.07. With solid research supporting the practices of using student data to determine how to respond to students who need additional time and support, collaborative teams should know their work in answering critical question 3 is worth the time and effort.

1

In chapter 2, we referenced Hattie's new thinking around collective teacher efficacy (Goddard et al., 2000; Hattie, 2017). If collective teacher efficacy means the "collective self-perception that teachers in a given school make an education difference to their students over and above the education impact of their home and communities," then high-performing collaborative teams in a PLC are the way to ensure all students learn at high levels (Tschannen-Moran & Barr, 2004, p. 190).

A coach focusing on the work of collaborative teams emphasizes the value of everyone working on the same things and heading in the same direction. Sometimes we find individual teachers want to keep their own students for the response because they believe they know their students better than their teammates. However, all students don't learn in the same way, and teachers are using their best instructional strategies during initial instruction. They *cannot* use that same strategy again and hope students will learn it at a deeper level. Instead, the value of sharing practices and even sharing students—that is, working collaboratively—has a greater chance of helping these students learn.

The following four actions support the work of PLC critical question 3: How will we respond when some students do not learn?

Action 1: Build Shared Knowledge About a System of Supports

When a school begins to develop a system of supports for students who need either intervention or extensions, the work moves from team response to a systematic response. The school must create a master schedule that ensures all students have access to the help they need and distribute resources in an effective way. In order to build shared knowledge about a system of supports, coaches must work with the staff to do the following.

 ▸ Understand the importance of culture and collective vision for supporting learners.

 ▸ Clarify schoolwide versus team-level responsibilities.

 ▸ Explain features of an effective system of supports.

Understand the Importance of Culture and Collective Vision for Supporting Learners

When we begin to work with teams who are getting started as a PLC, we often ask them to think about the children in their own lives. How do they wish for teachers to treat their own children if they need help and support with learning? If you are a coach who is working with a school just beginning to develop a systematic response, this question might provoke a good dialogue about what teachers want this response to look like. Although most schools spend time when they decide to become a PLC working on their mission and developing a positive school culture, we know that regularly going back and assessing their current status is an important task. A good time to do a culture check-in would be when the school begins building its systematic response.

Coaches will want to consider whether the current school culture supports the following important ideas:

▸ We know that all our students learn at different rates and with different levels of support.

▸ Because we believe that our purpose is to ensure that all students learn at high levels, we will proactively monitor their learning and respond swiftly and systematically with additional time and targeted support.

In a PLC where collective responsibility is critical for success, students must receive embedded and systematic supports, not supports that depend on individual teachers. The most effective interventions are those in which all stakeholders are engaged and partners in the support process. Those working with students who are struggling should have multiple instructional tools and effective strategies.

In chapter 1 (page 11), we recommended schools create a vision to make sure everyone agrees about what his or her ideal school should look like in the future. As the school builds a systematic response system, it may also want to create a vision for how this will impact its students. The school could use the same strategy as it did with its assessment vision by replacing the *Imagine* statements with the following.

▸ Imagine a school that takes collective responsibility for all students and has a systematic process in place to provide time and support.

▸ Imagine a school where the students know what they have to learn and all teachers believe that they can learn at high levels.

▸ Imagine a school that dedicates time and resources to provide additional time and support for students.

▸ Imagine a school that monitors the progress of students who are receiving this additional time and support so they know when students reach a level where they need more of this time and support or less of this time and support.

Then the groups work to develop the culture they need so this ideal school becomes reality.

Before answering PLC critical question 3, it makes sense to review the vision established for the school and the commitments made in support of student learning. If your staff haven't engaged in specific descriptors of their future school in terms of the type of support they provide to students who are struggling, it is critical to engage in conversations and build shared knowledge about the guiding principles of a system of supports. The following are some basic questions you can use to guide the conversation.

▸ What would we like to see happen when students struggle to learn?

▸ What evidence would tell us that we provided effective systematic support for all learners?

Clarify Schoolwide Versus Team-Level Responsibilities

Schools that are examining their system of supports often establish a schoolwide intervention-planning team to examine existing practices and make recommendations for their development. The books *Simplifying Response to Intervention: Four Essential Guiding Principles* (Buffum, Mattos, & Weber, 2012) and *Taking Action: A Handbook for RTI at Work* (Buffum, Mattos, & Malone, 2018) consider all the tasks related to how well a school responds to students and suggest who should be responsible for each of them. Studying these ideas together helps schools not only build an effective system of response but also helps staff see what they are responsible for in the process.

Figure 4.1 shows the RTI at Work™ pyramid divided into two halves. The right side focuses on *academic skills*, and the left side focuses on *academic and social behaviors* schools expect from students. The shaded section of the pyramid represents those things that should be systematic, meaning the entire school develops the process and is responsible for implementation. All three levels of academic and social behaviors are included in the systematic portion of the chart. This means the school has common behavior expectations for everyone. The school agrees that teaching and assessing academic behaviors should be everyone's responsibility. Collaborative teams have primary responsibility for Tier 1 and Tier 2 academic skills. This makes sense because classroom teachers are the most skilled at teaching and monitoring content.

Buffum et al. (2012) suggest that the work of building a systematic response is shared between three types of teams: (1) the leadership team, (2) the school intervention team, and (3) collaborative teams. Let's first examine the role of the leadership team.

Leadership Team

This team may also be called the guiding coalition and makes decisions that affect the entire school. Responsibilities of this team include developing a master schedule that allows equal access for all students to core

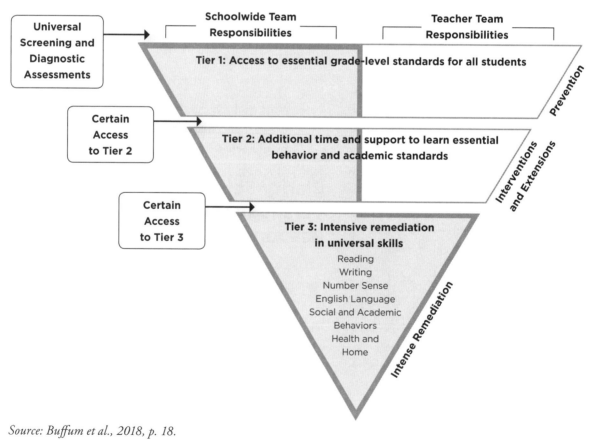

Source: Buffum et al., 2018, p. 18.

Figure 4.1: The RTI at Work™ pyramid.

instruction as well as interventions, evaluating the school's culture, developing school goals based on district goals and on identified areas of need, evaluating the effectiveness of core instruction, analyzing the effectiveness of benchmark assessments, leading Tier 1 behavioral interventions by establishing policies for behavior and attendance, and planning and executing universal screening. The leadership team's first step may be to explore the existing reality at a school. The following are some questions it may use to guide its work.

▸ How do we identify students needing additional support? Is it timely?

▸ Do we know from year to year who is struggling, or do we wait for the information to trickle down?

▸ Which students are consistently underperforming?

▸ Who is getting additional time and support? In what areas? How effective is it?

School Intervention Team

The second team the authors identify is the school intervention team. Team members could include literacy specialists, counselors, teachers who provide support for English learners (ELs), behavior specialists, and any individual whose roles and strengths would provide meaningful support to students. The responsibilities of this team include leading interventions for Tier 3 academic issues, determining the specific needs for students in Tier 3 academic interventions, revising student interventions based on progress monitoring, determining when special education assessment and identification are appropriate, and monitoring student progress in behavior intervention. The intervention team communicates in an ongoing fashion with the guiding coalition and provides information

regarding the status of student growth, program effectiveness, and other related issues. Following are some questions to guide the work of the school intervention team.

▸ What triggers initial interventions for students?

▸ How do we monitor progress during the interventions?

▸ What triggers remove interventions?

▸ How do we communicate progress for students who are in interventions to parents, other teachers, and students?

Collaborative Teams

Finally, we have grade-alike or course-alike collaborative teams. These teams are responsible for identifying and teaching essential standards, providing quality core instruction for Tier 1, using assessments to identify students who need more support or more extension, and taking primary responsibility for Tier 2 academic support (Buffum et al., 2012). When roles and responsibilities are clearly laid out, the response is more effective. The following questions drive the work of collaborative teams when discussing their responses.

▸ How do we use the information from end-of-unit assessments to support learning? From common formative assessments?

▸ Do our assessments of our students who are struggling give us specific diagnostic data?

▸ Are we targeting each student's specific needs, or are we using a "one-size-fits-all" approach?

▸ How do we monitor and evaluate our interventions?

Explain Features of an Effective System of Supports

When schools and their teams are developing systems to provide additional time and support to students who aren't achieving, we look for some key indicators.

▸ All staff, rather than individual teachers, take collective responsibility for the design and delivery of support for students.

▸ Teams provide systematic interventions to students on a timely basis based on the results of common assessments.

▸ Teams collect data throughout the interventions in order to monitor their effectiveness.

▸ Interventions reflect best instructional practices and use research-based programs whenever appropriate.

▸ Qualified educators implement interventions and devote resources to areas of critical need.

▸ Support is not invitational. Students receive additional time and support within their instructional program (rather than being invited to attend before and after school).

▸ Teachers do not exclude students from core instruction in order to provide intervention and support.

Use the Coaching Reflection on page 170 to reflect on the information you explored for Action 1.

Action 2: Use Common Assessments to Identify Students Who Struggle

Focusing on results, schools that operate as a PLC use data to make decisions rather than relying on instincts or opinions. Once they have collected data about what students have and have not yet learned, collaborative teams use those data to make decisions about how to respond. In order to use common assessments to identify students who struggle, coaches must work with teams to do the following.

▸ Understand the role of assessment data in the RTI process.

▸ Find the time.

▸ Use a protocol to analyze common formative assessment data.

▸ Use a protocol to analyze summative data.

Understand the Role of Assessment Data in the RTI Process

In chapter 3 (page 79), we recommend that coaches examine the school's assessment system to see if it's balanced to include a mix of both formative and summative assessments. Next, we'll focus on how the coach can ensure the school has an effective response system that uses these assessments with students. Schools generally plan their interventions in three levels of response.

The inverted pyramid in figure 4.2 illustrates the focus of each level and the percentage of students typically receiving support at that level. The first level is what happens for all students (Tier 1). Quality instruction includes teachers using effective instructional strategies and frequent assessment (both classroom formative assessments as well as common formative assessments) and then corrective instruction for students who didn't demonstrate mastery and

enrichment opportunities for those who did. In the PLC at Work model, this tier focuses on ensuring all students master the identified essential standards for a grade or course.

Pyramid RTI Model

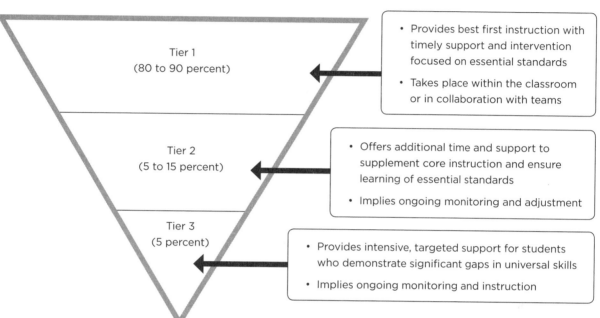

Tier 1
(80 to 90 percent)

- Provides best first instruction with timely support and intervention focused on essential standards
- Takes place within the classroom or in collaboration with teams

Tier 2
(5 to 15 percent)

- Offers additional time and support to supplement core instruction and ensure learning of essential standards
- Implies ongoing monitoring and adjustment

Tier 3
(5 percent)

- Provides intensive, targeted support for students who demonstrate significant gaps in universal skills
- Implies ongoing monitoring and instruction

Figure 4.2: Percentage of students receiving intervention at each level of the pyramid RTI model.

Coaches should investigate what classroom and common formative assessments the teams are currently using. Do teachers feel confident that they are able to identify when students master essential standards? Have collaborative teams built time into their pacing guides so they have time for corrective instruction after each common formative assessment?

Referencing the model of RTI in figure 4.2, approximately 80–90 percent of students should be proficient as a result of the school's solid core instructional program. If this isn't the case, the school must focus on refining that core instructional program. It does this by choosing essential standards and using common formative assessments to identify students who need help. Without a solid core program,

schools find it very difficult to support the larger numbers of students who need intervention at Tier 2 and Tier 3.

The second level of intervention (Tier 2) occurs when teachers identify students who didn't learn this year's essential standards even though they had corrective instruction based on the results of common formative assessments. We identify these students when we reassess after corrective instruction in Tier 1. The support for students in Tier 2 generally requires additional small-group instruction a couple of times per week. Teams should monitor these students frequently to determine if they no longer need this help or need more than this.

The third level of intervention (Tier 3) occurs when a teacher identifies a student needing intensive support. This intensive level of support is usually necessary because students haven't mastered the essential prerequisite standards from previous grades or courses. Students may need this additional help as frequently as five days a week, and teachers deliver these interventions in small groups or individually.

Some students may need Tier 1, Tier 2, and Tier 3 support. As a coach, it's important to determine whether these levels of support are available for all students and whether all teachers are involved in making this process effective. Coaches should also be alert for situations in which there is a lot of ambiguity about what kind of help students need. In some cases, schools mistakenly merge their Tier 2 and Tier 3 support systems, and then teachers have a difficult time making sure each student gets what he or she needs. For example, some schools might group all students together who are identified as being far below grade level from a benchmark assessment. Because the response isn't specific to the needs of each student, it may or may not meet each student's needs. In this chapter, we discuss how teachers can use benchmark assessments to identify students who need intensive time and support as well as monitor whether students are getting the right level of support—not too much or too little.

Figure 4.3 clarifies the relationship between the assessment data available to teams, as described in chapter 3 (page 79), and the tier of response with which it will be used.

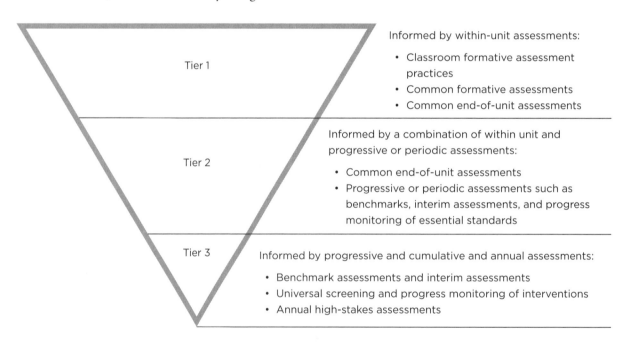

Figure 4.3: Connections between assessments and RTI tiers.

Find the Time

Coaches should also examine how the school allocates time for responding to students. Tier 1 response should occur during regular class time, as it is a component of good instruction. Some schools can't make this happen because teams haven't built time into their pacing guides to respond to common formative assessments. Those schools can rework their pacing guides to include time after each common formative assessment to respond to the data. Tiers 2 and 3 must happen at a time when students aren't missing new instruction around essential standards. Many schools build intervention time into their school day specifically designed for this kind of support. Coaches should double check to ensure students aren't missing instruction around essential standards when they receive interventions.

As a coach, determine the current reality regarding the resources and established expectations.

▸ How do students currently receive support if they are struggling?

▸ What is the expectation for providing support during core instruction?

Early in the PLC at Work process, teams may experience concerns about two ideas related to how they answer critical question 3. First, they may worry about the time they'll need to provide reteaching and response for students because they feel like they already have too much content in their curriculum and too many responsibilities for responding to student needs. Coaches can help teams see the value of learning together as they work through cycles around the four critical questions—identify and unwrap essential standards, write and use common formative assessments, and plan and execute effective responses. Realizing that this work is an ongoing process helps teams feel confident that they are making progress knowing they can't do everything in one year. Teams will also learn that the more experience they have with designing responses to data, the better they will get at designing effective differentiated responses. Coaches need to help teams see that a good response done a little less frequently is better than a poor response done every week.

Second, some team members might be more comfortable and feel more in control if they keep their own students for intervention. Experience

might be the most effective way to tame these concerns. Teachers will find that having a different voice and different instructional strategy coming from one of their colleagues may be the exact response a student needs.

Use a Protocol to Analyze Common Formative Assessment Data

In their article "One Step at a Time," Parry Graham and Bill Ferriter (2008) describe seven stages through which groups can engage in the PLC at Work process. Table 4.1 (page 142) summarizes these stages.

Stages 1, 2, and 3 represent teams who are struggling to find effective ways to collaborate, teams who may become stuck in what DuFour (2003) calls "collaboration-lite"—collaboration about issues and ideas that don't impact what happens in the classroom. Stage 4, developing common assessments, will impact classroom practices. What happens after this (stages 5–7) is about how the team responds to the information it receives from these assessments and what this chapter is about. In stage 5, teams analyze the information to find out not only which students still need support but also what kind of support they need. Stage 6 takes this to the next level when teams develop response plans for their students and take collective responsibility for student learning. During stage 7, teams begin to use their assessment results to answer questions about their practice.

In a PLC, teachers recognize that this emphasis on collective inquiry is a fundamental part of their work. Teams that learn together and have developed high levels of trust are always willing to question their current reality and push themselves to try new strategies and ways of teaching to improve student learning. These three levels don't always happen in a particular sequence but, rather, often develop

Table 4.1: Seven Stages of Collaboration

Stage	Characteristics
1. Filling the Time	Not knowing what to do; trying to do too much; focusing on creating agendas
2. Sharing Personal Practices	Helping make instruction transparent; being willing to share what happens in the classroom
3. Planning, Planning, Planning	Common pacing; sharing instructional strategies; delegating responsibilities; identifying essential standards
4. Developing Common Assessments	Unwrapping standards into learning targets; identifying what proficiency looks like; discussing what evidence we need
5. Analyzing Student Learning	Sharing our results; bringing student work to the table; relying on the data to determine what comes next
6. Differentiating Follow-Up	Responding to common formative assessments by providing additional time and support for students; taking collective responsibility
7. Reflecting on Instruction	Engaging in reflection about the impact of strategies on student learning; professional learning; continuous improvement

Source: Adapted from Graham & Ferriter, 2008, pp. 39–42.

*Visit **go.SolutionTree.com/PLCbooks** for a free reproducible version of this table.*

concurrently as teams become more familiar with the data-analysis process and more confident with understanding of how assessment information drives the work. In this chapter, we'll explore stages 5, 6, and 7 to see how teams can effectively use common formative assessment data to improve their own collaborative practices.

As a coach, it's important to know about the different types of data teams can successfully use to assess student learning as well as the norms guiding those data.

Different Types of Data

Early in our own work as teachers in the 1970s and 1980s, what little data we had focused solely on numbers. We had learned about standard scores, percentiles, stanines, and percentages as ways to interpret data. These numbers represented the total aggregate of what our students had learned. In turn, we reported student learning as a number translated into a grade that represented the average of all the scores students earned in our classes. Of course, some teachers included scores representing student behavior as well. For example, we scored a missed assignment as a zero, which didn't really reflect what the student learned, just that he or she hadn't completed the assignment. Many teachers lowered a student's grade by one level for every day the assignment was late. Again, this is not a reflection on learning but on behavior.

What has changed since this time is the idea that numbers aren't the only way to analyze student learning and, as a coach, this is an important concept to help teams understand. The primary purpose of designing and using common formative assessments is to determine whether students acquire the skills or concepts that are taught—and to *use* that information to take action that supports their learning.

Therefore, the information we seek goes beyond the numbers to determine which specific skills each student does or does not learn. Teams first analyze the results globally to identify items with which students struggle. Then, they dig down to determine whether there are patterns that show where or why the student struggles. Finally, they drill down to the student level to determine where each student is achieving on the measured targets.

For this to happen, the team needs to look at its results one learning target at a time. Team members must answer questions such as: How many students were not proficient? What errors do we see in their responses? Then, they plan how they will respond. In *Simplifying Common Assessment* (Bailey & Jakicic, 2017), we recommend the following protocol for analyzing the data (figure 4.4).

Steps	Team Notes
1. Set the stage. • Establish the purpose of the meeting. • Review norms (focusing on data norms).	Two minutes
2. Review the focus of the assessment. • Identify the essential learning targets we assessed and which questions are designed to assess each of them. • Review the expectations for proficiency (for example, two out of three correct on a multiple-choice assessment, or a level 3 on the rubric). • Discuss any questions we had when we scored student work.	Two minutes
3. Discuss the data. • For each target, identify how many students need additional time and support.	Five minutes Each team member must participate in this discussion.
4. Determine student misconceptions and errors. • For each target, identify which students need help. • Once we've identified the students who need help, regroup them by specific need (for example, students who made a calculation error versus students who chose the wrong solution pathway).	Ten minutes Be careful to do this step one essential learning target at a time.
5. Determine instructional strategies. • Decide whether we will develop small groups for reteaching or use a re-engagement lesson with the whole class. • Each teacher should share his or her original instructional strategy so we can see if one strategy works better for certain students. • For each target and for each mistake or misconception, develop a plan to help students move ahead on their learning of that target. • If necessary, go back to best practice information about how to teach the concept or about what strategies work best for students who are struggling. Consult instructional coaches or specialists if necessary.	Fifteen minutes Make sure that all team members have the same understanding of what this will look like.
6. Develop the items we will use to monitor whether students met the learning target after this response. This provides information about which students still need help on this essential target.	Ten minutes You may do this reassessment orally or create a version of the original assessment.

Source: Bailey & Jakicic, 2017, p. 82.

Figure 4.4: Protocol for analyzing common formative assessment data.

*Visit **go.SolutionTree.com/PLCbooks** for a free reproducible version of this figure.*

Following is an outline of the protocol in figure 4.4 (page 143).

1. Team members review the purpose of the meeting and their data norms.

2. They review the assessment information in their assessment plan, remembering which learning targets to assess and how to determine proficiency (how many correct items or what level on the rubric).

3. Team members work on one target at a time, determining how many students are or are not yet proficient. The purpose of this step is to get a sense of the number of students who need corrective instruction. If a significant percentage of the total number of students need support, the team may decide to reteach the learning target to the entire student group. If there are only a small handful of students, the team will likely not set aside a whole class period for corrective instruction. Teams also use this information later in the protocol (step 5) to consider whether a particular strategy works better in teaching this learning target.

4. Teams determine not only which students need corrective instruction but also precisely how teachers should best deliver it. There are a few specific ways teams do this work—pile and plan and error analysis, for example. However, we know that high-performing teams will likely use a variety of strategies to best fit their assessments. The outcome of this step is a specific plan teachers use to work with student groups.

5. Team members discuss how they will reassess after this corrective instruction to determine which students are not yet proficient. If some students are still not proficient, they will move into Tier 2 intervention.

6. Teams develop items to be used to check whether students have learned the target.

Teams can organize their information in various ways, but in general, they should examine data by teacher and by learning target. Figure 4.5 provides a sample template teams can use to examine their data.

Data Team Meeting

Team:

Assessment Description:

Targets Assessed	Type of Assessment	Proficiency Expectations

Target 1

	Number of Students Below Proficiency	Number of Students at Proficiency	Number of Students Above Proficiency
Teacher 1			
Teacher 2			
Teacher 3			
Teacher 4			

Target 2

	Number of Students Below Proficiency	Number of Students at Proficiency	Number of Students Above Proficiency
Teacher 1			
Teacher 2			
Teacher 3			
Teacher 4			

Target 3

	Number of Students Below Proficiency	Number of Students at Proficiency	Number of Students Above Proficiency
Teacher 1			
Teacher 2			
Teacher 3			
Teacher 4			

Which students need more time and support?

Target 1

	Students Identified for Intervention, Practice, or Enrichment	Planned Instructional Strategy
Additional time and support		
Additional practice		
Enrichment		

Source: Bailey & Jakicic, 2012, p. 111.

Figure 4.5: Template teams can use to examine their data.

continued →

Target 2

	Students Identified for Intervention, Practice, or Enrichment	Planned Instructional Strategy
Additional time and support		
Additional practice		
Enrichment		

Target 3

	Students Identified for Intervention, Practice, or Enrichment	Planned Instructional Strategy
Additional time and support		
Additional practice		
Enrichment		

Which questions do we need to review?

Question Number	Concern

Which teaching strategies or pacing issues do we need to discuss?

Strategy or Topic	Issue of Concern

*Visit **go.SolutionTree.com/PLCbooks** for a free reproducible version of this figure.*

Rather than simply looking at a spreadsheet of scores, we strongly recommend that teams examine actual student work when they are analyzing the results and planning the response. This helps move the conversation away from right or wrong answers to questions and on to what misunderstanding or misconceptions a student has around the learning target. It helps teams see that the concept of a cut score applied to an entire assessment gets in the way of deep diagnosis by learning target. Consider how this impacts the response. When the team looks at a cut score for the entire assessment, some students will have mastered some but not all the learning targets. When the team designed the common formative assessment, it included learning targets that were *essential* for students to learn. When that same team looks at the learning targets individually, they will identify students who didn't master one or more of them. Using figure 3.5 (page 92), teams should start their analysis by looking at the column labeled Expectations for Proficiency. This reminds team members what they agreed students would need to do to show proficiency (for example, three out of four multiple-choice questions or proficiency on the rubric).

Coaching the Issue

1. Using a protocol during data analysis helps teams keep the discussions on track. As a facilitator, you can enter data into the data template and ask the questions.

2. Make sure every team member participates in the process. We've seen situations in which a teacher is reluctant to share data and avoids participation.

3. If team members are new to this work, they may not have developed a trust level that allows them to discuss results without feeling uncomfortable. In fact, we've seen team members who didn't want to have the best results because they don't like to be singled out. Keep the discussion focused on how different instructional strategies affect results rather than how different teachers affect results.

Data Norms

Teams benefit from developing a list of norms to guide their work. One of the first things high-performing teams collaborate about is the behaviors they expect from each other in order to be able to work together efficiently and effectively. These norms often help teams develop trust with each other. Team members should take some time when they start working with common assessment data to discuss whether they need to add norms around their use of data, especially how comparisons are made between students as well as between teachers. We've found that early in the process teachers may be reluctant to compare results because they worry their scores won't be as good as the other team members' results. In fact, we also worked with teachers who don't want their scores to be better than others because that makes them uncomfortable.

Coaches can support teams through this process by using an activity in which teams consider both the positives and the negatives of sharing results. They start with a T-chart with one side titled *best hopes* and the other side titled *worst fears*. The coach then asks the team to privately brainstorm and write on sticky notes things that might go wrong if they share the results of common formative assessment data; that is, they pen their worst fears about the process. The coach collects the notes and lists the responses on the *worst fears* side. He or she then asks team members to go through the same process brainstorming best hopes for engaging in the work. After listing these ideas on the chart, the coach then asks, "What are the behaviors we would need from each other to ensure these outcomes will happen?" The team helps write what will become its data norms.

Sample data norms include:

▸ We will not compare scores with the intention of judging each other.

▸ We will use data to help each other and our team to get better at what we do.

▸ We will value data for what they tell us to do next, and we will not make excuses about them.

Use a Protocol to Analyze Summative Data

We know that when a school builds a systematic response system, common formative assessments are only one type of assessment it relies on. Let's consider how teams use end-of-unit, benchmark, and progress-monitoring data differently than formative data.

Generally, these summative data points provide a measure of where students are relative to grade-level proficiency expectations. Instead of focusing on learning targets, these items are designed to assess whether students can respond to questions and problems that may use multiple learning targets to answer. For example, in a formative assessment, an item might ask students to identify the author's point of view, but the summative assessment might ask students to analyze how the author's point of view impacts what facts the author includes (or excludes) in the text.

In addition, many of these assessments are designed to show whether students are growing

as expected so teams don't have to wait until the end of the year to see if their strategies are successful. This is especially useful for teams who are monitoring whether students are receiving the appropriate amount of intervention time and support. If students are not making expected progress, teachers can provide more or different intervention. If students have made progress, they may receive less intervention time.

We offer a different protocol for teams to use when they are analyzing summative data (see table 4.2).

This protocol will guide teams through the process of having a meaningful and productive conversation around the results in student learning at the end of a unit. Each step is designed to build toward the development of specific actions the team will take based on the results. Following are coaching tips for each portion of the process.

1. **Set the stage:** Teams identify the purpose for their meeting, that is, examining benchmark data for all students or progress-monitoring data for students in intervention. Beyond student monitoring, how else will team members use these data? For example, do they need to see if they are making progress on their team SMART goal?

2. **Review the assessment focus:** Teams elicit a discussion about the assessment itself and what data they are looking for during this meeting. Because teams use a variety of different assessments, it's important that team members take a few minutes to remind themselves about how this particular assessment organizes these data. Do they report out on strands or domains? Do they report on specific standards? During this step, it's also important that team

Table 4.2: Protocol for Analyzing End-of-Unit (Summative) Data for Critical Question 3

Steps	Facilitator Notes
1. Set the stage. • Establish the purpose of the meeting. • Determine the outcome. • Review data norms.	Three minutes
2. Review the assessment focus, addressing the following questions. • Determine how the data from this assessment are organized. • Determine what it is measuring (standards, domains, fluency, or all of these). • Decide how to determine proficiency.	Five minutes (Ensure input from all participants.)
3. Discuss the data. • Working individually, examine the data, looking for fact statements and avoiding drawing inferences or conclusions. • Take turns sharing the facts and take notes. • Once everyone lists the facts, begin developing inferences and conclusions. • Determine how many students were proficient, not proficient, and beyond proficient. • Discuss patterns in data such as how clusters of students (by subgroup, by teacher) performed, how any specific interventions affected growth, and how changes in pacing or instructional strategies affect performance. • If you are using this assessment for screening or progress monitoring, identify the students who need continued support and those who need less support.	Fifteen to twenty minutes (Record the facts first and then the inferences and conclusions.)
4. Develop the action plan. • Develop a plan for how you can use the data to work with flexible student groups, change pacing if needed, and consider any instructional strategies to add.	Fifteen to twenty minutes
5. Set goals for improvement. • Discuss what the team learns from these data and what follow-up assessments to use. • Consider any obstacles or stumbling blocks team members identify in the discussion. • Discuss ongoing efforts and strategies designed to ensure quality first instruction. • If appropriate, review the SMART goal this is measuring and tweak if needed.	Eight to ten minutes (Identify no more than three strategies to directly impact achievement in this area.)
6. Determine agreed-on actions and results indicators. • Discuss what indicators to use to determine the effectiveness of the results of this action plan. • Determine how you will know if the plan is effectively improving student achievement.	Five minutes to record decisions and summarize for the group

Source: Bailey & Jakicic, 2017, p. 81.

members understand the different reports to use and how to analyze data. Coaches can facilitate this step by making sure all team members understand the available reports and what information they include.

3. **Discuss the data:** Teams should consider this step as a framework to examine data. They should start with the facts. Taking time to do this can help team members slow down to consume and analyze the assessment information before they begin making inferences about its meaning. For example, facts might include statements like: "We see a larger number of students having difficulty with vocabulary rather than with other reading strands," or "Our students are doing well with geometry but not as well with fractions."

This step also helps teams think more carefully about the inferences they make and whether they are built on facts. When teams start with inferences, they don't always make sure their inferences fit the facts. Consider for example the inference: "Our students always do poorly on numbers and operations because they aren't fluent with mathematics facts," or "Our students struggle with reading the text on the screen because they don't always scroll down to the bottom of the text." These hypotheses are just guesses. It's important for teams to see the difference between the facts and their hypotheses.

As teams generate facts, they should list them for everyone to consider. During this time, a coach should ensure teams looks for patterns in their data. Are there subgroups who are scoring especially well or having

unusual difficulty? Have there been any significant changes, good or bad, since they last administered the assessment? After they exhaust the facts they see, the team then begins to share inferences based on the facts.

Some teams get stuck on this step because they look at their results too broadly. Many teams see all the students who score in the lowest level from their benchmark or end-of-the-year testing as their most at-risk students but don't always know how to dig deeper into this information to see the differences in the needs of individual groups. Therefore, teams put all these students together in one intervention group and use the same strategies for additional time and support even if they don't all need the same help.

Coaches who can look at these data prior to the meeting can plan to lead this discussion by knowing which reports will be most helpful during this step. Prior to the team meeting they can plan out specific questions to ask which might help guide the team to see some inferences they've missed. These assessments often allow teams to identify prerequisite skills that students haven't mastered, so having a list of the essential standards from the prior grade or course might be helpful. The more specific teams can be about the gaps in student learning, the more effective the interventions.

4. **Develop the action plan:** Teams use these inferences to create an action plan about their next steps for students. Just as they do with common formative assessments, the team needs to decide which teachers will work with which students and what strategies they will use to intervene.

5. **Set goals for improvement:** Teams connect these data to their collaborative practices. They consider if data provide support for or questions about their instructional practices. High-performing teams often use these data for their action research. Consider a science team who believes that providing students class time to design and carry out their own experiments based on identified hypotheses will show better results than they have been seeing when the experiments are teacher directed. Not wanting to wait a full year to see if they are correct, the team examines the benchmark data for indicators that student learning is improving. Teams can then decide to continue what they're doing or make changes to their practices.

6. **Determine agreed-on actions and results indicators:** Teams agree to specific actions or times that they will check to see if their new strategies are effective. Is there any other evidence or data they should monitor to make sure the action plan is effective? What other actions might be needed to adjust the curriculum or pacing in this area?

Summative assessments also allow teams to set and monitor their team goals. If they've set a yearlong SMART goal for improvement, they can use their benchmark assessments to determine the effectiveness of their action plan several times during the year. This way, the team can make adjustments throughout the year as it sees which strategies are working.

One consideration we hear from teachers is that benchmark or interim assessments do not always totally align to the pacing or curriculum they are using. This means that assessments might ask students a question about content that they haven't yet been taught. We know that this can be frustrating for teachers who want to make sure their students are learning at high levels. Discrepancies will happen unless a school or district writes a benchmark assessment. Coaches can ensure teachers that this doesn't have to impact the way the team responds. That is, if the concept hasn't been taught yet, the team doesn't worry about it during intervention time.

On the other hand, these summative assessments help teachers determine if students are able to put together the multiple learning targets and standards to make sense of what they are learning. Consider all the individual skills that students are taught in their writing curriculum. Students haven't met the goal if they can't put these skills together to develop well-written text. Summative assessments also help teams identify general areas of student weakness in their pacing or curriculum. For example, if vocabulary is problematic for a large percentage of students, the English language arts reading assessment will indicate this.

Use the Coaching Reflection on page 171 to reflect on the information you explored for Action 2.

2

Coaching the Issue

Sarah is the reading instructional coach for a third-grade team at an elementary school. This team has been working collaboratively in its school PLC for three years and is really proud of what it has accomplished. The team members are Sally, a ten-year veteran of the third grade; Alison, a new addition to the team as

continued →

well as the teaching profession; and Adam, a six-year veteran who has been teaching third grade for four of those years. These teachers have been confidently using their benchmarking assessment system to identify students who need help in reading by using the four-color levels of proficiency—red (far below), yellow (below), blue (proficient), and green (beyond proficient). They have set aside a half-hour block each day to respond to those students who need extra help and enrich students who can benefit. Last year, they began to write and use common formative assessments around their essential learning targets.

Coach Sarah helped them unwrap their essential standards into learning targets and plan and write common formative assessments to match the rigor of those targets. In the beginning, it seems like each assessment took forever to write and use, but they will willingly share how successful they are feeling as team members get more comfortable with the process.

However, the one thing that they're having problems with is the response time. Originally, team members kept their own students during this time but have recently decided to group students by the color levels from their benchmarking assessment during intervention time. They have four groups because the special education teacher uses that intervention time to provide service to her students. They are struggling because there are often students in the red who don't receive special education services, and they feel the other groups are too large to get the attention they need. The team asks Sarah to come to an upcoming meeting to help them work through this problem.

- **Coach's role:** Sarah believes that the team really only needs her to help facilitate their decisions because of the experience the members have in the process and in teaching in general.

- **Team meeting:** Sarah begins the team meeting by asking members to share what they feel is going well with intervention time and then list the problems they are having. The problems, as expected, involve large group sizes and the amount of time for intervening. Sarah shares the purposes of each of the three tiers of RTI and asks team members to connect to their current reality. While talking about Tier 1, she references the generic unit plan (figure 3.4, page 88) to discuss how important it is to respond immediately after the common formative assessment on the essential learning targets.

As the team discusses its current practices, members realize they are using their half-hour intervention time to respond to common formative assessments as well as to the benchmarking data. The idea of separating the two (calling the response to common formative assessments as corrective instruction and the other responses intervention) helps the team get more clarity about how to organize both response times. Sarah reminds the team members that the common formative assessments are written around this school year's essential standards, and that they'll use Tier 3 support time to teach essential standards from prior years that students didn't learn.

Sarah then asks what teachers are working on during the intervention block. This leads to an interesting discussion! For the red-, yellow-, and blue-level students, the teachers chose reading materials at the average grade level students were able to read in the group. Teachers planned lessons based on data from the benchmarking assessment. However, one teacher asks, "I know I'm supposed to use the benchmarking data to know what to teach, but the students have so many different needs. Just because they're in yellow doesn't mean they all need the same support. I know I should be able to help them move forward, but I'm so busy moving from group to group, I don't have enough time to do anything well."

Sarah suggests they consider what these data are telling them as well as what they know from working with students. She asks, "What are the most pressing needs you see for students reading below grade level?" Adam says he is most concerned about three of his students who are still learning phonics. The other members concur, and they agree to put together a small group of seven students they call the phonics group.

Sally then raises the issue of fluency. She describes students in her class who are making progress in reading but who need practice on fluency. Once identified, this group totals ten students. Then, Sarah asks about the next issue. Alison shares what they are all thinking. If they have two groups this small, the other two groups will be too large to even have enough desks in the classrooms. Adam joins in but shares an idea he has been thinking about. He has used literature circles before in his classroom with some success.

"What if we run literature circles for the students who are at or above grade level in reading? We could plan them so at the end of each cycle, we consider what issues to address next for students who need support. We can plan a time to re-assess all students and change groups at that time based on need. And I have the materials from last year that I used to teach literature circles so we don't have to start from scratch."

Adam's colleagues are enthusiastic to try this out. They realize that they need to continue to use their assessments to diagnose what students need but now feel they have a system in place to use time more effectively. They are also pleased to know that the best readers will be engaged in quality work.

3

Action 3: Develop the Response

There are probably as many ways to respond to the information that teams get from their common formative assessments as there are learning targets. However, the factor that has the most influence on the quality of the response is whether teams use actual student work to help them plan their responses. If a team can more accurately diagnose where a student's learning has stopped or what misunderstanding or misconception is getting in the way, the planned response will be much more effective. Teams who bring actual student work to the table can collaborate about the qualities of both correct and incorrect answers. Let's examine some strategies coaches can use to facilitate and illuminate this team learning.

In order to develop the response to assessment data, coaches must work with teams to do the following.

- Select from various strategies to plan the response.

- Identify which teacher will work with which group.

- Use data to reflect on instruction.

- Include singletons in the process.

Select From Various Strategies to Plan the Response

Consider an eighth-grade English language arts team that develops a common formative assessment around one of its standards: "Determine an author's point of view or purpose in a text and analyze how the author acknowledges and responds to conflicting information or viewpoints" (RI.8.6). When the team unwraps this standard, the first thing it notices is that the first phrase (learning target) is exactly the same for grades 6, 7, and 8. (Determine an author's point of view or purpose in a text.) However, the second explicit learning target is different at each grade level, so the team decides to use a learning progression model to determine what students needed to learn to master this target at eighth grade. To do this, the team looks at the seventh-grade learning target as the prerequisite skill it could expect students to already know. Members consider this target a bookend of the progression. The team then considers the learning target written for proficiency, which becomes the other bookend of the progression. See figure 4.6.

| Target | Bookend | | Bookend | |
	Prerequisite Target (Seventh Grade)	Simpler Targets	Proficiency Target (Eighth Grade)	Extended Targets
Analyze how the author acknowledges and responds to conflicting evidence or viewpoints.	Analyze how the author distinguishes his or her position from that of others.		Analyze how the author acknowledges and responds to conflicting evidence or viewpoints.	

Source for standards: Adapted from NGA & CCSSO, 2010a.

Figure 4.6: Sample bookends of progression for an eighth-grade team.

Team members then realize that their task was to help students move from the seventh-grade learning target to become proficient on the eighth-grade learning target. To do this, they discuss what other skills or concepts students might need to learn to be able to transfer what they already know to bridge the gap to mastery on this year's target. One strategy they use is to look at their list of DOK levels in reading. They recognize that the proficiency target is a DOK 3, so they examine the DOK 2 student skills. They list these simpler targets on their progression. Once team members identify the simpler targets, they discuss what it will look like if students go beyond proficiency on the target and write this target in the last column of their learning progression. See figure 4.7.

Target	Bookend Prerequisite Target (Seventh Grade)	Simpler Targets	Bookend Proficiency Target (Eighth Grade)	Extended Targets
Analyze how the author acknowledges and responds to conflicting evidence or viewpoints.	Analyze how the author distinguishes his or her position from that of others.	Targets are: • Identify clues the author provides about his or her position or purpose by looking at specific vocabulary and word choice. • List evidence the author uses to support his or her point of view. • Identify conflicting evidence or viewpoints the author includes.	Analyze how the author acknowledges and responds to conflicting evidence or viewpoints.	Use the techniques from the analysis to produce a piece of writing with differing points of view or conflicting evidence.

Figure 4.7: Sample bookends for eighth-grade students who exceed learning targets.

When they start to write the common formative assessment for this target, team members decide to use a state legislator's recent article about gun control. They develop a graphic organizer for students to complete as they analyze the text. They ask students to determine what strategies the author uses to acknowledge and respond to conflicting information.

When the team comes to the data meeting to plan its response, members bring student work with them. The team uses the pile and plan strategy (see the following section) to organize the data based on what it sees in students' work. First, it realizes that some students aren't proficient because they can't identify the author's point of view, which is the prerequisite target. To address that need, the team plans to work with those students by having them highlight any words or clues in the article that reveal the author's point of view. A teacher models this strategy using the first paragraph and then asks students to work in pairs to complete the rest of the article.

Another student group isn't proficient because even though the students can identify the author's point of view and find conflicting evidence, they are not able to analyze the technique the author uses to acknowledge and respond to this information. For these students, the team chooses three additional sample texts (short excerpts) containing conflicting information and viewpoints. The team uses one of the texts with a document camera and shows students how to look for the techniques the author uses. The students then work in pairs to complete the same process with the second piece of text. Finally, they independently annotate the third piece of text, which the team decides it can use as a reassessment to identify which students are now proficient.

3

Teams can use various strategies to analyze the data they get back from their assessments and develop effective ways to respond. These strategies include pile and plan with constructed-response questions, error analysis with multiple-choice questions, and re-engagement or reteaching.

Pile and Plan With Constructed-Response Questions

When a team uses a constructed-response question to assess a learning target, they gather information about student thinking from the students' written responses. For the pile-and-plan strategy, the team uses student answers to plan how to respond. Typically, there is only one question that aligns to a specific learning target, which may or may not be the only learning target that this common formative assessment assesses.

Following is the complete protocol for the pile and plan strategy.

1. Identify the essential learning target for the question and what proficiency looks like on the rubric.

2. Separate student work samples into two piles—those who are proficient (or beyond) and those who are not yet proficient.

3. For students who are not yet proficient, consider what evidence you have to help create a hypothesis about what the students misunderstood or where the learning stopped. Create separate piles for each hypothesis.

4. For each pile, collaboratively plan what the corrective instruction looks like.

5. Plan how to extend the learning for students who are proficient on the learning target.

As team members engage in this work, they start by sorting student responses into two categories—(1) students who are proficient (or beyond) on the target and (2) students who aren't yet proficient. In order to facilitate this step, we recommend that teachers "score" student work prior to the meeting. That is, they read responses and provide some feedback about the level of response. For a constructed-response question this may mean circling the level reached on the rubric and making note of the misconception or mistake. Feedback can also include questions for reflection and specific comments about a correct answer. When we've worked with teams using this protocol, we often see lots of conversation happen at this point. For example, "Did you notice that some students missed the central idea and that's where they went wrong?" Or, "I had a student who solved the problem correctly but didn't use the process we were expecting." Coaches should encourage this kind of discussion, as this is where team learning happens.

Once teams sort the students who aren't proficient, the next step is to determine whether these students had more than one mistake or misunderstanding. Coaches should remind teams that they don't want to give everyone the same response if they have different diagnoses. Sometimes one teacher on the team sees a mistake that others don't see. This teammate helps everyone be a better diagnostician. Once team members sort the work the second time, they decide how to respond to students in that group. For example, for a mathematics assessment, a team may notice that some students can apply an algorithm to a simple mathematics task but are unable to apply that same algorithm to a task based on a real-life situation. These students don't need help on the algorithm but do need help on reading and understanding a real-life problem.

During this discussion, the team also needs to consider the students who have reached proficiency. What will these students be doing while the teacher is working with the other groups? We will investigate these practices in more depth in chapter 5 (page 175).

Error Analysis With Multiple-Choice Questions

When teams write multiple-choice questions, they often choose the distractor options based on common mistakes or misunderstandings students might have about the learning target. For example, a mathematics problem might include distractors that would be the correct answer *if* students use an incorrect solution pathway. When team members analyze student work (data), they group together students who choose the same wrong solution or answer choice. Using the following error-analysis protocol, teams can gather evidence of misconceptions and develop a plan of action that might correct the misconception or error.

1. Identify the multiple-choice questions connected to an essential learning target.

2. Consider the distractors (incorrect answer choices in a multiple-choice question) the student chose for his or her incorrect questions.

3. Determine what this choice or choices reveals about what the student was thinking or misunderstood.

Consider how the question writer for this released item from *Exemplar Grade 3 Mathematics Test Questions* from ACT Aspire (2017, p. 13) for third graders has chosen the five answer choices:

The number of students who attended summer camp during each of the two weeks is listed below.

- Week 1: 289

- Week 2: 347

Andrea estimated the total number of students by correctly rounding each number to the nearest 100 and then adding the rounded numbers. What is Andrea's estimated total?

    a. 500

    b. 550

    c. 600

    d. 640

    e. 700

The correct answer choice is, of course, *c*. Answer *b* isn't a number rounded to the nearest 100, so students who choose *b* don't understand how to round to a specific place value number. Students who chose answer *d* may have added the two numbers without rounding and then rounded the answer to the nearest 10. Students who chose answer *a* or *e* rounded to 100 but calculated incorrectly. These clues can help the team plan a more accurate response based on mistakes the students made. Coaches can help teams work through this protocol by asking questions such as the following.

▶ "How might a student have arrived at that answer?"

▶ "How did you teach that concept?"

▶ "Are there other problems for the same target the student misses?"

Re-engagement or Reteaching

In each of the previous strategies for responding, the team decided to use small groups of students who made a similar mistake as the structure for the response. We often think about this structure when we consider developing a differentiated response. However, there is another strategy a team can use to respond; one that keeps the entire class together, called a re-engagement lesson. A *re-engagement lesson* uses student work from a formative assessment for the purpose of uncovering misconceptions, providing feedback on student thinking, and helping students to go deeper into the learning.

We were first introduced to the concept of re-engagement through the work of David

3

Foster and Audrey Poppers (2009). Their work in mathematics instruction with teachers who were reteaching lessons led them to coin the term *re-engagement lesson* (Foster & Poppers, 2009):

> We realized that even when teachers were reteaching concepts, they often were not appreciating the need to engage their students in thinking about the concepts in a new way—the need to *re-engage* them differently in the mathematical ideas. In order to distinguish this type of lesson design from more traditional reteaching or review, we began to talk with teachers about this idea of re-engagement and to develop tools to support the practice of designing lessons that were directly tied to the results of formative assessments. (p. 12)

During the re-engagement lesson, a teacher typically places students into heterogeneous cooperative groups and gives each group two or more examples of student work showing how students accurately solved a problem. The teacher asks these groups specific questions about the examples, and the group works together to determine the answer. During this small-group discussion, students who weren't proficient are able to hear another student explain his or her reasoning and ask questions. This is often exactly what students need to understand the correct solution.

For students who are proficient, the questions require them to go more deeply into why these proficient students chose the solution pathway they did or to see another possible solution pathway. By doing this activity, students realize that solving a problem correctly is only one part of the work, as being able to explain, critique, and justify either their or others' reasoning are equally important.

Teams can use re-engagement effectively in other content areas besides mathematics. The key to the success of this strategy is to determine circumstances when this strategy would work well with students, choosing student work samples that will promote student dialogue, and writing quality questions to ask the class as well as student groups. Teams may decide to include both incorrect and correct answers so groups have to figure out why certain answers are incorrect.

Consider, for example, what this might look like for a social studies teacher who asks students to interpret a political cartoon created during a specific historical time period. Students must interpret the cartoon based on what they know about the history of that period. There may be different correct interpretations or an incorrect one students can use to spark dialogue about how to fix it.

Coaches can be especially helpful to teams who want to use this strategy by helping them identify opportunities where it might be particularly effective. They can also help teams select student work samples that will encourage student thinking and help these teams write quality questions for the lesson.

In our book *Simplifying Common Assessment* (Bailey & Jakicic, 2017), we offer the following protocol for teams to follow.

1. Determine if a re-engagement lesson will work in this situation. For example, there must be learning targets that allow multiple right answers or solution pathways. Student work from the assessment must contain at least two strong examples of correct answers that student groups can compare.

2. The team determines which learning targets it will emphasize during the re-engagement lesson and identifies at least two student work samples it will use.

3. The team designs the lesson considering how large the groups will be, what it will ask groups to do, what questions it will ask, and how and when whole-group instruction will occur. Team members plan how to begin the lesson and write the initial questions or prompts. For example, "Examine these two answers from different students to make sense of their thinking and the strategy they use. Compare their responses and decide if they are correct or incorrect."

4. Team members develop strong questions (assessing or advancing) they can pose to assist student groups who might get stuck or to ensure students make progress throughout the lesson.

5. The team plans how it will reassess students at the end of the lesson to determine whether the students who were not yet proficient prior to this lesson reach proficiency.

Coaching Tips

1. Unless they have experience with student work as their data, teams may feel the process is overwhelming when they first begin. This may be an important time for coaches to facilitate this process explicitly using the data-analysis protocol.

2. Many teachers still want to grade their papers by putting a percent or overall score at the top. Be prepared to remind team members that the purpose of this formative assessment is to identify students who need additional time and support.

3. If a team doesn't carefully discuss its answer guide, you'll see the team tend to score responses differently. For example, one teacher might give half credit for a student who has an incomplete answer. It's important to make sure every team member applies the rubric in the same way.

Identify Which Teacher Will Work With Which Group

Common formative assessments and their responses are part of good core instruction and should be available to all students (see chapter 3, page 79). Therefore, teams should respond during regular class time as part of the Tier 1 instruction. Teachers often ask us if students should stay with their assigned classroom teacher for this response or if the team should separate students according to needs, with each team member taking a different group. Both of these strategies can be effective. If the team agrees to separate students by specific need, then it assigns each teacher to a group of students with the same needs. Teams sometimes assign the teacher who had the most initial success on the learning target to the students who had the most difficulty. When teams use this strategy to respond, each teacher is working on only one lesson plan for the response. Because of the way schools lay out master schedules, this plan is often easier for elementary schools than secondary schools. The other way that teams might plan to respond is to have each teacher keep his or her students and differentiate the lesson within that group.

For example, let's consider a second-grade team of two teachers who use a common formative assessment covering two learning targets: (1) identify the main topic in a multi-paragraph text, and (2) identify the focus of specific paragraphs within the text. There are a total of thirty-eight students in both classes. For the assessment, students read a multi-paragraph text about elephants and must answer two questions: What is the main topic of this text? and What is the focus of the first paragraph?

The two teachers will use student responses to identify three groups of students: those who are proficient on both learning targets (Group A), those who aren't able to identify the main topic of the text (Group B), and those who can identify the main topic but not the focus of the first paragraph (Group C). The team asks Group A (students who are proficient on both learning targets) to work independently after the initial instruction.

In this example, fifteen students are proficient. The team organizes them into smaller cooperative groups and asks them to create a group writing project on a topic related to the science materials students are studying. The team reminds students that they need to write paragraphs that have a specific focus.

In this example, eight students are in Group B (those who aren't proficient on either target). During data analysis, the team discovers that most students who don't find the correct main topic listed the first sentence of the first paragraph as the main topic. With Group B, the assigned teacher shares two different text excerpts, one in which the main topic appears in the first sentence and one in which it doesn't. After some discussion, the teacher feels comfortable that students are seeing the difference. The teacher then moves on to the second learning target requiring students to identify the focus of each paragraph. He or she asks students to look at each paragraph and highlight words and ideas that relate to the main topic and helps them identify the category that these words fit into.

Finally, Group C has fifteen students (those who were able to identify the main topic but not the focus of each paragraph). When the assigned teacher begins this lesson, he or she models for the group how to find the main topic so they all agree. The teacher then asks the group to focus on the first paragraph and use a highlighter to look for specific details that link to the main topic it identifies. While these students do this, the teacher encourages them to explain their thinking aloud as they highlight. After students finish highlighting the paragraph, the teacher asks them what these details have in common. For the second paragraph, the teacher asks students to work with a partner using the same process. Once the teacher is comfortable that they understand the process, he or she asks students to work independently to find the focus of the third paragraph. He or she uses this as the reassessment to know which students will still need Tier 2 support on this essential standard (Burke, 2013).

In this example, the team planned the responses for Groups A, B, and C together. The teacher who had Group B also had Group A in his or her classroom. The other teacher worked with Group C. Teams often rotate which teacher takes which group and will sometimes choose a teacher who has had more success teaching a target take the group who needs more help. Sometimes, there's an additional teacher or aide available to make the response groups smaller.

Coaching Tips

Many teams we've worked with are using resources that provide not only information about what the standards mean but also suggest instructional strategies teachers can use, including some for English learners. We've found that this sometimes jumpstarts conversations about instruction as well as corrective instruction. Some good resources include the following:

Blauman, L., & Burke, J. (2014). *The Common Core companion: The standards decoded, grades 3–5*. Thousand Oaks, CA: Corwin Press.

Burke, J. (2013). *The Common Core companion: The standards decoded, grades 6–8*. Thousand Oaks, CA: Corwin Press.

Marzano, R. J. (2017). *The new art and science of teaching*. Bloomington, IN: Solution Tree Press.

Nickelsen, L., & Dickson, M. (2018). *Teaching with the instructional cha-chas: Four steps to make learning stick*. Bloomington, IN: Solution Tree Press.

Taberski, S., & Burke, J. (2014). *The Common Core companion: The standards decoded, grades K–2*. Thousand Oaks, CA: Corwin Press.

Coaching Insight

It's important for anyone involved in data analysis of common formative assessments to avoid the four most common mistakes we see.

1. Don't average students' scores on the assessment. It's important to consider each essential learning target by itself. A student could master one but not the other.

2. Don't rely on class averages. If all students but one master a target, that student still needs additional time and support.

3. Avoid making excuses for the data. "You have the special education cluster in your classroom" doesn't resolve the fact that *all* students must learn at high levels.

4. Don't draw conclusions that may not be based on facts. "My students don't like to write, so I don't expect them to do well on constructed-response questions."

Coaches can remind teams to avoid these mistakes if they are working with them during data analysis.

3

Use Data to Reflect on Instruction

If someone wrote a book on the one best way to teach the standards, we'd all want a copy of that book! However, we know that there isn't one best way to teach a concept that works for all students. In a PLC, teams are always trying to learn more about what strategies work best for each of their students. Using the results of common formative assessments, teams can learn what strategies are most effective. In our protocol for using the results of common formative assessments, we suggest team members share their strategies with each other. There are two reasons for this. The first is to determine if there is one particular strategy that seems to be more effective than another. The second is to ensure all corrective instruction for students is different from the initial instruction.

In addition, we've seen some high-performing teams use their data as action research for learning together about effective strategies. A team might agree to look at a particular question of practice and then use the common formative assessment results to determine if the strategy is effective. For example, a mathematics team might question the amount of student discourse it's using in the classrooms to know how much and what kind of discourse works best. The team notices that students are reluctant to fully explain their work and their reasoning. The team agrees it will increase the amount of time dedicated to student discourse and plan some lessons together with common questions it will use to engage students in discussion. The team also agrees its members will use their next common formative assessment to see if this practice affects student learning in a positive way. The team plans to ask two constructed-response questions, one which requires students to explain their solution and one requiring students to critique the response from another student. They hope to see improvement in the overall responses they get from students.

Include Singletons in the Process

When a school uses collaborative teams in different configurations because of the number of singletons on the staff, it sometimes gets stuck in the first of Graham and Ferriter's (2008) stages of collaboration (see table 4.1, page 142), trying to figure out its purpose and how to have meaningful partnerships. When

teams are able to effectively work together to answer the question "What do we want students to know and be able to do?," and then "How will we know if they have learned it?," they find their purpose. The meaningful partnerships they develop reside in the answers to those questions. Making sure all students learn their essential standards is their purpose.

As these teams move into stages 5–7, how they configure their teams will affect how they are able to respond to data. Consider, for example, a vertical team makeup of three elementary teachers who teach grades 3–5. These teachers may have been working together on standard one for writing (writing opinions). As they think about how to work with students experiencing difficulty with this standard, they may choose to share students, regardless of grade level, among the three teachers and flexibly group students according to their specific needs. One teacher may work with any students who need help brainstorming ideas and structuring their writing. Another might work with students having difficulty with supporting their opinions and the third with students struggling with developing strong conclusions. They may also each keep a group of proficient students. For these students, teachers can begin the class with a short minilesson to get them started on developing their writing and then focus more intensely on the students who are not yet proficient.

Consider, also, a small high school whose ninth-grade teachers work together as an interdisciplinary team. The team creates a SMART goal to improve student success with reading complex text in all subject areas and has been focusing this quarter on disciplinary reading. The science and history teachers decide to write a common formative assessment around standard seven for reading, which they have been teaching in class (NGA & CCSSO, 2010a).

- **Standard Seven in Science, Grades 9–10:** Translate quantitative or technical information expressed in words in a text into visual form (such as, a table or chart) and translate information expressed visually or mathematically (such as, into an equation) into words (RST.9–10.7).

- **Standard Seven in History / Social Studies, Grades 9–10:** Integrate quantitative or technical analysis (such as, charts, research data) with qualitative analysis in print or digital text (RH.9–10.7).

When they get together to look at their common formative assessment results, team members identify that the misunderstandings of nonproficient students fall into two groups. The first are students who make mistakes when teachers ask them to accurately analyze quantitative information, and the second are those who are able to analyze the information but unable to translate that information into visual or written form. For their corrective instruction, team members decide to share students—the science teacher takes the students who aren't able to analyze the information, and the history teacher takes those who aren't able to translate that information into a written or visual form. They plan their responses together, building on each other's instructional strengths.

A third scenario may exist in which each team member is solely responsible for his or her content. For example, a high school electives team may comprise one teacher teaching agriculture, another teaching orchestra, and another teaching visual arts. When teams don't share content or even students, they can still use their collective expertise to support student learning. Team members can provide feedback in terms of what he or she sees in student work and quality instructional practices. They can pose questions to their colleagues that lead to

clarification and focus. In other words, they function as a critical friend to other members of the team. Individually, they teach unique content, but collectively, they examine the impact and results of instruction and provide input about next steps. These mixed-content conversations, while unique and not without their challenges, can be powerful and build on shared knowledge of effective instructional practices. However, these conversations need structure to make them focused and productive. Following is a mixed-content and single-team assessment analysis protocol, using a critical friend approach.

Divide total meeting time into equal parts and rotations to allow each team member to share and seek input. Allow sufficient time at the end of the meeting to reflect on the process.

Members should come prepared with their students' results organized by proficiency level, for example, in categories such as advanced; meets, does not meet, or exceeds expectations; understands the concept but has some mistakes; and struggling.

For each rotation (approximately fifteen minutes per teacher), do the following.

1. **Set the stage:** This step should last no more than two minutes. The presenting teacher shows the assessment item (using a document camera or providing samples to each team member) and describes the focus of the assessment (for example, the standard and specific learning targets being assessed). The teacher limits questions from remaining team members to getting information about how students completed the assessment.

2. **Do the what? so what? now what? strategy:**

   a. *What?*—For about three minutes, the presenting teacher discusses his or her observations of the results (for example, general success rate, strengths or surprises, common errors, misconceptions) and asks team members for other observations. Note: The teacher shares examples using the document camera or by distributing work of representative students.

b. *So what?*—For two minutes, members share what they notice or learn from by looking at the students' responses and the assessment items, pacing, and so on. They can discuss questions about the strategies used to achieve the results (for example, what works).

c. *Now what?*—For approximately six to eight minutes, all teachers discuss potential strategies to reteach the skill or concept to students who are struggling *or* if the data imply, re-engage the whole class to reinforce the skill or concept.

The presenting teacher shares final thoughts about the strategies he or she will use and any changes to the assessment item or curriculum that would be appropriate for the next time. Repeat the process for each presenting teacher.

Use the Coaching Reflection on page 172 to reflect on the information you explored for Action 3.

Coaching the Issue

The seventh-grade English team is composed of three teachers—Jared, Keisha, and Jessica. They have all been teaching middle school English for ten years or more and are confident they can keep their students engaged by choosing interesting and motivating literature and text for them. However, they are concerned about the number of students who are unable to comprehend complex pieces of seventh-grade text. While their students most in need have time built into their schedules to work with either a special education teacher or an interventionist to improve their reading comprehension, many other students aren't being pulled out for support, leaving the intervention to the English teachers. As there is no instructional coach at this school, they have asked their principal to help them solve this problem.

- **Coach's role:** Carlos's background is middle school English, but he doesn't feel he knows all the answers to this problem. He decides that he will facilitate the discussion but also put together some resources to bring to the team.

- **Team meeting:** Carlos starts the meeting by recognizing that this is a schoolwide problem that crosses into other curricular areas. He suggests that the team focus on its own students with the idea that what they are able to learn together may be shared with the rest of the staff in the future. The first thing he asks the team to do is consider what strategies it uses as readers when its members encounter difficult text. The list includes things like: look up unknown vocabulary, reread difficult paragraphs, chunk the text into smaller pieces, and annotate the text with questions and reflections. Team members mention that they have taught their own students some of these strategies but haven't necessarily built them into routine practices.

Carlos then asks the team about whether they have been using close reading strategies in their classes with complex text relying on text-dependent questions. Two of them have but not routinely. Carlos shares some of the close reading resources he's pulled together, including some specific examples of text appropriate to the seventh-grade curriculum with close reading lessons. The team agrees to use one of the examples in the next week and then come back together to gauge the effectiveness of this strategy. Carlos encourages team members to use their common formative assessments in the next unit to see whether they see improvement for the students who generally struggle with seventh-grade text.

- **Next steps:** The team agrees it will identify additional materials that support the use of a close reading strategy and learn more about how to support students with complex text. Members realize that they are doing real action research and will review the data from their common formative and benchmark assessments to determine how effective this work is for students. They want to be able to answer some of the questions they're thinking about: How often should they do this? How many strategies should they focus on at a time? Should they allow students to choose strategies, or should they be more directive? The team feels energized that it finally has a plan in place.

Action 4: Take Into Account Other Considerations for Effective Responses

Some schools may have developed and used intervention systems for a period of time before realizing these systems are not as effective as they hoped they would be. A coach new to a system may want to throw everything out and start over, but it would be far more effective to spend some time supporting and facilitating teams as they identify the pieces that are working or not working. Then the goal becomes streamlining or tweaking the system. Most teachers are far more willing to modify a program than start completely over.

In order to take into account other considerations for effective responses, coaches must work with teams to do the following.

- Evaluate the current response system.

- Make the system mandatory rather than invitational.

- Respond to academic and social behavior issues.

- Take a proactive stance.

Evaluate the Current Response System

As in any system interested in continuous improvement, schools must continuously examine their practices. Teams can use the checklist in figure 4.8 (page 166) as a tool to periodically focus efforts on the next steps toward the school's vision for systematically supporting students.

4

Teams can use this checklist to determine whether their school has considered the important components of their response system. These ideas may suggest ways to more effectively provide support to students.

How do we find time?

☐ Response to common formative assessments happens during regular class time.

☐ Tier 2 and Tier 3 responses occur when no new instruction is being delivered.

☐ Response happens quickly after we give any assessment.

Who delivers the response?

☐ The most qualified staff work with the students most in need.

☐ Team members work best with Tier 1 and Tier 2 academic response.

☐ Academic and social behavior responses match students with teachers who can develop positive relationships with them.

How do we use data?

☐ Common formative assessments provide data about students learning the essential learning targets.

☐ The response is student by student, learning target by learning target.

☐ Summative assessments provide data around standards, strands, or domains.

☐ Data aren't always numbers—observations, checklists, and student work pieces are also effective data.

☐ Students in interventions are frequently monitored using progress monitoring tools.

☐ Data are the foundation of the planned response.

Is the intervention mandatory?

☐ Before and after-school interventions can't be mandatory and, therefore, may not be effective.

☐ Teams don't allow students to opt out of interventions.

☐ All teachers must participate in the intervention system.

Do we respond to academic and social behaviors?

☐ Some students are capable of doing the work but are unmotivated.

☐ Schools should have a systemwide behavior plan.

☐ Teams teach students correct behaviors.

☐ Students who need academic help are not in the same group as students who need behavioral help.

Figure 4.8: Checklist to evaluate the effectiveness of our systematic support system.

*Visit **go.SolutionTree.com/PLCbooks** for a free reproducible version of this figure.*

Make the System Mandatory Rather Than Invitational

When we work with teams to find time to respond to student learning, we sometimes see that they are using time before and after school for interventions. While this solution ensures students aren't missing core instruction, it also is flawed because schools can't make student attendance mandatory. In other schools, we've seen intervention time built around lunch time, but they make attendance invitational. We know that it's vital for schools to create a system of response in which students are required to attend interventions. This, then, means that the school must build this time into the school day. In addition to ensuring students attend interventions, having a dedicated time also demonstrates to all students the school's commitment to providing the time students need to learn.

4

Respond to Academic and Social Behavior Issues

Most of us have worked with students who aren't completing assignments that we know they are able to do. These students are sometimes more frustrating to teachers because it's often easier to remediate academics than motivate students who don't want to do the work. In figure 4.1 (page 136), we lay out a response system that accounts for these students on the left side of the pyramid. As noted previously, this side is generally the school's responsibility rather than individual teams because it's important for a school to have campuswide expectations for behavior as well as a well-designed response when students have academic or social behavior issues that impact their learning. This doesn't mean teachers aren't involved in implementing this support; it means they implement the overall process in a systematic way so students know it doesn't matter to which teacher they are assigned—they will be accountable at the same level.

Again, there are lots of examples of how schools design these interventions; the key is the same for responding to academic gaps. There needs to be a core program and a core response for all students. For example, some schools implement a "lunch and learn" program during their lunch hour. Students who don't complete their work go to a location away from the lunch room where they can eat and also work on missing assignments. As a coach, you'll want to prepare for implementing this kind of program by making sure all teachers know they must participate in this program to make it effective.

Also, schools need to prepare for a large number of students early in implementation. For the first week or so, staff may feel overwhelmed because so many students are used to not being held accountable. Once students understand that this is a priority for staff, the number of students they assign to a "lunch and learn" program becomes easily manageable.

Finally, a note about collective responsibility. When schools build intervention time during the school day for Tier 2 *academic* support, they must also implement a different intervention for students who need Tier 2 *behavior* support. Usually the teachers who work with these students play an important role because they send the message that every staff member participates. For example, when sport coaches, performance arts teachers, and physical education teachers work with these students, they often have different relationships with students who have not been successful in other classes; these relationships can make the response more effective. Students see that the school is uniform in making sure students complete their work when everyone participates.

Take a Proactive Stance

Teams don't always need to wait for assessment results to know that some students will need additional time and support. As teams engage in the planning process (part of the PDSA cycle, see figure 1.1, page 13), they can anticipate students' needs and build in instructional supports and scaffolds from the beginning of the learning process. For example, if they observe that many students don't possess prerequisite skills for learning a new concept or skill set they're going to teach, they can design their preassessments to measure students and gather specific information up-front. Teachers can use that information quickly to catch students up through intentional front-loading, guided group work, and other strategies. Additionally, they can provide scaffolds from the beginning of instruction to provide support for specific goals. This *does not* mean teachers should reduce the level of rigor or engagement

4

students experience through challenging tasks. But it does mean they should have a set of strategies ready to go when students struggle.

Another example of this proactive process might be to preteach vocabulary that focuses on providing support for English learners or students who need more background information prior to the introduction of a new concept. When teams can anticipate and design their instruction to meet various student needs from the beginning of instruction, they move beyond simply functioning in a reactive or catch-up mode.

In addition to designing instruction proactively, coaches can build in routine check-ins to review the progress of students who are struggling. For example, coaches can schedule these check-ins every six to eight weeks. Each team member provides an update on his or her targeted students, providing artifacts as needed. Collectively, the team can brainstorm ideas for supporting students. Ideally, other available site resources, such as a reading specialist, can be present during these periodic meetings to offer recommendations and be part of the solution as appropriate.

The school's goal is to support all students toward proficiency of those things deemed most essential. Through team engagement in a systematic approach of monitoring all students and supporting them in a timely basis, the results will be evident in student learning. The next chapter focuses on meeting the needs of students who are exceeding the standards.

At the beginning of this chapter, we shared Graham and Ferriter's (2008) seven stages of collaboration. These stages focused on how successful teams use assessment data to effectively respond to student needs. Stages 5–7 in Graham and Ferriter's list (see table 4.1 on page 142) determine how teams use data to respond so students are all learning at high levels. While these stages don't always occur in the same order, we know that the highest-performing teams are effective at the final stage, which is where teams *learn together*. These high-performing teams use data to set and plan action research projects about their own work. They know that collective inquiry is a foundational characteristic of PLCs. As coaches, you can help every team improve his or her work by creating opportunities for teams to learn together as a team as well as from other teams.

Use the Coaching Reflection on page 173 to reflect on the information you explored for Action 4.

Conclusion

This chapter focused on how coaches support teams as they answer critical question 3 (How will we respond when some students do not learn?), the basis for providing students with the support, feedback, and responses they need to succeed. By implementing the four actions in this chapter, teams accomplish the following.

▶ Build shared knowledge about a system of supports on both a schoolwide and team level.

▶ Use common assessments to identify students who struggle, including a protocol to analyze common formative and summative assessment data.

▶ Develop effective responses and strategies for promoting student learning and achievement based on assessment results.

▸ Consider various issues that influence effective responses, such as academic and social behaviors.

By focusing on these actions and doing the right work, teams can provide students with various levels of support, specific to students' individual needs, ensuring no one is left behind and *all* students have the opportunity to learn. The last chapter turns its focus from students who are struggling to those who are already achieving but need more challenge. It explores PLC critical question 4 (How will we extend the learning for students who are already proficient?).

Coaching Reflection for Action 1: Build Shared Knowledge About a System of Supports

Use the questions in this chart to reflect on the information you explored in Action 1.

What do I need to consider about the context of the teams in my school? What is their current practice in responding to the needs of students based on assessment results? Are there specific school- or district-established guidelines about this practice?	What role (facilitator, consultant, coach) should I play with each team?
Do the teams take collective responsibility for student learning? If not, what steps should I take?	What issues or concerns do I need to anticipate and plan for?
Are there schools or districts that have an effective systematic process in place that might provide guidance for us in this action?	What is a reasonable time line for completing this step?

Coaching Reflection for Action 2: Use Common Assessments to Identify Students Who Struggle

Use the questions in this chart to reflect on the information you explored in Action 2.

What do I need to consider about the context of the teams in my school? Are teachers comfortable sharing data and discussing results?	What role (facilitator, consultant, coach) should I play with each team?
Are each of my teams comfortable with how to analyze data from each assessment?	What issues do I need to anticipate and plan for?
Are my teams familiar with the various reports available to them? Can I model the use of several to get them started?	What is a reasonable time line for completing this step?

Coaching Reflection for Action 3:
Develop the Response

Use the questions in this chart to reflect on the information you explored in Action 3.

Do all teams have the same needs? Is it more effective to model different strategies for each team one at a time or for the entire staff at the same time?	What role (facilitator, consultant, coach) should I play with each team?
Will my teams need help generating responses? What questions can I anticipate?	What issues do I need to anticipate and plan for?
Do my teams use data to reflect on their instruction? How can I help them with this?	What is a reasonable time line for completing this step?

Coaching Reflection for Action 4: Take Into Account Other Considerations for Effective Responses

Use the questions in this chart to reflect on the information you explored in Action 4.

What are the most effective components of our current systematic response? What changes do we need to make?	What role (facilitator, consultant, coach) should I play with each team?
Are all our interventions mandatory? Are we effectively helping students who need academic support or behavior support?	What issues do I need to anticipate and plan for?
What ideas or strategies can I find that might help teachers and teams get better at this work?	What is a reasonable time line for completing this step?

Coaching focus for PLC critical question 4:
How will we extend the learning for students who are already proficient?

1

ACTION 1: Build Shared Knowledge About Team Responses That Extend Learning

▸ Establish common language and a shared vision around supporting advanced learners.
▸ Clarify schoolwide versus team responsibilities.

▼

2

ACTION 2: Identify Students Who Would Benefit From Extensions or Advanced Learning Opportunities

▸ Understand the implications for a growth mindset in advanced learners.
▸ Use multiple data sources to identify advanced students.
▸ Define what *beyond proficiency* looks like.
▸ Develop assessments to identify students who can benefit from extensions.
▸ Follow a team protocol to collaboratively identify students who need learning extension based on results.

▼

3

ACTION 3: Select Strategies to Extend Learning

▸ Align extensions to the essential standards.
▸ Select and use a strategy to create learning extensions.
▸ Work collaboratively to develop specific activities that extend the learning of essential standards.

▼

4

ACTION 4: Deliver and Monitor the Impact of Extension Activities

▸ Deliver learning extensions during a specific time frame or segment of the day.
▸ Take a proactive stance through collaborative planning.
▸ Develop team members' mindsets.

ACTIONS

How Will We Extend the Learning for Students Who Are Already Proficient?

Effective collaborative teams in a PLC analyze their assessment results to ensure every student learns essential skills and concepts. In the last chapter, we explored how teams take this information and develop a timely response when students demonstrate difficulties or gaps in their learning. A team's examination of critical question 4, How will we extend the learning for students who are already proficient? actually becomes an extension of that exact same process.

PLCs use this final critical question to ensure teams consider the needs of *all* students and promote higher levels of learning, even when they already demonstrate proficiency. In other words, teams not only discuss strategies for supporting learners who are struggling but they collectively and strategically plan their response for students who are already considered proficient while analyzing the results from common formative or summative assessments. This chapter focuses on coaching strategies that guide teams to collectively respond by adjusting their instruction to support and advance student learning.

Coaches should understand the following.

▸ Some students come to school knowing more than others, and some learn much

more quickly than others. It's important to keep all students motivated to learn more.

▸ Just like the pyramid model we use to examine a school's system of supports for students who are struggling, there are schoolwide responsibilities for ensuring students receive challenging yet supportive learning environments. However, teams are responsible for providing direct support to challenge and extend the learning of their advanced students as they teach their core curriculum, emphasizing what is most essential.

▸ The decision to provide an extension activity is based on evidence of student learning. When teams know which students have mastered the essential standards in a unit of instruction by examining their assessment results, they can plan opportunities for those who are advanced to learn more.

▸ Just as there isn't a right way to do interventions, there also isn't one right way to do extensions and enrichment.

Explore Your Context

While this chapter focuses primarily on team conversations and actions, coaches should be aware of the schoolwide structures and course offerings that advance student learning. Additionally, knowledge of the existing culture and general practices for providing support to advance learners will benefit your coaching efforts. The following are some questions to guide your study.

▸ What formal programs and services exist to identify and provide support to students who are advanced? In elementary school, does the school need to identify students as gifted and talented in order to receive challenging activities? How do these students receive support? Do teachers place students in clusters within classrooms, or do they receive pull-out services from designated staff?

▸ Are students getting equal access to these programs, or are certain student subgroups underrepresented? For example, are students whose primary language is one other than English represented proportionally when compared to the school's general population? In high school, the question might turn to data for advanced placement (AP) classes. Do more students engage in AP classes over the prior year?

▸ When, if appropriate, are students engaging in an accelerated curriculum? Can a student get both acceleration and enrichment? Acceleration and extension?

To gain more specific insights regarding instructional practices to support advanced learners, the following are some recommended guiding questions.

▸ What background knowledge and experiences related to extending learning or differentiation exist among the staff?

▸ How do teachers currently gather information that informs them of student needs for differentiation or extension?

▸ What currently takes place with students who demonstrate mastery on the common formative and end-of-unit assessments?

▸ What practices are currently in use across classrooms? What opportunities currently exist for enrichment and extension?

Many teachers feel overwhelmed with the idea of differentiating their instruction for all students in their classroom. They worry about the great disparity among students, especially as they enter the secondary level. As a coach, it will be helpful to explore the training teachers have already had in this area and build on that training.

We advocate the idea that classroom instruction using assessment to provide a differentiated level of support is the most effective. Consider a high school teacher who just scored a common formative assessment on how well students can read an argument and understand the facts and details the author uses to support this argument. If that teacher can easily group or cluster students by what they know (or don't yet know) about supporting an argument, the differentiation he or she plans as a result is likely to be much better than if the teacher just planned a lesson with differentiated activities based on what he or she *thought* students knew.

As kindergarten teacher Lisa May from Willow Grove Kindergarten Center in Buffalo Grove, Illinois notes:

> It's just as important for me to know specifically what my proficient readers need as those who might struggle. I have a student this year who entered kindergarten as a reader, however, after further diagnosis it seemed as if he was "word calling." He struggled to identify the main topic of a piece of text and recall important details, so this is something we needed to work on together. (L. May, personal communication, May 4, 2018)

The following four actions support the work of PLC critical question 4: How will we extend the learning for students who are already proficient?

Action 1: Build Shared Knowledge About Team Responses That Extend Learning

As a coach, you may realize it's difficult to guide teams forward without first giving everyone the opportunity to come from a common baseline of information. In the case of PLC critical question 4, you may find that there are misconceptions or a lack of common knowledge about advanced learners and strategies for meeting their needs. Additionally, you may find competing beliefs or philosophies among team members that could potentially roadblock meaningful collaboration. By engaging in conversations about common terminology and concepts, team members can clarify their shared vision for learners.

In order to build shared knowledge about team responses that extend learning, coaches must work with teams to do the following.

- Establish common language and a shared vision around supporting advanced learners.

- Clarify schoolwide versus team responsibilities.

Establish Common Language and a Shared Vision Around Supporting Advanced Learners

During her keynote at the PLC institutes, Rebecca DuFour frequently quoted Mike Schmoker's (2004) advice: "Clarity precedes competence" (p. 85). She shared that some schools call themselves professional learning communities but aren't really engaged in the work of answering the four critical questions. With that in mind, it's important for coaches to help teams get clear on key terms related to the notion of differentiation. Sometimes the terms are used interchangeably, and yet the intent of each is quite different. Additionally, not all approaches are applicable to the work of collaborative teams. Let's look at the three most common terms associated with differentiation.

1. **Acceleration:** This is the process of progressing through education at a rate faster than typical. This can occur through grade skipping or subject acceleration (for example, a fifth-grade student taking sixth-grade mathematics) (National Association for Gifted Children, n.d.). Generally, district and school policies determine acceleration

1

in conjunction with social considerations and best instructional practices.

2. **Enrichment:** These activities add to or go beyond the existing curriculum. They may occur in the classroom or in a separate setting such as a pull-out program (National Association for Gifted Children, n.d.).

3. **Extension:** These activities do what the name describes. They extend the learning of essential standards. For example, if students are learning fractions, they may extend their learning by finding fractions represented in their world. Teachers may level extension activities depending on students' needs. Effective collaborative teams in a PLC codesign these extension activities and use them specifically to support student learning.

As in every aspect of the PLC process, we suggest that coaches engage teams in clarifying their vision for students. Teams can discuss the type of evidence that would be in place if they pose the question "What would it look like if we were responsive to the needs of advanced students in our classes?" If, as a coach, you are working in a school that provides all intervention levels (Tiers 1, 2, and 3) during only one designated intervention time, or at a school in which the only opportunity for differentiation occurs in advanced classes, you must guide people to think more deeply about their purpose and all the possibilities open to them. A conversation to build shared knowledge about differentiation can set the stage for next steps.

In the last chapter, we referenced Tomlinson and Murphy's (2015) five quality indicators of differentiated classrooms that meet all students' learning needs. Teachers could use these five indicators to frame conversations around a school or team's vision for providing

differentiated support to students. As always, we can use the question about what educators would want for their own child to trigger reflection on the topic.

Clarify Schoolwide Versus Team Responsibilities

If you could hold up a mirror to your current RTI pyramid (see figure 5.1), the reflection that appears in the mirror shows the levels of differentiation or enrichment schools should provide for students who are able to learn more than the essential grade-level standards. This means that there should be a Tier 1 response for all students who demonstrate mastery of essential learning targets established for the current grade or course on common formative assessments. You can use figure 5.1 to review your current RTI practices.

Schools should provide a Tier 2 response for students who can benefit from learning extensions on a short-term basis and Tier 3 for those who would benefit from more intensive enrichment opportunities. We recognize that there is a difference between offering students *enrichment* opportunities (content not available in the regular curriculum), *extension* opportunities (content that aligns to the curriculum but offered with high DOK-level learning targets), and *acceleration* (content within the next grade-level or course-level curriculum).

Teachers often offer extension during regular class time for students who have demonstrated proficiency on a common formative assessment. They may work with small groups to provide extra support on essential learning targets, offering them the opportunity to work on materials with higher-level content. On the other hand, consider a middle school who has accelerated mathematics classes available for students. Sixth graders receive a course in the seventh-grade curriculum, seventh graders

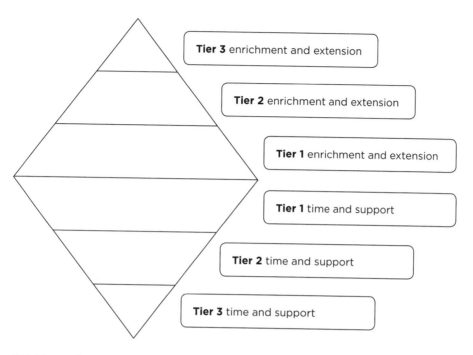

Figure 5.1: Form for teams to review current RTI practices.

*Visit **go.SolutionTree.com/PLCbooks** for a free reproducible version of this figure.*

a course in the eighth-grade curriculum, and eighth graders a course in the ninth-grade curriculum. They use acceleration to meet their students' needs. Teachers typically make the decision to accelerate a student through a process that school policy outlines; policy that

addresses a more global need to challenge a particular student.

Use the Coaching Reflection on page 198 to reflect on the information you explored for Action 1.

Action 2: Identify Students Who Would Benefit From Extensions or Advanced Learning Opportunities

The response to students who need more time and support to learn essential standards must be systematic, and similarly, it's equally important that enrichment and extensions for students who can benefit also be systematic. Sometimes schools become so engaged in helping their neediest students that they don't consider what they should be doing for students who have already learned the essential standards and need more challenge. In order to identify

students who would benefit from extensions or advanced learning opportunities, coaches must work with teams to do the following.

▶ Understand the implications for a growth mindset in advanced learners.

▶ Use multiple data sources to identify advanced students.

▶ Define what *beyond proficiency* looks like.

- ▶ Develop assessments to identify students who can benefit from extensions.

- ▶ Follow a team protocol to collaboratively identify students who need learning extension based on results.

Understand the Implications for a Growth Mindset in Advanced Learners

The work of Carol Dweck on the concept of mindset has swept the education community. In her book *Mindset* (2006), Dweck shares the results of her research regarding how mindset affects our view of the world and, more important, what we may ultimately accomplish. She identifies two mindsets—fixed mindset and growth mindset. People with a fixed mindset believe that their intelligence is set at a certain level. People with a growth mindset believe that with hard work, their intelligence evolves over time.

Contrary to what we typically think of as advanced learners, these learners may not always invite challenge. Many of them have experienced success with minimal effort. In the world of a growth mindset, they may actually have a fixed mindset—stuck on the concept that they are smart and already know the information. They may not be inclined to do what they perceive as more work, nor do they always value feedback that implies they could do better. Some advanced students with a fixed mindset are afraid to tackle new challenges because they fear they will fail. We clearly need to undo that mindset and foster a growth mindset for all students.

In this chapter, we explore the idea of mindset as it affects students who are able to demonstrate mastery of grade-level standards. We want to offer these students activities and opportunities for challenge, and we need to think about how students with a fixed mindset approach challenges differently than students with a growth mindset. Students with a fixed mindset may avoid challenges because they worry they may not be successful. Because they believe that intelligence is set, a missed challenge appears to demonstrate they aren't as intelligent as they hoped. Students with a growth mindset, on the other hand, enjoy challenges. They don't worry about not being successful because they believe with hard work, they will be successful in the future.

Students who perceive they have fixed intelligence may decide that giving more effort isn't necessary. While students who struggle are often exerting a lot of effort without success, advanced learners might have experienced a lot of success without much effort. They may be complacent because of this experience. In their view, getting the grade is enough. Effective differentiation keeps students' success-to-effort ratios balanced. The key is to find that balance to ensure that they are challenged and continue to grow (Tomlinson, 2014).

Following are some strategies teachers might use to promote learning of their advanced students. They offer suggestions for encouraging a growth mindset in students.

- ▶ Provide feedback with questions that advance the thinking students have demonstrated.

- ▶ Ensure grades reflect student learning no matter how long it took students to learn the content.

- ▶ Use formative assessment to move student learning ahead. If students already demonstrate proficiency, provide more challenging assignments.

▶ Use summative assessments to determine which students would benefit from accelerated coursework.

▶ Make sure all assignments have a purpose and design them to move student learning forward; no busywork.

▶ Work together to develop opportunities for student choice in which there is more than one way to demonstrate proficiency.

Use Multiple Data Sources to Identify Advanced Students

The purpose of giving students formative assessments is to gather information about students' learning. Teams can design their assessments to get specific information for every student's level of learning on specific targets—the essential standards. Teams can use three types of assessments to gather evidence of student learning.

1. **Preassessments:** Teams can use these diagnostically to identify students who possess prerequisite skills as well as students who are already proficient and therefore should be challenged through learning extensions. Teams can use this information to proactively plan to meet the needs of these students. As the name suggests, preassessments are timed prior to initial teaching.

2. **Common formative assessments:** Teams can use common formative assessments throughout the learning process to validate student proficiency of specific targets that comprise the essential standards. Teams collect formative data at specific times as the unit of study progresses.

3. **Common end-of-unit and summative assessments:** Teams use these assessments to assess the essential standards the unit addresses. While teams often give them on the last day of a unit of instruction, they can use them a few days before the last day and then use the remaining days to provide targeted support or extensions based on student needs.

It's important to remember that all these assessments can provide evidence of student learning in general as well as specific evidence of learning that aligns to current curricula. For example, we know that not all students who are able to learn more will be able to do this during every unit of instruction. That makes the process of identification more complicated because to be more effective, teams will want to flexibly group students for extension. Just as we don't want a student who needs Tier 2 intervention to be in that intervention forever, a student who is capable of learning more during one unit of instruction may have more difficulty reaching mastery in another unit.

Define What *Beyond Proficiency* Looks Like

The better a team gets at being able to describe what it looks like for a student to learn beyond the expected proficiency level, the easier it will be for it to develop effective lessons to make that happen for its students. In chapter 2 (page 35), we described processes for teams to use to identify essential learning targets from their essential standards and emphasized that teams have to agree on what proficiency looks like on those targets. The same is true when a team wants to describe what beyond proficiency looks like on those targets.

2

In his book *Formative Assessment and Standards-Based Grading*, Marzano (2010) recommends that schools and districts develop scales for their standards so they can create a standards-based reporting system more accurate than the traditional one hundred–point scale. Instead of reporting a percentage (typically linked to a letter grade), which is an average of all the work the student has done during that reporting period, a standards-based reporting system allows teachers to report out on each standard the student is working on. The system is based on a four-point scale with 3.0 being proficiency, and 4.0 being beyond proficiency.

Not all the schools we work with are using a standards-based reporting system, but many still want to define what it looks like when students are able to learn more. So, when we work with teams who want to develop differentiated lessons, we use a similar idea for defining what it looks like for students to go beyond proficiency on their learning targets. The process of defining proficiency remains the same as described in chapter 2 (page 35), but the team takes an additional step to determine what it looks like for students to go beyond that.

Consider a biology team that has unwrapped one standard to identify the following learning target: Explain the transfer of light energy into chemical energy through photosynthesis. The team decides that this target is a DOK 2 because there is an expectation that students can explain the relationship between the types of energy and the chemical formula that explains the change that occurs. The team builds a scaled representation of this learning target. For the beyond proficiency target, team members ask themselves, "If the proficiency target is a DOK 2, what would that target look like as a DOK 3?" They come up with figure 5.2.

Now the team knows what students must learn on this target to be proficient as well as what it looks like if they go beyond proficiency.

Develop Assessments to Identify Students Who Can Benefit From Extensions

Just as students won't always need interventions, they won't always need extensions either. That means we must develop common formative assessments to guide our work around extensions in the same way we do around students who need additional help to be proficient.

Consider the biology team in the previous scenario that defines what beyond proficiency looks like for a learning target. This team first writes the questions it will use to determine whether students are proficient on this DOK 2 target. The team also agrees to include an additional question for its common formative assessment on photosynthesis that requires

Beyond Proficiency (4.0)	The student can use his or her understanding of photosynthesis to make predictions about what happens when the amount of light energy changes.
Proficiency (3.0)	The student can explain how light energy is transferred into chemical energy during photosynthesis.
Partial Proficiency (2.0)	The student can define light energy and chemical energy but can't explain what happens to that energy during photosynthesis.
No Proficiency (1.0)	The student can't define light energy or chemical energy.

Figure 5.2: Sample scaled representation of learning target.

students to think strategically at the DOK level of thinking. Based on its scaled learning target, the team adds the following to its common formative assessment: Develop an experimental design to answer the question of how light intensity affects photosynthesis.

A coach working with this biology team might take a few different roles depending on the experience team members have with differentiation. If a team has little experience, the coach likely needs to be a consultant to explain both the process and how team members might use this information with their students. If members have more experience, the coach may choose to be a facilitator as the team defines *beyond proficiency* and develops the questions it will use on the common formative assessment.

As part of the process outlined in the protocols in chapter 4 (page 131), teams organize their students based on their proficiency level. Figure 5.3 summarizes the co-planning that takes place, including the response teams will provide to students who require enrichment.

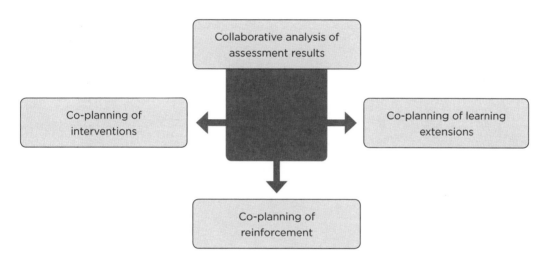

Figure 5.3: Summary of team co-planning for students who need enrichment.

When considering learning extensions, can assessments give us complete insight on what students really know and can do? If we only design our assessments to see if students are proficient, we may not identify students who can actually go beyond proficiency. As teams become more efficient in designing common assessments, they can begin to embed items that give students an opportunity to go beyond the bar. These are typically constructed items that ask advanced-level questions as a vehicle to identify higher-level thinking. An example of this type of question might be, "What if we change the variable in this problem? What might be the result?" or "How might you design an experiment to test this theory?" By designing assessments that give students an opportunity to go beyond expectations, we automatically gather meaningful, not limited, evidence about student learning.

One strategy we've seen high-performing teams use is to make sure they are asking higher-level-thinking questions of *all* students during classroom instruction. In fact, they often plan these questions collaboratively to make sure they are well designed and all team members participate in the process.

Teams can use additional ways to examine data to identify which students need and are ready for extended instruction. For example, some schools use leveled benchmark assessments designed to allow students to show mastery beyond their own grade-level standards.

Teams can use these assessments to identify students who could benefit from more rigorous and complex learning. Teams could also examine performance levels on high-stakes assessments and classroom observations as evidence. In general, teams use multiple sources of evidence to identify potential students who require instruction that extends learning.

Follow a Team Protocol to Collaboratively Identify Students Who Need Learning Extension Based on Results

The protocol in figure 4.4 (page 143) is the same process we use when discussing PLC critical question 4. In fact, it's simply an extended portion of the conversation. We've added two additional sub-steps (see boldfaced statements in steps 3 and 5 in figure 5.4). These additional sub-steps will help guide the teams in addressing the needs of advanced learners.

Use the Coaching Reflection on page 199 to reflect on the information you explored for Action 2.

Steps	Team Notes
1. Set the stage. • Establish the purpose of the meeting. • Review norms (focusing on data norms).	Two minutes
2. Review the focus of the assessment. • Identify the essential learning targets we assessed and which questions are designed to assess each of them. • Review the expectations for proficiency (for example, two out of three correct on a multiple-choice assessment, or a level 3 on the rubric). • Discuss any questions we had when we scored student work.	Two minutes
3. Discuss the data. • For each target, identify how many students need additional time and support. • **Determine which students demonstrate the need for extended learning.**	Five minutes Each team member must participate in this discussion.
4. Determine student misconceptions and errors. • For each target, identify which students need help. • Once teams identify the students who need help, regroup them by specific need (for example, students who made a calculation error versus students who chose the wrong solution pathway).	Ten minutes Be careful to do this step one essential learning target at a time.

Steps	Team Notes
5. Determine instructional strategies. • Decide whether we will develop small groups for reteaching or use a re-engagement lesson with the whole class. • Each teacher shares his or her original instructional strategy so we can see if one strategy works better for certain students. • For each target and for each mistake or misconception, develop a plan to help students move ahead on their learning of that target. • If necessary, go back to best practice information about how to teach the concept or about what strategies work best for students who are struggling. Consult instructional coaches or specialists if necessary. • **Brainstorm strategies for extending the learning for advanced students and strategies.**	Fifteen minutes Make sure that all team members have the same understanding of what this will look like.

Teams may chart the following responses:

Support for Students Not Proficient	Reinforcement for Students at or Near Proficiency	Extensions for Students Above Proficiency

Steps	Team Notes
6. Develop the items we will use to monitor whether students met the learning target after this response. This provides information about which students still need help on this essential target.	Ten minutes You may do this reassessment orally or create a version of the original assessment.

Source: Adapted from Bailey & Jakicic, 2017, p. 82.

Figure 5.4: Protocol for analyzing common formative assessment data for critical question 4.

Coaching the Issue

Four kindergarten teachers at an elementary school know they have students each year who enter school already reading. In the past, each teacher individually adjusted the literacy curriculum to accommodate these students. However, all teachers agree that it's time for them to develop their pyramid of differentiation with specific enrichment and extension strategies so their response is consistent for all students. They ask Madison, their literacy coach, to work with them on this process.

• **Coach's role:** For the first meeting, Madison decides she will use both a presenting and facilitating role with this team. She wants to make sure the teachers thoroughly understand the three tiers they will build together, as well as how they will use their data in the process. She knows that she also needs to facilitate conversations around their current reality to ensure they don't throw away things that are already successful.

continued →

- **Team meeting:** Madison starts the meeting with a large graphic reminding the team of the meaning of the three tiers of extension and enrichment and answering any questions they have about the process. She asks the team to avoid making immediate decisions based on their current process and resources so they don't eliminate any possible new ideas. Madison then explains the three ways the group can consider working with these students: acceleration, extension, and enrichment. The next question surprises the team: "Do you have the information you need to identify students who would benefit from different instruction or curriculum?" In response, they list kindergarten screening, the NWEA MAP test, AIMSweb, district benchmarks, and their team's common formative assessments. Everyone acknowledges that he or she has a lot of information.

Madison then suggests that the team consider what kinds of time and support would make sense for each of the three tiers. As the team begins to explore Tier 1 possibilities, it realizes the importance of looking at its essential standards and developing specific extension targets to guide its work with these students. Team members discuss how they can add questions on their common formative assessments around these extension targets to help identify students ready to move beyond proficiency.

The next discussion explores the idea of what the team does as a whole group versus the strategies it uses during flexible groups. One of the teachers, Kristin, suggests that they keep whole-group reading time but plan to explicitly ask all their students higher DOK-level questions during that time so students can benefit from higher-level thinking whether or not they're identified for extension. This conversation leads to discussion around their flexible groups. Currently, during their literacy time, members work with small groups based on their assessment data. When developing these flexible groups, they try to be as diagnostic as possible about what each student group needs to learn. While the teachers work with these small groups, the other students work in centers or stations developed around their word work, writing, or daily five instructional strategies. The team feels like this is the area in which it's been most successful in providing extensions and enrichment, however, it would like to get feedback from Madison to see if she has other ideas for this time.

Sharise, another teacher on the team, has been teaching kindergarten for many years. She asks the question they've all been avoiding. Is there an expectation that they will use acceleration for Tiers 2 and 3? After team members offer opinions, they realize they have already been using acceleration for some students without calling it that. Some student groups use texts beyond typical kindergarten level and are being taught grade 1 learning targets. Other students are writing at levels that allow teachers to use what are typically first-grade standards. They decide that it may be time now to formalize this process in a collaborative way so they know which students are working above grade level on which targets. They plan to build consensus around the criteria they will use to identify and monitor students and know they will need to include questions on their common formative assessments to identify students who can go beyond proficiency on their learning targets. They also discuss the possibility of grouping students who need the same extensions across their classes instead of having each teacher provide the same lessons. As the meeting ends, team members agree they have some work ahead but feel like they are effectively moving forward.

- **Next steps:** Madison plans to visit each classroom during the literacy block when teachers are using flexible groups. She will document what she sees and explore other ideas for the highest-performing students. Sharise, the team leader, puts an action step on the next agenda to develop extension learning targets for the team's upcoming essential standards. She also makes a note for members to examine their upcoming common formative assessments to see what questions they must add to identify students who can benefit from acceleration, extension, and enrichment.

Action 3: Select Strategies to Extend Learning

Although multiple instructional strategies are available to teachers, the conversation teams engage in should focus on clearly identifying a specific game plan to impact advanced students so they actually advance their learning. The decision to take a specific action should be based on alignment and sound instructional practice. As a coach, you will engage teams keeping this focus in mind.

In order to select strategies to extend student learning, coaches must work with teams to do the following.

- ▸ Align extensions to the essential standards.

- ▸ Select and use a strategy to create learning extensions.

- ▸ Work collaboratively to develop specific activities that extend the learning of essential standards.

Align Extensions to the Essential Standards

The goal in designing activities to extend learning is not simply to come up with something for advanced students to do to stay busy while we work with other student groups.

Our intention is to deepen student learning or understanding on essential standards. Whenever we design an extension for students, we must be clear about the specific skill we are trying to extend through the activity.

Carol Ann Tomlinson (2014) talks about having high expectations for all and providing lots of "ladders" to help everyone climb to new levels of success. If we visualize a ladder of learning, we can envision each rung as a step closer to the end in mind. We know some students might be lower on the ladder, others might be further along, and some might already be at the top rung. Now, visualize revising that learning ladder to an *extension* ladder that allows every student who meets proficiency to keep moving forward in the learning process. Our goal for PLC critical question 4 is to design those rungs on the extension portion of the ladder.

Select and Use a Strategy to Create Learning Extensions

Let's look at four general practices teams can use when designing activities (see step 5 in figure 5.4, Protocol for Analyzing Common

3

Formative Data for Critical Question 4, pages 184–185) to extend student learning. Each practice integrates the use of evidence obtained from common assessments and is clearly connected to essential standards targeted in instruction. These practices include the: (1) skill progression approach, (2) re-engagement approach, (3) student need for advancement approach, and (4) rigor progression approach.

Skill Progression Approach

When teams unwrap standards into learning targets, they often realize that a target may be interpreted differently depending on who is interpreting. Some teams rely heavily on the verbs in the standard. While the standard verbs are often intended to indicate the rigor of the standard, this isn't always the case. Some standard verbs aren't in any of the well-known taxonomies of learning. Take for example, "*Delineate* and evaluate the argument and specific claims in a text" (RI.8.8, emphasis added); or "*Determine* an explicit expression, a recursive process, or steps for calculation from a context" (HSF.BF.1.a, emphasis added). Teachers might interpret the verb *determine* as having various levels of rigor. In chapter 2 (page 35), we recommend that teams consider what comes *after* the verb when determining rigor. This helps

teams understand that the concepts are also important in understanding what the standard means as well as the rigor of the learning targets. So, what does this mean to a team that needs clarity about the expectations they are setting for students?

In chapter 4 (page 131), we discussed a process teams can use to better understand how teams can use learning progressions to evaluate where students are in their understanding of a new concept. By examining what student learning looks like as students move from the prerequisite skill to the proficiency learning target, teams can identify simpler targets they can teach that might help them identify where student learning stops if students don't reach proficiency. We use the example of a Reading standard for eighth grade: "Determine an author's point of view or purpose in a text and analyze how the author acknowledges and responds to conflicting information or viewpoints" (RI.8.6).

In chapter 4, we also focused on what happens between the first bookend learning target from seventh grade and the eighth-grade proficiency target. Now we examine what happens after students reach the proficiency target. See figure 5.5.

| Target | Bookend | Simpler Targets | Bookend | Extended Target |
	Prerequisite (Seventh grade)		Proficiency Target (Eighth grade)	
Analyze how the author acknowledges and responds to conflicting evidence or viewpoints.	Analyze how the author distinguishes his or her position from that of others (DOK 3).	Targets: • Recognize conflicting information. • Recognize conflicting viewpoints.	Analyze how the author acknowledges and responds to conflicting evidence or viewpoints (DOK 3).	Use techniques from the analysis to produce a piece of writing with differing points of view or conflicting evidence.

Source for standards: Adapted from NGA & CCSSO, 2010a.

Figure 5.5: Sample bookend learning target after students reach proficiency.

As the team plans what it will do for students who were proficient on this target, it can design an activity for them to work on independently while working with students who aren't proficient. Or the team may decide to cluster all the advanced students together with one teacher. In this case, team members might ask these students to choose a topic for a letter to the editor and write a letter based on their point of view. Teachers can challenge students to use some of the techniques they learn to provide effective evidence to support their point of view.

Teams can use a similar idea with mathematics learning targets. The team can start with the learning target and identify the prerequisite skills or concepts the student should have learned in the previous grade. Kanold et al. (2018) explain how a team can effectively use different types of problems in mathematics. They suggest two levels of problems teachers should use: lower-level-cognitive-demand tasks and higher-level-cognitive-demand tasks. *Lower-level-cognitive-demand tasks* are those that "typically focus on memorization by performing standard or rote procedures without attention to the properties that support those procedures" (Kanold et al., 2018, p. 22). They contrast these problems to what they call *higher-level-cognitive-demand tasks*, defined as "those for which students do not have a set of predetermined procedures to follow to reach a resolution or, if the tasks involve procedures, they require that students justify why and how to perform the procedures" (Kanold et al., 2018, p. 22). The range for the mathematics concepts goes from the prerequisite skill to students being able to use the target to solve simple problems, then more complex problems, and then even problems that require students to explicitly use a mathematics practice.

Figure 5.6 shows how teams might create a fifth-grade learning target on adding fractions.

Target (Fifth-grade mathematics)	Prerequisite Skill (Fourth-grade mathematics)	Simpler Problem	Real-Life or Realistic Complex Problem	Additional Mathematics Practice
Solve word problems involving addition and subtraction of fractions referring to the same whole, including cases of unlike denominators.	Generate equivalent fractions and compare them.	Problems: • Add fractions with unlike denominators • Subtract fractions with unlike denominators	Solve word problems involving addition and subtraction of fractions.	Critique the reasoning of others in explaining a real-life problem involving subtraction of fractions.

Figure 5.6: Fifth-grade learning target on adding fractions.

In this case, the team might decide to use both simple tasks requiring students to demonstrate proficiency on the algorithm and complex tasks requiring students to choose a solution pathway and solve the problem on a common formative assessment. The team can then use the results to understand which students need help with the algorithm and which students can do the algorithm but need help determining the solution pathway or solving the problem. For students who show proficiency on this assessment, the team may provide some additional tasks that ask students to add a mathematics practice. For example, the team can ask students to critique a solution from a student with examples or counterexamples to explore the student's reasoning. When teams attempt to find or create these more complex problems, it's often easier to find well-designed tasks online than to write them from scratch. Two of our favorite websites for these kinds of tasks are Illustrative Mathematics (www.illustrativemathematics.org) and Inside Mathematics (www.insidemathematics.org). (Visit **go.SolutionTree.com/PLCbooks** to access live links to the websites mentioned in this book.)

Re-Engagement Approach

In chapter 4 (page 131), we discussed a strategy teams can use when responding to common formative assessment data during which they keep the whole class together. It's beneficial for students to examine several different approaches to solving a problem or answering a question. In chapter 4, we focused on students who weren't successful having the opportunity to see several different correct solutions. During the re-engagement lesson, these students can learn the ways others answer the question from their peers. They also have time to ask questions and talk through ambiguous ideas until they reach clarity.

This chapter looks at ways to extend the learning of students who are already proficient. For these students, during a re-engagement lesson, they will see at least one additional way to solve the problem or answer the question. They may also be asked to explain to the class their thinking about their own solution or answer. If the team provides a weak answer or solution as one of its examples, students work with their peers to improve the answer or solution from the student sample. This means that these already proficient students are seeing the question or task from a different perspective. The Common Core ELA and mathematics emphasize the importance of student discourse both orally and in writing. By creating these re-engagement lessons, teams are increasing the opportunities for student discourse in the classroom as students use content-specific language in their cooperative groups.

We like the comparisons from mathematics education consultant and former president of the National Council of Teachers of Mathematics Diane Briars and her colleagues Harold Asturias, David Foster, and Mardi Gale (2013) made as they reviewed the benefits of both reteaching and re-engagement as shown in table 5.1.

Student Need for Advancement Approach

As discussed in the previous chapter, teams develop intervention plans based on student progress in their attainment of specific learning targets. They typically identify groups of students who need specific support. Teams can apply this same process when identifying students who are proficient but who would benefit from specific strategies to advance the quality of their work or depth of understanding. Teams can still use the pile and plan approach when engaging in this process.

For example, they'll put students into the following groups.

▶ **Group A—Students who struggle with organization of their writing:** Planned support is to provide a graphic organizer and work with students on the structure of their writing.

▶ **Group B—Students who struggle with word choice and sentence quality:** Planned support is to examine strategies and linking words for combining sentences. Edit anonymous examples to improve word choice and sentence quality. Students then revise sentences within their own writing.

▶ **Group C—Students who are proficient but would benefit from refining the quality of their work by enhancing their "voice" as a writer:** Planned support is to guide students as they examine and annotate text exemplars to identify author styles.

Table 5.1: Reteaching Versus Re-Engagement Lessons

Reteaching	Re-Engagement
Teach standards in the unit again, the same way as the original presentation.	Revisit student thinking using focused tasks that represent content standards for the unit.
Address basic skills that are missing.	Address conceptual understanding that is missing.
Do the same or similar problems over.	Examine the same or new tasks from different perspectives.
Practice more to make sure students learn the procedures.	Critique student approaches and solutions to make connections to the tasks.
Focus mostly on students in need of additional support.	Focus on engaging both students in need of support and students in need of enrichment.
Lower the cognitive-demand expectations of the students.	Raise the cognitive-demand expectations of the students.

Source: Briars et al., 2013, p. 146.

Engage in peer editing and feedback sessions. Students revise their work to enhance a particular style.

Rigor Progression Approach

For this approach, teams can use the cognitive rigor matrixes (Hess, 2013) to identify levels above and below the level being targeted in core instruction. They can identify potential strategies for differentiation by examining the DOK level below (which points to the intervention focus) or above (which points to activities designed to deepen or extend the learning).

For example, a sixth-grade mathematics team might be working with students on using information in a chart to solve multistep problems. Looking at this excerpt from Hess's (2013) cognitive rigor matrix for mathematics and science (figure 5.7, page 192), we can see that this is a level 2 task. The team might challenge students who are already proficient in this task by creating a DOK 3 task (solving nonroutine problems), providing a partially complete set of data in the charts, and having students use their knowledge of the concepts to complete them. (Visit www.karin-hess.com/free-resources to access the full cognitive rigor matrix.)

Work Collaboratively to Develop Specific Activities That Extend the Learning of Essential Standards

As with all collaborative work of a team implementing the PLC process, developing and choosing activities to extend student learning is far more effective when done in a collaborative way. While each teacher on the team brings ideas and suggestions to this work, a true collaboration means that the final product or decision is often a composite of several ideas that get better as the team shares its thinking and learning. PLC critical question four is often the one that teams leave until last to implement. This means the team likely has already found the benefits of collaboration in making sure all their students are learning at high levels. As a coach, it may fall to you to remind teams of the successes they've had in their work so they don't lose momentum in this process.

Use the Coaching Reflection on page 200 to reflect on the information you explored for Action 3.

3

DOK 1	DOK 2	DOK 3	DOK 4
Students should be able to: • Follow simple procedures • Calculate, measure, apply a rule (such as, rounding) • Apply algorithm or formula (for instance, area, perimeter) • Solve linear equations • Make conversions among representations or numbers, or within and between customary and metric measures	Students should be able to: • Select a procedure according to criteria and perform it • Solve a routine problem applying multiple concepts or decision points • Retrieve information from a table, graph, or figure and use it to solve a problem requiring multiple steps • Translate between tables, graphs, words, and symbolic notations (for instance, graph data from a table) • Construct models given criteria	Students should be able to: • Design investigation for a specific purpose or research question • Conduct a designed investigation • Use concepts to solve nonroutine problems • Use and show reasoning, planning, and evidence • Translate between problem and symbolic notation when not a direct translation	Students should be able to: • Select or devise an approach among many alternatives to solve a problem • Conduct a project that specifies a problem, identifies solution paths, solves the problem, and reports results

Source: Adapted from Hess, 2013.

Figure 5.7: Cognitive rigor matrix.

Coaching the Issue

A sixth-grade mathematics team has been collaborating to write common formative assessments this year. The team comprises two veteran mathematics teachers who generally feel pretty confident about both instruction and assessment. As the two collaborate to plan the response to their data, they benefit from the experience they both bring to their work. They are feeling really good about how things are going except for one issue, that is, how to provide enrichment for the students who demonstrate proficiency on the common formative assessment.

• **Coaching role:** Adriana is the instructional coach for the entire staff. While her background is middle school English language arts, the staff highly regard her because she was one of them before last year when she transitioned into the coaching role. She is confident that the mathematics teachers will be able to solve their problem with some facilitation by her.

• **Team meeting:** Adriana asks the two teachers to describe what they've been doing up to now for students who are already proficient. They admit with a bit of embarrassment that they aren't happy with what's been happening but have felt greater pressure to help students who need extra time and support. Thus, they often let these students catch up on their homework or sometimes ask them to help other students who are struggling. Adriana suggests that they take some time to explore all the ways they can extend the learning for these students in both the regular classroom as well as during intervention time the school has set aside for Tier 2 and Tier 3 support. She encourages them to think about extension (going to a more rigorous level of thinking) rather than acceleration (going into the next grade-level concepts). During this discussion, they talk about the fact that they have an accelerated mathematics class for sixth grade that uses the seventh-grade mathematics standards. In this course, the teacher focuses on more complex problems than those that would generally be expected for mastery. The team also discusses how it asks its best mathematics students to take turns during the Tier 2 and Tier 3 mathematics time to be available to any student who needs help on an assignment or homework.

Adriana then asks the team to consider the DOK chart for the four levels in mathematics and suggests that one way to design an extension activity is to look one level higher on the chart than the learning target being taught. She asks them to consider the DOK level of the following learning target: "Understand the concept of a unit rate a/b associated with a ratio $a{:}b$ with $b \neq 0$ and use rate language in the context of a ratio relationship" (NGA & CCSSO, 2010b).

The team determines the learning target is DOK 2, because it calls for students to be able to look at realistic situations in word problems and choose the correct information and solve whatever questions are asked. As team members look at the criteria for a DOK 3 problem, they consider how requiring students to generalize a pattern and provide mathematical justifications could be related to this target. They dig into the performance tasks on the Inside Mathematics website (www.insidemathematics.org/assets/common-core-math-tasks/truffles .pdf) and find a problem that requires students to look at how they might use ratios to plan the best strategy to win a race. They will place students who have reached mastery into cooperative groups and give them this more complex problem to solve.

- **Next steps:** The team agrees that each time it plans a response it will search for complex problems related to the learning target it assesses. Team members agree to think about some of the mathematics practices they want students to learn as they choose more complex tasks, for example, critiquing the response of others, making or justifying conjectures, and so on. They also consider how they could work with other departments to build in some cross-curricular tasks. For example, they could work with the science teachers to look at how the speed of an object changes in different situations.

3

Action 4: Deliver and Monitor the Impact of Extension Activities

In chapter 4, we discussed how a team determines the best way to provide additional time and support for students who are struggling to learn the essential standards as well as how important it is to monitor whether the support worked. In a similar way, in order to deliver and monitor the impact of extension activities on students, coaches must work with teams to do the following.

▸ Deliver learning extensions during a specific time frame or segment of the day.

▸ Take a proactive stance through collaborative planning.

▸ Develop team members' mindsets.

Deliver Learning Extensions During a Specific Time Frame or Segment of the Day

How might this process look within a unit of study? The structure of a school's system will typically drive how this works. Schools that have a daily time designated for differentiated support provide smaller pieces of differentiated instruction based on common formative assessments. Schools that don't employ a common time may co-plan the differentiated support, but each teacher delivers that support within their own schedule. Some teams time the administration of their end-of-unit assessment before the scheduled end of the unit (rather than the last day of the unit's time frame), and then use the final few days to provide support and extensions based on the data. For example, figure 5.8 shows how such a plan might look for a five-week instructional unit.

Take a Proactive Stance Through Collaborative Planning

Most teachers don't need to wait for the results of a classroom assessment to know there are some students who are already proficient in a particular skill or concept. Just as we know that we can anticipate students who need additional time and support, teams would benefit from proactively designing their instruction to meet their needs. Teams can reference the approaches outlined in this chapter as a jumping-off point to differentiate instruction in terms of content

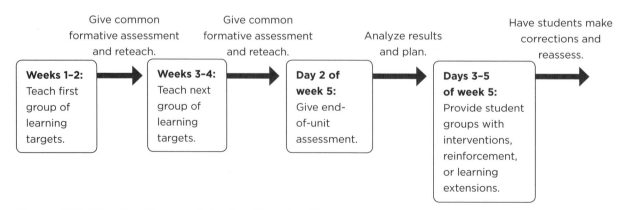

Figure 5.8: Plan for five-week instructional unit.

and instructional process, paying particular attention to promoting higher-level thinking.

As they refine their instructional units from year to year, teams can also embed more student choice of the products they create to show their proficiency. Our experience is that, just as with trying to write and use all their common formative assessments in one year, trying to differentiate for all different kinds of students using all different kinds of strategies can't happen in one year. Instead, we recommend teams set goals to try out a new strategy and then evaluate the results for their students. As they get more proficient, they add new strategies slowly and monitor their effectiveness.

Develop Team Members' Mindsets

Earlier in this chapter, we discussed the research around fixed mindset and growth mindset and how a person's mindset might affect how he or she approaches learning. How might a coach get a team thinking about its own view of mindset, and what might he or she do to help students develop a growth mindset? We've used a round-robin brainstorming activity with schools to engage the staff in conversation and make decisions about the following topics: use of feedback, grading practices, formative assessment, summative assessment, instructional practices, and student choice. We hang six pieces of chart paper around the room, and label each with one topic. The teams get two to three minutes at each piece of chart paper to brainstorm as many ideas as they can about what they could do to encourage a growth mindset for students related to the topic. When teams return to their original chart paper, they read all the ideas other teams list and choose the best idea to report out to the staff. From this list, all teams can then decide which ideas they want to focus on for their students. Some

ideas we've seen teams generate include the following.

▶ Use feedback rather than grades on a formative assessment.

▶ Make sure students know the answer to Sadler's (1989) three questions: Where am I going? Where am I now? How can I close the gap?

▶ Make sure grades reflect actual student learning and allow students the opportunity to show this growth by retaking a test after they've actively tried to learn more.

▶ Provide all students with access to all different activities, not just those designed for their learning level.

▶ Use more rigorous questions during instruction as well as assessments.

▶ Increase opportunities for student discourse.

Of course, there's also often a need for teams to build shared learning about a topic such as mindset. Kathy Liu Sun (2018) warns teachers that, while many of them use the language of having a growth mindset (everyone can learn), their classroom practices don't always support this belief. Consider, for example, teachers who move quickly away from a student who has answered a question incorrectly during a class discussion. Sun suggests a better response is to help the student reveal his or her thinking and, therefore, the misunderstanding or misconception. This, of course, means that the questions students are discussing must be rigorous. Teachers who respond to misunderstanding by inviting the opportunity to discuss thinking send the message that perseverance matters and learners don't always get it right the first time. Sun (2018) also suggests that teachers avoid simplifying the ideas and the work provided to

4

certain students when they start to struggle, as that sends the message they are not as capable as others.

Finally, we've worked with teams who collectively have a mindset about their ability to learn together. We have seen teams at the very end of a continuum when it comes to learning together. There are teams who believe they already know how students learn. We sometimes think these teachers are afraid to admit they don't have all the ideas they need to help their students. They seem afraid to try new ideas because they might not be successful. At the other end of the continuum are teams that relish trying new strategies, reading new books, and learning new ideas. And, of course, some teams have members with both types of mindsets.

As a coach, you might find it helpful to consider the mindset of the teams you're working with. We began this book by identifying several different roles coaches can take: facilitator, presenter, consultant, or coach. When working with teachers or teams who have a fixed mindset about themselves as learners, you might consider working with them on how they view their own ability and the need to be a continuous learner. A coach might ask questions to help teams examine their work and how it affects their results, and offer to support them as they try out new strategies. Dweck (2006) claims that mindsets aren't set in stone. The

coach's goal is to move teachers and teams further along the continuum to a growth mindset.

A coach should be aware that a teacher's beliefs about the concept of mindset can affect how that teacher works with or avoids working with the idea of mindset. There are some teachers who believe that intelligence is fixed and some students will never be successful in academics. Some teachers believe that most students will only do the minimum. Interestingly, these teachers also tend to have a fixed mindset about their own learning, believing that they have learned what they need to know. Teachers with a growth mindset question their assumptions about students. They are careful to use questions and feedback to let students know they are capable of accomplishing more. These teachers are more likely to engage in new learning for themselves.

What can a coach do to help? The first thing is to model the behavior and the language you want teachers to use. Emphasize stories and examples of students who successfully display a growth mindset. Share Dweck's (2006) research and ideas at staff and team meetings. Help teams develop rigorous and engaging activities. Share examples of ways that other teachers build choice into their curriculum.

Use the Coaching Reflection on page 201 to reflect on the information you explored for Action 4.

Conclusion

This chapter focused on how coaches support teams as they answer critical question 4 (How will we extend the learning for students who are already proficient?), which compels teams to inspire and challenge advanced learners. By implementing the four actions in this chapter, teams accomplish the following.

▸ Build shared knowledge about team responses that extend learning, establishing a common language and shared vision for advanced learners.

▸ Identify students who would benefit from extension and advanced learning, defining what proficiency looks like and using multiple data sources.

- ▸ Work collaboratively to select effective strategies to extend learning, aligning extensions to the essential standards.

- ▸ Deliver and monitor the impact of extension activities through collaborative planning and a growth mindset.

By implementing these actions, teams can inspire advanced learners to achieve at higher levels and be clear that they have high expectations for *all* the students in their classrooms.

Throughout this book, we have purposefully used the term *actions* because we know how important it is for teams to get started with this work. Our experience has also shown us that once teams get started and work through the four critical questions in a few cycles, they learn more about best practices than if they spent that same amount of time planning and considering what they should be doing. Coaches can help the teams they support by focusing on these actions. As a coach, you will guide teams to understand the why of these actions, move through a clear process, navigate through those "muddy" places that occur from time to time, and build common clarity and, ultimately, build collective efficacy in the process. You will learn. Your teams will learn. But it's how we move forward and help our students that makes the real difference.

We also encourage you to be a learner yourself. Be comfortable with being uncomfortable! Take some time to reflect on your own learning, and consider how you might work with other coaches and leaders to learn together.

Coaching Reflection for Action 1: Build Shared Knowledge About Team Responses That Extend Learning

Use the questions in this chart to reflect on the information you explored in Action 1.

How are teachers and teams currently providing opportunities for students who have reached proficiency to go beyond those expectations?	What role (facilitator, consultant, coach) should I play with each team?
Do teams recognize the differences between acceleration, enrichment, and extension? How can I help them think broadly about supporting already proficient students?	What issues do I need to anticipate and plan for?
Do teams have access to materials and resources to use for these students? How can I help direct them to these resources?	What is a reasonable time line for completing this step?

Coaching Reflection for Action 2:
Identify Students Who Would Benefit From
Extensions or Advanced Learning Opportunities

Use the questions in this chart to reflect on the information you explored in Action 2.

How are teachers currently identifying students who can benefit from enrichment, extension, or acceleration? How does the schedule support this work?	What role (facilitator, consultant, coach) should I play with each team?
Are teachers confident in how to use their assessment data to identify these students? If not, how can I help them?	What issues do I need to anticipate and plan for?
Is the current assessment system effective in identifying students who can benefit from extension?	What is a reasonable time line for completing this step?

Coaching Reflection for Action 3:
Select Strategies to Extend Learning

Use the questions in this chart to reflect on the information you explored in Action 3.

How has this school built in time to respond to advanced students, and do teams feel confident they have the expertise to develop strong responses?	What role (facilitator, consultant, coach) should I play with each team?
Do teams see their responsibility for this work? Do they want someone else to take care of this?	What issues do I need to anticipate and plan for?
How can I support teams in this process by finding appropriate resources, materials, and websites to help teams with this work?	What is a reasonable time line for completing this step?

Coaching Reflection for Action 4:
Deliver and Monitor the Impact of Extension Activities

Use the questions in this chart to reflect on the information you explored in Action 4.

Do we have anything currently in place to help us use results to monitor this work? If not, what might that look like?	What role (facilitator, consultant, coach) should I play with each team?
Have my teams made a commitment to do this work over time? Do they recognize this isn't something that happens all at once?	What issues do I need to anticipate and plan for?
How can I support teams in evaluating their successes? How can I build in celebrations?	What is a reasonable time line for completing this step?

Epilogue:
Maintaining the Momentum
and Sustaining the Process

● ● ● ●

To someone who hasn't engaged in the process of working as a PLC, there may be a tendency to simplify the process. It probably seems straightforward and easy to navigate. There are four questions to answer and a reasonable list of products to create. Simple, right? The reality is, this is complex work. And because of this complexity, it's easy to fall into some difficulty. It takes insightful and responsive navigation, taking into account the different cultural, structural, and external factors that impact a school and its learners.

We have seen a number of schools and districts that believe they are doing the right work but don't see the results they hope for. Some schools falling into this category have taken some dangerous shortcuts in their work. For example, we've seen schools that simply use the same pacing guide they've always used. Maybe they highlighted the standards they believe are essential in the document, but they made no other changes in their practices as a result. Other schools take the stance that all their standards are important and that they can't possibly cut any. They don't vary the emphasis or time they dedicate to teach a standard. Or, we see schools that believe that they don't have the skills to create effective assessments, so they

purchase a program or use the tests that come from their curriculum materials as their common formative assessments.

Once in a while, we'll see schools that believe the best way to help students who are struggling is to pull them out of class to work with special teachers or to provide them with an alternate curriculum that is less rigorous than the one used for the rest of the students. And we're sad to say that in some schools, there is little time left over after all the work of helping students who are struggling for teams to plan ways to engage those who can benefit from learning beyond the expected proficiency level.

In this epilogue, we offer some specific ideas about how to keep your school moving in the right direction while still feeling successful about what you've accomplished and excited about what's still to come.

We first set the stage for powerful collaboration focused on student learning. We ensure student learning by building a schoolwide culture that values all students and emphasizes the collective responsibility of every single person in the school—each person commits to working together to ensure that all students learn.

Celebrating Success

Let's start by being honest that this work is difficult, and if we want to keep participants motivated to do the work, it's important that everyone plans for regular celebrations of his or her successes. Traditionally, schools have been good about celebrating student success with honor banquets, awards assemblies, honor roll lists, and so on. They have not always been as good about celebrating teachers and teams.

In *Learning by Doing*, DuFour et al. (2016) make four suggestions for schools wanting to incorporate celebrations.

1. **Be explicit about the purpose of the celebration:** This is especially important when schools celebrate actions and adults as well as students.

2. **Make sure everyone is responsible for celebrations:** Some of the most powerful awards we've seen are those recognizing something a teacher or team did with very specific information about the impact of that action. For example, team members might recognize someone for helping them become better assessment writers.

3. **Tie recognitions to specific behaviors or commitments the school encourages:** This means that the school considers its mission, vision, collective commitments, and goals as it establishes what it wants to celebrate. It's important that the recognition for teachers or teams be specific and include the details about both the action and the results. In one school we worked with, the teachers wore T-shirts on opening day with their collective commitments printed on the back. Imagine how their students felt to see the unity of purpose.

4. **Provide opportunities for lots of winners:** Limiting recognition to the best or the first reduces the impact on school culture. It's better to recognize too many actions than not enough actions.

Coaches can be especially helpful in identifying areas for celebration. Because teachers are often reluctant to mention their own successes, others may not be aware of actions that warrant recognition. Coaches who are regular participants at team meetings can share stories that provide information about who and what to celebrate. By intentionally building in celebrations, particularly those that link team efforts to an impact on student learning, schools strengthen the *collective efficacy*—the knowledge that their hard work has paid off.

Taking Stock of the Team's Current Reality

When we work in schools over a period of time, we recommend that they regularly take stock of their current reality using surveys and questionnaires that ask teachers to reflect about a given situation or step in the work. Take, for example, figure E.1, Collaborative Team Reflection. The school's leadership team may use this survey to determine what kinds of professional development it may want to provide based on how teachers or teams respond. For example, it may find that teams are struggling with using SMART goals in their work. The team may decide to have an upcoming staff meeting in which some teams share examples of how they are successfully using SMART goals. Or, a team might feel like it's stuck in a cycle of not moving forward. It can use this survey to identify the steps its members might take to get started again. By having individual teachers respond and then looking at the aggregated data, the leadership team might see that other teams aren't following norms or aren't successful in using common formative assessment data. By identifying the problem, a coach can be more effective in helping the collaborative process.

Please rate your agreement with these statements using the one to five scale, with one meaning strongly disagree and five meaning strongly agree.					
Statement	**1** Strongly disagree	**2** Disagree	**3** Somewhat agree	**4** Agree	**5** Strongly agree
1. Our team has established specific commitments about the work it will do in support of the school's mission and vision.					
2. Our team members hold themselves and each other accountable to these norms and commitments during our collaborative time.					
3. Our focus during collaborative time is on student learning of essential standards.					
4. Our team uses data to establish clear annual and unit-based SMART goals for student learning.					
5. We run our collaborative meetings efficiently and follow the plan-do-study-act model of continuous improvement.					
6. Our team collaboratively designs units of study, including: • End-of-unit and formative assessments to monitor the learning of essential standards • Effective instructional strategies we'll use					
7. We regularly collect, review, and analyze evidence and data throughout the instructional process using formative and end-of-unit assessments.					
8. Our team uses the data from formative assessments to make instructional adjustments and identify specific students who require additional time and support or extensions for learning.					
9. Our team willingly shares best practices across its members and celebrates successes in student learning.					
10. Our team organizes and continuously updates its work products.					

Figure E.1: Collaborative team reflection.

*Visit **go.SolutionTree.com/PLCbooks** for a free reproducible version of this figure.*

At other times, it is important for teams to take stock of what they've accomplished so they can see what their next steps should be. One of our favorite strategies is for teams to use the reproducible "Critical Issues for Team Consideration" (DuFour et al., 2016). See figure E.2. We recommend teams use this list of eighteen critical issues to evaluate their effectiveness at least once per year (before the year starts or at the end of the year when teams are planning next steps for the new year) to keep themselves on the right track.

Critical Issues for Team Consideration

Team Name:

Team Members:

Use the following rating scale to indicate the extent to which each statement is true of your team.

1	2	3	4	5	6	7	8	9	10

Not True of Our Team   **Our Team Is Addressing This**   **True of Our Team**

1. _____ We have identified team norms and protocols to guide us in working together.

2. _____ We have analyzed student achievement data and established SMART goals to improve on this level of achievement we are working interdependently to attain (SMART goals are specific and strategic, measurable, attainable, results oriented, and time bound. SMART goals are discussed at length in table 1.1 on page 25).

3. _____ Each team member is clear on the knowledge, skills, and dispositions (that is, the essential learning) that students will acquire as a result of our course or grade level and each unit within the course or grade level.

4. _____ We have aligned the essential learning with state and district standards and the high-stakes assessments required of our students.

5. _____ We have identified course content and topics we can eliminate to devote more time to the essential curriculum.

6. _____ We have agreed on how to best sequence the content of the course and have established pacing guides to help students achieve the intended essential learning.

7. _____ We have identified the prerequisite knowledge and skills students need in order to master the essential learning of each unit of instruction.

8. _____ We have identified strategies and created instruments to assess whether students have the prerequisite knowledge and skills.

9. _____ We have developed strategies and systems to assist students in acquiring prerequisite knowledge and skills when they are lacking in those areas.

10. _____ We have developed frequent common formative assessments that help us determine each student's mastery of essential learning.

11. _____ We have established the proficiency standard we want each student to achieve on each skill and concept examined with our common assessments.

12. _____ We use the results of our common assessments to assist each other in building on strengths and addressing weaknesses as part of an ongoing process of continuous improvement designed to help students achieve at higher levels.

13. _____ We use the results of our common assessments to identify students who need additional time and support to master essential learning, and we work within the systems and processes of the school to ensure they receive that support.

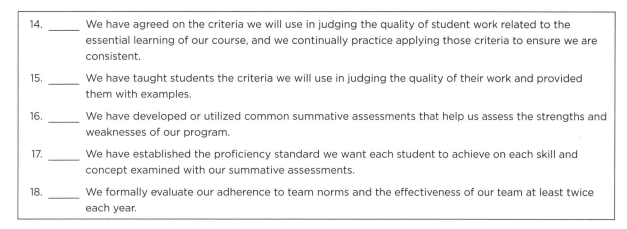

14. _____ We have agreed on the criteria we will use in judging the quality of student work related to the essential learning of our course, and we continually practice applying those criteria to ensure we are consistent.

15. _____ We have taught students the criteria we will use in judging the quality of their work and provided them with examples.

16. _____ We have developed or utilized common summative assessments that help us assess the strengths and weaknesses of our program.

17. _____ We have established the proficiency standard we want each student to achieve on each skill and concept examined with our summative assessments.

18. _____ We formally evaluate our adherence to team norms and the effectiveness of our team at least twice each year.

Source: DuFour et al., 2016, pp. 69–70.

Figure E.2: Critical issues for team consideration.

Visit **go.SolutionTree.com/PLCbooks** for a free reproducible version of this figure.

Sometimes teams are overwhelmed when they first look at the list, and we've seen other teams use it simply to check off items that they need to complete. To prevent either reaction, we recommend teams use this list to help them when they are writing their SMART goals. To this end, figure E.3 (page 208) consists of a set of cards teams can use with one issue or activity on each card. We ask teams to sort the cards into three piles: (1) items they have accomplished, (2) items they are working on, and (3) items they haven't had time to begin. The cards that represent items they have accomplished might appear on their SMART goal action plan (see figure 1.10, page 27) as current strengths; the cards that represent items they are working on can become steps in their action plan. The third set of cards is items they haven't begun but want to work on in the future.

Another variation is for teams to take all the cards that represent ideas they haven't yet started and prioritize the next two or three they should work on. This helps teams see that they aren't expected to accomplish everything at the same time.

Coaches can be helpful with these activities in two ways. If a team tends to look at this as a checkoff list, ask team members to create a list of products for the items they list as accomplished. For example, for the item "We have taught students the criteria we will use in judging the quality of their work and provided them with examples," teams should be able to show examples of strong and weak work for those lessons and rubrics written in student-friendly language for students.

Finally, we always recommend that teams can generate good information about their current reality using the various continuums in the book _Learning by Doing, Third Edition_ (DuFour et al., 2016). Team members can read each descriptor and determine which is the closest to their current reality. They then consider, based on the next level in the continuum, what they need to do to get better.

We have identified team norms and protocols to guide us in working together.	We have analyzed student-achievement data and established SMART goals to improve on this level of achievement we are working interdependently to attain.	Each team member is clear on the knowledge, skills, and dispositions (that is, the essential learning) that students will acquire as a result of our course or grade level and each unit within the course or grade level.
We have aligned the essential learning with state and district standards and the high-stakes assessments required of our students.	We have identified course content and topics we can eliminate to devote more time to the essential curriculum.	We have agreed on how to best sequence the content of the course and have established pacing guides to help students achieve the essential learning.
We have identified the prerequisite knowledge and skills students need in order to master the essential learning of each unit of instruction.	We have identified strategies and created instruments to assess whether students have the prerequisite knowledge and skills.	We have developed strategies and systems to assist students in acquiring prerequisite knowledge and skills when they are lacking in those areas.
We have developed frequent common formative assessments that help us determine each student's mastery of essential learning.	We have established the proficiency standard we want each student to achieve on each skill and concept examined with our common assessments.	We use the results of our common assessments to assist each other in building on strengths and addressing weaknesses as part of an ongoing process of continuous improvement designed to help students achieve at higher levels.
We use the results of our common assessments to identify students who need additional time and support to master essential learning, and we work within the systems and processes of the school to ensure they receive that support.	We have agreed on the criteria we will use in judging the quality of student work related to the essential learning of our course, and we continually practice applying those criteria to ensure we are consistent.	We have taught students the criteria we will use in judging the quality of their work and provided them with examples.
We have developed or utilized common summative assessments that help us assess the strengths and weaknesses of our program.	We have established the proficiency standard we want each student to achieve on each skill and concept examined with our summative assessments.	We formally evaluate our adherence to team norms and the effectiveness of our team at least twice each year.

Source: DuFour et al., 2016, pp. 69–70.

Figure E.3: Cards for eighteen critical issues for team consideration.

*Visit **go.SolutionTree.com/PLCbooks** for a free reproducible version of this figure.*

Forming High-Performing Teams

High-performing teams are a hallmark of the PLC process. When teams function well, the work they accomplish will, without a doubt, lead to higher achievement for their students. As a coach, you may be able to have the greatest impact in this area because you will likely participate in and observe many team meetings. As we work in schools, we see teams in the same school or district who have widely different styles of working together and also widely different outcomes for their students. Some recommendations for successful team collaboration include the following.

▸ **High-performing teams have norms of behavior that include how they will monitor their interactions during meetings:** We've worked with dysfunctional teams, and when we ask to see their norms, they have them posted on team agendas. Norms won't work if the team ignores evidence that members aren't following them. Effective norms establish the expectations team members have for working together. Norms should be built around the team's needs. If the team has a strong person who tends to dominate the discussion, it needs a norm that makes sure everyone participates in all discussions.

Some teachers ask us if teams with only two members need norms. The answer is *yes*! If these partners never discuss what they expect from each other, they may find they are silently steaming about what happens during their meetings. There should be a norm that describes how the team will react if a member violates a norm. For example, a team might have a picture of Norm from the television show *Cheers* on a popsicle stick in the middle of the table. If someone violates a norm, another member holds it up and calls, "Norm!" Whatever the team agrees on must be something all team members are comfortable with and willing to do. In his book *The Five Dysfunctions of a Team*, Patrick Lencioni (2007) establishes trust as the first problem teams must address. Norms help teams develop trust for each other.

While teams should be responsible for monitoring themselves, a coach may be the first to notice when a team is having trouble working together. If this is the case, it's important to focus on how specific behaviors are affecting the work rather than calling out individual team members.

▸ **High-performing teams use protocols for tackling discussions:** Protocols help teams maximize their use of time during their meetings, as well as keep teams on track during discussions. When teams simply use agenda items such as "Review the common formative assessment data," the meeting can move in many directions, sometimes without accomplishing much. With a protocol, teams know that they are answering the right questions and getting to the correct issues. Without a protocol, teams might easily avoid topics that feel uncomfortable.

▸ **High-performing teams produce specific products and use these products to monitor their successes:** For example, we've seen teams who have periodically looked back over their agendas and minutes to determine if they are focused on the four critical questions. In fact, we have audited schools in which all we had to do was establish agendas and ask the question, "Are your team meetings focused on the four critical questions of a PLC?" to see if they've gotten off track. Many teams find that keeping the products they create in a shared electronic folder works best to allow everyone access. For example, a team member might check the minutes from a previous meeting to check a date for a common formative assessment or to remember what he or she is supposed to prepare for the next meeting.

▶ **High-performing teams regularly use results and build shared knowledge to make decisions:** As teachers, we can remember meetings in which we discussed topics such as homework or grades. Each team member shared an opinion, and often the person with the loudest voice or the most seniority won the debate. In a PLC, teams look to research and examples of successful schools as ways to increase their knowledge about an upcoming decision. When they do so, the final decision is much easier because everyone is making the decision based on the same information.

Responding to Team Dysfunction

When team members are struggling to get along and accomplish their work, they often prefer to have an outsider, such as a coach or an administrator, get involved. This can often contribute to discord because team members may feel betrayed. Teams must first confront their own problems. So how might this happen? As we mentioned previously, one of the roles of the leadership team is to monitor the products of collaboration. During its meetings, the leadership team often shares products and problem solves together. During this process, it might discover that one of the teacher teams is having some difficulty in its work. The leadership team can then help this team solve the problem. If the team hasn't developed norms, this would be the first place to start. If it has norms, the question is whether it has norms that address the areas of concern. If so, is the team willing to hold members accountable? If not, the team needs to review its norms and add one or more to address the current issues.

If the team continues to have difficulty, it should investigate how to have a conversation with that member who is causing the issue. In *Crucial Conversations*, authors Kerry Patterson, Joseph Grenny, Ron McMillan, and Al Switzler (2012) make a number of recommendations for how to best accomplish this. For example, they recommend planning the conversation ahead of time to prepare the initiator. They suggest starting with heart. This means presenting a clear and focused conversation. The initiator should start with the following so that the hearer is less likely to react defensively: "I want our meetings to run more smoothly so we can be more effective in the way we respond to our students." On the contrary, the following would likely be met with defensiveness: "You are constantly disrupting our meetings, and everyone is frustrated with you!" The conversation can then turn to specific examples of what this member is doing that's getting in the way. The more specific the initiator can make these examples, the less likely this will disintegrate into a battle of examples. It's also important to give the team member an opportunity to explain how he or she sees the problem. If both participants in the conversation can see he or she is working to the same end, the results are likely to be better for the team. Finally, the conversation must feel safe to both participants. The entire team shouldn't gang up on one of its members; choose one or two people to be the representatives. The location of the conversation is important; if it's held in the teacher's own classroom, the initiator can easily leave at the end without anyone else being aware of what was happening. We know that the foundation of high-performing teams is trust. It's very important that this process maintains the trust of all participants.

The leadership team might respond to team dysfunction by doing the following.

▸ Monitor the products together and discuss what products have been most effective. Support each other by providing suggestions and feedback when one team is struggling.

▸ Role-play responses in difficult situations. We know how hard it is for colleagues to confront or have difficult conversations with one of the team members. We've found that

by role-playing the conversation, the discussions are better because they're planned and thought out. Have your leadership team make suggestions to improve the conversation during the role play.

▸ Model the discussions teams should be having around their data. Some team dysfunction is the result of teachers being reluctant to be honest about the facts when looking at data. If, as a leadership team, you've had those conversations, it will be much easier to do this with your own team.

So, if teams respond to their own difficulties, what is the coach's role? As an observer, the coach can help define the dysfunction teams are having. We have encountered situations in which teams know they're not working effectively but can't articulate the problem. A coach can take notes and share back what he or she has seen during a meeting without drawing conclusions or determining fault. Coaches can also help members by supplying resources and ideas the team hasn't had time to explore. For example, if a team hasn't established electronic agendas and minutes, the coach can set up the folders and provide sample templates. Coaches can share between teams any ideas and resources that might be helpful to other teams they're working with.

Using the Guiding Coalition Effectively

The most successful PLC schools and districts are those having a leadership team or guiding coalition that embraces the idea of continuous improvement. These schools regularly share products with each other as well as feedback and ideas for improvement. DuFour et al. (2016) explain that the guiding coalition

or leadership team should take time to examine the work products of teams to ensure that each team is functioning well. While not every team will always be at the same point in its journey, all teams should have evidence of their work around similar issues. DuFour (2015) discusses the idea of having a simultaneously loose-tight leadership style. He lists the six things every school must be tight (fixed) about; these are essential (DuFour, 2015):

> These six elements of the culture are nondiscretionary, and every member of the faculty is expected to hone and observe these core practices of a PLC, which include the following.
>
> 1. Educators work collaboratively rather than in isolation and have clarified the commitment they have made to each other about how they will work together.
>
> 2. The fundamental structure of the school becomes the collaborative team in which members work interdependently to achieve common goals for which all members are mutually accountable.
>
> 3. The team establishes a guaranteed curriculum, unit by unit, so all students have access to the same knowledge and skills, regardless of which teachers they are assigned.
>
> 4. The team develops common formative assessments to frequently gather evidence of student learning.
>
> 5. The school creates systems of intervention to ensure students who struggle receive additional time and support for learning in a way that is timely, directive, diagnostic, and systematic.
>
> 6. The team uses evidence of student learning to inform and improve the individual and collective practices of its members. (p. 230)

Monitoring Products Through the Leadership Team

One role of the leadership team as the guiding coalition is to monitor the products of collaboration. The leadership team makes sure that all collaborative teams are making progress in their work but also provides support to any teams who are struggling. As a coach, you may be asked to provide that support so it's important you are part of the monitoring process. Coaches don't need to monitor all these products, nor do they need to monitor them all at the same time. Figure E.4 shows some of the typical products a team generates as well as the characteristics the leadership team should monitor.

When working with leadership teams, we sometimes ask them to complete the graphic organizer shown in figure E.5 (page 215) to help focus teams on the right work. The first step is to agree on what products the leadership team believes teacher teams should be generating. Once they've created the list of products (column two), they can identify the characteristics they should look for in each product. Finally, they discuss the support they might be able to provide if a team is struggling on a particular product.

Figure E.6 (pages 216–217) shows an example of how a leadership team might complete the graphic organizer for the right work using sample products and monitoring items.

Product	Characteristics for Leadership Team to Monitor
Commitments	• Commitments are few in number. • Commitments focus on team behaviors, not on what others will do. • If a team member doesn't follow the norms, teams have established a way to react.
Agendas	• Items focus on the four critical questions of a PLC. • Teams build consensus for critical decisions. • All team members participate.
SMART Goals	• Goals meet the SMART criteria. • Goals are stretch goals (they require collaboration from everyone to be successful). • The action plan is specific enough to likely result in success.

Products from PLC critical question 1: What do we want students to know and be able to do?

Product	Characteristics for Leadership Team to Monitor
Essential Standards	• Standards come from the required state (or province) standards. (We recommend the teams keep the standard language until standards are ready to use with students.) • Standards represent approximately one-third of the curriculum. • Standards align vertically.
Pacing	• Team members have a pacing guide or curriculum map that establishes when they will administer common formative assessments. • The pacing guide has time after each common formative assessment for teams to respond. • The essential standards are evident, and more time is allocated in the pacing guide to ensure all students are learning.
Unwrapping	• Teams unwrap each essential standard to identify the learning targets members must teach. • Teams agree on what proficiency will look like for each learning target.

Figure E.4: List of team-generated products and characteristics the leadership team monitors.

continued

Products from PLC critical question 2: How will we know if they have learned it?

Product	Characteristics for Leadership Team to Monitor
Common Formative Assessments	• The assessment is short. • The assessment focuses on one to three learning targets. • Assessments show evidence of rigor. (Look for constructed-response questions rather than multiple-choice questions.)
Student Involvement	• Teams post learning targets in student-friendly language. • Teams list learning targets on assessments. • Students have some responsibility in responding to the results.
Use of Benchmark or Interim Assessments	• Teams use these assessments to identify students who haven't mastered all the previous years' essential standards. • Teams use the information to judge their own effectiveness. They ask themselves, "Have we paced the curriculum correctly? Are our instructional practices working to get students to proficiency?"

Products from PLC critical questions 3 and 4: How will we respond when some students do not learn? and How will we extend learning for students who are already proficient?

Product	Characteristics for Leadership Team to Monitor
Use of Time	• Teams provide time for corrective instruction after common formative assessments. • Teams develop a way to identify students needing Tier 2 and Tier 3 instruction. • All students have access to all three tiers of intervention.
Effective Response	• Teams can demonstrate how they differentiate based on the results after a common formative assessment. • Teams challenge proficient students to go beyond.

*Visit **go.SolutionTree.com/PLCbooks** for a free reproducible version of this figure.*

Six Actions	Products to Monitor	What the Leadership Team Should Look For	What Support Teams Might Need
1. Educators work collaboratively rather than in isolation and have clarified the commitments about how they will work together.			
2. The fundamental structure of the school is the collaborative team in which members work interdependently to achieve common goals for which all members are mutually accountable.			
3. The team establishes a guaranteed and viable curriculum, unit by unit, so all students have access to the same knowledge and skills, regardless of which teacher they are assigned.			
4. The team develops common formative assessments to frequently gather evidence of student learning.			
5. The school creates systems of intervention to ensure students who are struggling receive additional time and support for learning in a timely, directive, diagnostic, and systematic way.			
6. The team uses evidence of student learning to inform and improve its members' individual and collective practices.			

Source: Adapted from DuFour, 2015, p. 230.

Figure E.5: "Are we focused on the right work?" graphic organizer.

*Visit **go.SolutionTree.com/PLCbooks** for a free reproducible version of this figure.*

Six Actions	Products to Monitor	What the Leadership Team Should Look For	What Support Teams Might Need
1. Educators work collaboratively rather than in isolation and have clarified the commitments they made to each other about how they will work together.	Norms	The team's norms are few in number, focus on participants' behaviors, include a way to call out someone not following them, and establish a definition or way of reaching consensus.	Share ideas for how each team is handling conflict and offer ideas for making all members active participants in the work.
2. The fundamental structure of the school is the collaborative team in which members work interdependently to achieve common goals for which all members are mutually accountable.	SMART goals	The team's goals are measurable, attainable, results-oriented, and time bound. The action plan is focused on interdependent activities that everyone is accountable for.	Provide the team with specific examples and ideas of how other teams have developed their action plans.
	Agendas and minutes (no need to monitor each of them, just periodically)	Agendas and minutes are focused on the four critical questions of a PLC.	Share specific ideas for creating effective agendas and minutes, including having the team build the agenda for the next meeting at the end of a meeting. For example, suggest that team members assign a recorder to take minutes during the meetings.
3. The team establishes a guaranteed and viable curriculum, unit by unit, so all students have access to the same knowledge and skills, regardless of which teacher they are assigned.	Pacing guides highlighting the power standards Time built into each unit for responding to the results of a common formative assessment	Pacing guides are organized unit by unit.	Suggest that the team discusses how to build a pacing guide. It can share templates as well as ideas of how to effectively monitor how well the pacing guides are working.
4. The team develops common formative assessments to frequently gather evidence of student learning.	Common formative assessments	Common formative assessments are short. They are focused on one to three learning targets. They include rigorous questions for all DOK 3 and 4 targets.	Offer help in how to develop quality assessments and how to unwrap standards.

5. The school creates systems of intervention to ensure students who are struggling receive additional time and support for learning in a timely, directive, diagnostic, and systematic way.	Evidence that the plan is being effectively used—for example, lists of students in each tier Examples of how the team uses data to progress monitor students	The team demonstrates evidence that it is responding in a timely way for every student; evidence that it has allocated time for Tier 1 response immediately after the common formative assessment; assurance that it is setting aside time for interventions (Tier 2 and Tier 3) when no new instruction is taking place; evidence of using both benchmarking and common formative assessment data in planning for response.	It's important that all teachers and each team use the systematic response plan in the same way. Confirm the expectations at the beginning of each school year and make sure all new staff members understand why and how the process works.
6. The team uses evidence of student learning to inform and improve its members' individual and collective practices.	Agendas, minutes, or meeting protocols that include team members comparing their instructional strategies or setting action research goals in which all team members try a new strategy and examine the results with a common formative assessment	At a minimum, the team examines the effect of instructional strategies on student learning by sharing practices and results. The team chooses new strategies it believes will positively impact student learning and uses its own assessment data to determine the effectiveness of these strategies.	Ask each team to share out how it is developing its own action research.

Figure E.6: "Are we focused on the right work?" graphic organizer example.

*Visit **go.SolutionTree.com/PLCbooks** for a free reproducible version of this figure.*

Final Thoughts

Guiding the work of collaborative teams is an exciting process. While each step in the journey can contain potential challenges, living the process will strengthen your skills as an instructional leader and broaden your perspectives. We would like to end this book with four final recommendations.

1. **Be sure to take care of yourself:** It's easy to become excited about the work sometimes at the expense of those natural balances we need in life. Whatever those balances are, make sure you take time for them.

2. **Always view this as a work in progress:** Setbacks in a particular process or a colleague's comments may frustrate you, but sometimes we need to encounter those challenges in order to build more clarity and collective commitment to the work.

3. **Take time to reflect:** We've included coaching reflections throughout the book to help you clarify your thinking. We agree with the quote from Pete Hall and Alisa Simeral (2017), "The more reflective we are, the more effective we are" (p. 21). Use these reflections to take some quiet time and gather your thoughts. Reflection is also likely to inspire some great ideas.

4. **Don't be an island:** Just like PLCs promote a collaborative culture, you need to engage with others involved in similar roles. If you don't have other instructional coaches in your school or district, find them online. Use the resources through AllThingsPLC (www.allthingsplc.info) to connect to others in similar contexts. (Visit **go.SolutionTree.com/PLCbooks** to access live links to the websites mentioned in this book.) Don't be worried about asking questions. Everyone who has been working in a similar capacity has learned and continues to learn from others doing the work.

Before his passing, our dear friend and mentor in this work, Richard DuFour, gave each of us a simple but incredibly special message. This message continues to touch our hearts, and when the going gets tough, it reminds us to keep focusing on the right work for the right reasons. We'd like to share his simple message with you in hopes that it will produce the same empowerment and encouragement: "I believe in you. Godspeed."

References and Resources

● ● ● ●

ACT Aspire. (2017). *Exemplar grade 3 mathematics test questions.* Iowa City, IA: Author. Accessed at http://actaspire.pearson.com/_documents/exemplars/AS1007AspireExemplarMathgr3_web_secure .pdf on March 13, 2018.

Aguilar, E. (2014, November 13). *Tips for coaching teacher teams* [Blog post]. Accessed at www.edutopia .org/blog/tips-coaching-teacher-teams-elena-aguilar on May 22, 2018.

Ainsworth, L. (2004). *Power standards: Identifying the standards that matter the most.* Englewood, CO: Advanced Learning Press.

Ainsworth, L. (2010). *Rigorous curriculum design: How to create curricular units of study that align standards, instruction, and assessment.* Englewood, CO: Lead + Learn Press.

Ainsworth, L. (2013). *Prioritizing the Common Core: Identifying specific standards to emphasize the most.* Englewood, CO: Lead + Learn Press.

Ainsworth, L., & Viegut, D. (2006). *Common formative assessments: How to connect standards-based instruction and assessment.* Thousand Oaks, CA: Corwin Press.

Bailey, K., & Jakicic, C. (2012). *Common formative assessment: A toolkit for Professional Learning Communities at Work.* Bloomington, IN: Solution Tree Press.

Bailey, K., & Jakicic, C. (2017). *Simplifying common assessment: A guide for Professional Learning Communities at Work.* Bloomington, IN: Solution Tree Press.

Bailey, K., Jakicic, C., & Spiller, J. (2014). *Collaborating for success with the Common Core: A toolkit for Professional Learning Communities at Work.* Bloomington, IN: Solution Tree Press.

Black, P., & Wiliam, D. (1998). Inside the black box: Raising standards through classroom assessment. *Phi Delta Kappan, 80*(2), 139–144.

Blauman, L., & Burke, J. (2014). *The Common Core companion: The standards decoded, grades 3–5.* Thousand Oaks, CA: Corwin Press.

Briars, D. J., Asturias, H., Foster, D., & Gale, M. A. (2013). In T. D. Kanold (Ed.), *Common Core mathematics in a PLC at Work, grades 6–8.* Bloomington, IN: Solution Tree Press.

Brookhart, S. M. (2008). *How to give effective feedback to your students.* Alexandria, VA: Association for Supervision and Curriculum Development.

Buffum, A., Mattos, M., & Malone, J. (2018). *Taking action: A handbook for RTI at Work.* Bloomington, IN: Solution Tree Press.

Buffum, A., Mattos, M., & Weber, C. (2012). *Simplifying response to intervention: Four essential guiding principles.* Bloomington, IN: Solution Tree Press.

Burke, J. (2013). *The Common Core companion: The standards decoded, grades 6–8.* Thousand Oaks, CA: Corwin Press.

Butler, R., & Nisan, M. (1986). Effects of no feedback, task-related comments, and grades on intrinsic motivation and performance. *Journal of Educational Psychology, 78*(3), 210–216.

California Department of Education. (2000, May). *History–social science content standards for California public schools: Kindergarten through grade twelve.* Sacramento: Author. Accessed at www.cde.ca.gov /be/st/ss/documents/histsocscistnd.pdf on May 25, 2018.

Conzemius, A. E., & O'Neill, J. (2014). *The handbook for SMART school teams* (2nd ed.). Bloomington, IN: Solution Tree Press.

Creighton, S. J., Tobey, C. R., Karnowski, E., & Fagan, E. R. (2015). *Bringing math students into the formative assessment equation: Tools and strategies for the middle grades.* Thousand Oaks, CA: Corwin Press.

Daggett, B. (2012). *Rigor/relevance framework.* Accessed at www.leadered.com/rr.html on September 1, 2012.

Darling-Hammond, L. (1997). *Doing what matters most: Investing in quality teaching.* New York: National Commission on Teaching and America's Future.

DeWitt, P. (2018, August 26). *Has instructional coaching become a dumping ground?* [Blog post]. Accessed at http://blogs.edweek.org/edweek/finding_common_ground/2018/08/has_instructional_coaching _become_a_dumping_ground.html?cmp=eml-contshr-shr on September 4, 2018.

Donohoo, J. (2017). *Collective efficacy: How educators' beliefs impact student learning.* Thousand Oaks, CA: Corwin Press.

DuFour, R. (2003). Leading edge: 'Collaboration-lite' puts student achievement on a starvation diet. *Journal of Staff Development, 24*(3), 63–64.

DuFour, R. (2015). *In praise of American educators: And how they can become even better.* Bloomington, IN: Solution Tree Press.

DuFour, R., DuFour, R., & Eaker, R. (2008). *Revisiting Professional Learning Communities at Work: New insights for improving schools.* Bloomington, IN: Solution Tree Press.

DuFour, R., DuFour, R., Eaker, R., & Karhanek, G. (2004). *Whatever it takes: How professional learning communities respond when kids don't learn.* Bloomington, IN: Solution Tree Press.

DuFour, R., DuFour, R., Eaker, R., Many, T. W., & Mattos, M. (2016). *Learning by doing: A handbook for Professional Learning Communities at Work* (3rd ed.). Bloomington, IN: Solution Tree Press.

DuFour, R., Reeves, D., & DuFour, R. (2018). *Responding to the Every Student Succeeds Act with the PLC at Work process.* Bloomington, IN: Solution Tree Press.

Dweck, C. S. (2006). *Mindset: The new psychology of success.* New York: Random House.

Elmore, R. F. (2002). *Bridging the gap between standards and achievement.* Washington, DC: Albert Shanker Institute. Accessed at www.shankerinstitute.org/resource/bridging-gap-between-standards -and-achievement on May 22, 2018.

Every Student Succeeds Act of 2015, Pub. L. No. 114-95 § 114 Stat. 1177 (2015).

Ferriter, W. (2011, June 5). *Twitter for singletons in a PLC* [Blog post]. Accessed at http://blog .williamferriter.com/2010/10/30/twitter-for-singletons-in-a-plc on March 12, 2018.

Foster, D., & Poppers, A. (2009). *Using formative assessment to drive learning: The Silicon Valley Mathematics Initiative—A twelve-year research and development project.* Palo Alto, CA: Noyce Foundation. Accessed at www.svmimac.org/images/Using_Formative_Assessment_to_Drive _Learning_Reduced.pdf on March 11, 2018.

Gareis, C. R., & Grant, L. W. (2008). *Teacher-made assessments: How to connect curriculum, instruction, and student learning.* Larchmont, NY: Eye on Education.

Garet, M. S., Porter, A. C., Desimone, L., Birman, B. F., & Yoon, K. S. (2001). What makes professional development effective? Results from a nation sample of teachers. *American Educational Research Journal, 38*(4), 915–945.

Garmston, R. J., & Wellman, B. M. (2009). *The adaptive school: A sourcebook for developing collaborative groups.* Norwood, MA: Christopher-Gordon.

Goddard, R. D., Hoy, W. K., & Hoy, A. W. (2000). Collective teacher efficacy: Its meaning, measure, and impact on student achievement. *American Educational Research Journal, 37*(2), 479–507.

Gojak, L. M., & Miles, R. H. (2015). *The Common Core mathematics companion: The standards decoded, grades K–2.* Thousand Oaks, CA: Corwin Press.

Gojak, L. M., & Miles, R. H. (2016). *The Common Core mathematics companion: The standards decoded, grades 3–5.* Thousand Oaks, CA: Corwin Press.

Graham, P., & Ferriter, W. (2008). One step at a time. *Journal of Staff Development, 29*(3), 38–42.

Guskey, T. R. (2003). What makes professional development effective? *Phi Delta Kappan, 84*(10), 748-750.

Hall, P., & Simeral, A. (2008). *Building teachers' capacity for success: A collaborative approach for coaches and school leaders.* Alexandria, VA: Association for Supervision and Curriculum Development.

Hall, P., & Simeral, A. (2017). *Creating a culture of reflective practice: Capacity-building for schoolwide success.* Alexandria, VA: Association for Supervision and Curriculum Development.

Hanover Research. (2015). *Best practices in instructional coaching: Prepared for Iowa Area Education Agencies.* Accessed at www.educateiowa.gov/sites/files/ed/documents/Best%20Practices%20in%20Instructional%20Coaching%20-%20Iowa%20Area%20Education%20Agencies.pdf on May 22, 2018.

Hattie, J. (2009). *Visible learning: A synthesis of over 800 meta-analyses relating to achievement.* New York: Routledge.

Hattie, J. (2012). *Visible learning for teachers: Maximizing impact on learning.* New York: Routledge.

Hattie, J. (2017, December). *Hattie ranking: 252 influences and effect sizes related to student achievement.* Accessed at https://visible-learning.org/hattie-ranking-influences-effect-sizes-learning-achievement on March 28, 2018.

Hattie, J., Masters, D., & Birch, K. (2016). *Visible learning into action: International case studies of impact.* New York: Routledge.

Hess, K. K. (2013). *Hess cognitive rigor matrix (math-science CRM): Applying Webb's depth-of-knowledge levels to Bloom's cognitive process dimensions.* Accessed at http://media.wix.com/ugd/5e86bd_1f5398ca7d5049daa1f96bc60d3bbc75.pdf on May 25, 2018.

Hill, H. C. (2009). Fixing teacher professional development. *Phi Delta Kappan, 90*(7), 470–476.

Hirsh, S. (2005). Professional development and closing the achievement gap. *Theory Into Practice, 44*(1), 38–44.

Joyce, B., & Showers, B. (1981). Transfer of training: The contribution of 'coaching'. *Journal of Education, 162*(2), 163–172.

Joyce, B., & Showers, B. (1995). *Student achievement through staff development: Fundamentals of school renewal* (2nd ed.). New York: Longman.

Kane, B. D., & Rosenquist, B. (2018). Making the most of instructional coaches. *Phi Delta Kappan, 99*(7), 21–25.

Kanold, T. D. (2011). *The five disciplines of PLC leaders.* Bloomington, IN: Solution Tree Press.

Kanold, T. D., Schuhl, S., Larson, M. R., Barnes, B., Kanold-McIntyre, J., & Toncheff, M. (2018). *Mathematics assessment and intervention in a PLC at Work.* Bloomington, IN: Solution Tree Press.

Killion, J., & Harrison, C. (2006). *Taking the lead: New roles for teachers and school-based coaches.* Oxford, OH: National Staff Development Council.

Killion, J., Harrison, C., Bryan, C., & Clifton, H. (2012). *Coaching matters.* Oxford, OH: Learning Forward.

Knight, J. (2007). *Instructional coaching: A partnership approach to improving instruction.* Thousand Oaks, CA: Corwin Press.

Lencioni, P. (2007). *The five dysfunctions of a team: Team assessment.* San Francisco: Pfeiffer.

Lexile Framework for Reading. (n.d.). *Matching Lexile measures to grade ranges.* Accessed at https://lexile .com/educators/measuring-growth-with-lexile/lexile-measures-grade-equivalents on March 12, 2018.

Many, T. W., & Sparks-Many, S. K. (2015). *Leverage: Using PLCs to promote lasting improvement in schools.* Thousand Oaks, CA: Corwin Press.

Marzano, R. J. (2003). *What works in schools: Translating research into action.* Alexandria, VA: Association for Supervision and Curriculum Development.

Marzano, R. J. (2010). *Formative assessment and standards-based grading.* Bloomington, IN: Marzano Research.

Marzano, R. J. (2017). *The new art and science of teaching.* Bloomington, IN: Solution Tree Press.

Mattos, M., DuFour, R., DuFour, R., Eaker, R., & Many, T. W. (2016). *Concise answers to frequently asked questions about Professional Learning Communities at Work.* Bloomington, IN: Solution Tree Press.

Medrich, E., & Charner, I. (2017). *Educator-centered instructional coaching practices that work: Lessons from PIIC research.* Durham, NC: FHI 360. Accessed at www.fhi360.org/sites/default/files/media /documents/resource-piic-ed-coaching.pdf on May 22, 2018.

Miles, R. H., & Williams, L. A. (2016). *The Common Core mathematics companion: The standards decoded, grades 6–8.* Thousand Oaks, CA: Corwin Press.

Miller, A. (2015, September 15). *Righting your RtI/MTSS triangle* [Blog post]. Accessed at www.mcrel .org/righting-your-rtimtss-triangle on August 30, 2018.

National Association for Gifted Children. (n.d.). *NAGC position statements and white papers.* Accessed at www.nagc.org/about-nagc/nagc-position-statements-white-papers on May 22, 2018.

National Governors Association Center for Best Practices & Council of Chief State School Officers. (2010a). *Common Core State Standards for English language arts and literacy in history/social studies, science, and technical subjects.* Washington, DC: Authors. Accessed at www.corestandards.org/assets /CCSSI_ELA%20Standards.pdf on March 8, 2018.

National Governors Association Center for Best Practices & Council of Chief State School Officers. (2010b). *Common Core State Standards for mathematics.* Washington, DC: Authors. Accessed at www.corestandards.org/assets/CCSSI_Math%20Standards.pdf on March 8, 2018.

NGSS Lead States. (2013). *Next Generation Science Standards: For states, by states.* Washington, DC: National Academies Press.

Nickelsen, L., & Dickson, M. (2018). *Teaching with the instructional cha-chas: Four steps to make learning stick.* Bloomington, IN: Solution Tree Press.

No Child Left Behind (NCLB) Act of 2001, Pub. L. No. 107-110, § 115, Stat. 1425 (2002).

Noyce Foundation. (2012). *Performance assessment task: Truffles grade 6.* Accessed at www .insidemathematics.org/assets/common-core-math-tasks/truffles.pdf on August 27, 2018.

Partnership for Assessment of Readiness for College and Careers. (n.d.). *Passage selection guidelines for the PARCC summative assessments, grades 3–11, in ELA/literacy.* Accessed at https://parcc-assessment.org /content/uploads/2017/11/passageselectionguidelines07_15.pdf on March 12, 2018.

Partnership for Assessment of Readiness for College and Careers. (2014). *PARCC model content frameworks: A companion to the Common Core State Standards—Mathematics, kindergarten through grade 2.* Accessed at https://parcc-assessment.org/content/uploads/2017/11/PARCC-K2-MCF-for -Mathematics-9-24-14-2.pdf on March 12, 2018.

Partnership for Assessment of Readiness for College and Careers. (2017). *PARCC model content frameworks for mathematics, grades 3–11: Version 5.0.* Accessed at https://parcc-assessment.org /wp-content/uploads/2018/01/PARCC_MCF_Mathematics-12-11-2014-v4-2017.pdf on March 12, 2018.

Patterson, K., Grenny, J., McMillan, R., & Switzler, A. (2012). *Crucial conversations: Tools for talking when stakes are high.* New York: McGraw-Hill.

Popham, W. J. (2003). *Test better, teach better: The instructional role of assessment.* Alexandria, VA: Association for Supervision and Curriculum Development.

Popham, W. J. (2007). The lowdown on learning progressions. *Educational Leadership, 64*(7), 83–84.

Popham, W. J. (2008). *Transformative assessment.* Alexandria, VA: Association for Supervision and Curriculum Development.

ReadWorks. (2016). *The Age of Exploration.* Accessed at www.readworks.org/article/The-Age-of -Exploration/d408fcd3-1738-4fd0-83d6-ad3dea1cc2b7#!articleTab:content/contentSection :45a25cf7-312b-487f-9286-79b045d49af3 on July 18, 2018.

Reeves, D. (Ed.). (2007). *Ahead of the curve: The power of assessment to transform teaching and learning.* Bloomington, IN: Solution Tree Press.

Rutherford, P. (2005). *The 21st century mentor's handbook: Creating a culture for learning.* Alexandria, VA: Just ASK.

Sadler, D. R. (1989). Formative assessment and the design of instructional systems. *Instructional Science, 18*(2), 119–144.

Schmoker, M. (2004). Learning communities at the crossroads: A response to Joyce and Cook. *Phi Delta Kappan, 86*(1), 84–89.

Smarter Balanced Assessment Consortium. (2015a). *Content specifications for the summative assessment of the Common Core State Standards for mathematics.* Accessed at https://portal.smarterbalanced.org /library/en/mathematics-content-specifications.pdf on March 12, 2018.

Smarter Balanced Assessment Consortium. (2015b). *English language arts and literacy computer adaptive test (CAT) and performance task (PT) stimulus specifications.* Accessed at https://portal .smarterbalanced.org/library/en/ela-stimulus-specifications.pdf on March 12, 2018.

Stiggins, R. J., Arter, J. A., Chappuis, J., & Chappuis, S. (2004). *Classroom assessment for student learning: Doing it right—Using it well.* Portland, OR: Assessment Training Institute.

Sun, K. L. (2018). Beyond rhetoric: Authentically supporting a growth mindset. *Teaching Children Mathematics, 24*(5). Accessed at www.nctm.org/Publications/Teaching-Children-Mathematics/2018 /Vol24/Issue5/Beyond-rhetoric_-Authentically-supporting-a-growth-mindset on March 14, 2018.

Sweeney, D. (2011). *Student-centered coaching: A guide for K–8 coaches and principals.* Thousand Oaks, CA: Corwin Press.

Sweeney, D., & Harris, L. S. (2017). *Student-centered coaching: The moves.* Thousand Oaks, CA: Corwin Press.

Taberski, S., & Burke, J. (2014). *The Common Core companion: The standards decoded, grades K–2.* Thousand Oaks, CA: Corwin Press.

Tomlinson, C. A. (2014). *The differentiated classroom: Responding to the needs of all learners* (2nd ed.). Alexandria, VA: Association for Supervision and Curriculum Development.

Tomlinson, C. A., & Moon, T. R. (2013). *Assessment and student success in a differentiated classroom.* Alexandria, VA: Association for Supervision and Curriculum Development.

Tomlinson, C. A., & Murphy, M. (2015). *Leading for differentiation: Growing teachers who grow kids.* Alexandria, VA: Association for Supervision and Curriculum Development.

Tschannen-Moran, M., & Barr, M. (2004). Fostering student learning: The relationship of collective teacher efficacy and student achievement. *Leadership and Policy in Schools, 3*(3), 189–209.

U.S. Department of Education. (n.d.). *Every Student Succeeds Act.* Accessed at www.ed.gov/ESSA on March 12, 2018.

Valdez, M., & Broin, A. (2015). *Untapped: Transforming teacher leadership to help students succeed.* New York: New Leaders. Accessed at http://newleaders.org/research-policy/untapped on November 10, 2017.

Webb, N. L. (2002). *Depth-of-knowledge for four content areas.* Accessed at www.hed.state.nm.us/uploads/files/ABE/Policies/depth_of_knowledge_guide_for_all_subject_areas.pdf on May 25, 2018.

Wei, R. C., Darling-Hammond, L., Andree, A., Richardson, N., & Orphanos, S. (2009). *Professional learning in the learning profession: A status report on teacher development in the U.S. and abroad.* Dallas, TX: National Staff Development Council.

West Virginia college- and career-readiness standards for social studies. (2016). Accessed at https://apps.sos.wv.gov/adlaw/csr/readfile.aspx?DocId=27577&Format=PDF on September 4, 2018.

Wiliam, D. (2011). *Embedded formative assessment* (2nd ed.). Bloomington, IN: Solution Tree Press.

Williamson, G. L. (2008). A text readability continuum for postsecondary readiness. *Journal of Advanced Academics, 19*(4), 602–632.

Index

Common Formative Assessment
Kim Bailey and Chris Jakicic
The catalyst for real student improvement begins with a decision to implement common formative assessments. In this conversational guide, the authors offer tools, templates, and protocols to incorporate common formative assessments into the practices of a PLC to monitor and enhance student learning.
BKF538

Simplifying Common Assessment
Kim Bailey and Chris Jakicic
Discover how to develop effective and efficient assessments. The authors simplify assessment development to give teacher teams the confidence to write and use team-designed common formative assessments that help ensure all students master essential skills and concepts.
BKF750

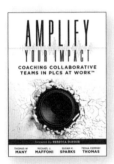

Amplify Your Impact
Thomas W. Many, Michael J. Maffoni, Susan K. Sparks, and Tesha Ferriby Thomas
Now is the time to improve collaboration in your PLC. Using the latest research on coaching and collaboration, the authors share concrete action steps your school can take to adopt proven collaborative coaching methods, fortify teacher teams, and ultimately improve student learning in classrooms.
BKF794

Everyday Instructional Coaching
Nathan D. Lang
Discover seven drivers you can use to improve your daily coaching practices: collaboration, transparency, inquiry, discourse, reverberation, sincerity, and influence. Each of the book's chapters defines, describes, and offers tips for implementing one of the seven drivers.
BKF802

Creating a Coaching Culture for Professional Learning Communities
Jane A. G. Kise and Beth Russell
This practical resource provides activities designed to meet a wide variety of needs so you can choose the ones that fit your leadership style, the learning styles of team members, and the particular needs of the school.
BKF350

a division of

Solution Tree | Press   Visit SolutionTree.com or call 800.733.6786 to order.

GL🄌BAL **PD**

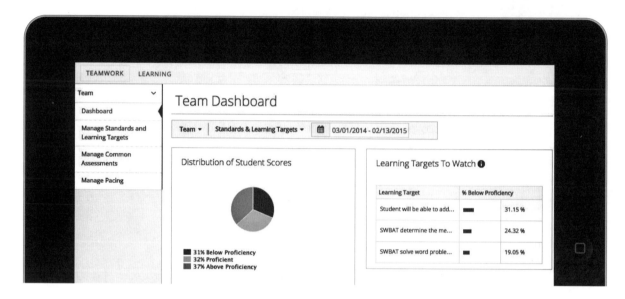

The **Power to Improve**
Is in Your Hands

Global PD gives educators focused and goals-oriented training from top experts. You can rely on this innovative online tool to improve instruction in every classroom.

- Get unlimited, on-demand access to guided video and book content from top Solution Tree authors.

- Improve practices with personalized virtual coaching from PLC-certified trainers.

- Customize learning based on skill level and time commitments.

▶ **REQUEST A FREE DEMO TODAY**
SolutionTree.com/GlobalPD